REAL PROPERTY

IN A NUTSHELL

FOURTH EDITION

By

ROGER BERNHARDT

Professor of Law

Golden Gate University, School of Law

ANN M. BURKHART

Professor of Law

University of Minnesota Law School

WEST
GROUP

ST. PAUL, MINN.

2000

For Christine and Chris

*

INTRODUCTION

No other course in the first year of law school seems to involve as many rules as does Real Property. Students suffer under the sheer number of rules thrown at them, and professors chafe at the amount of class time consumed in the brute articulation of all these rules. This book attempts to remedy that a little. For the students, it offers a brief compilation of all or most of the rules that are covered in the standard casebooks on the subject, organized so as to minimize their seeming randomness and arbitrariness. For the professors, it offers an opportunity to free up class time for an exploration of how the rules came to be, how they operate (or how to operate around them), and whether they work. Our goal is to make the mechanical statement of the rules the beginning, rather than the end, of the study of Property in law school

Anyone who finds this book helpful should thank Jo Walker whose editorial assistance converted a lot of random notes into a coherent first edition.

*

OUTLINE

OUTLINE

OUTLINE

Page

Page

PART TWO. CONVEYANCING

OUTLINE

Page

*

TABLE OF CASES

References are to Pages

LI

TABLE OF CASES

REAL PROPERTY

IN A NUTSHELL

FOURTH EDITION

*

PART ONE

INTERESTS IN LAND

CHAPTER ONE

POSSESSION AND OWNERSHIP

Real property (realty) consists of land and objects that are permanently affixed to land, such as trees and buildings. Real property generally is immovable. Personal property (personalty) consists of movable objects. Personal property can be tangible, such as a book or car, or intangible, such as an idea or the good will of a business. Most of the law of property consists of issues relating to real property, rather than to personal property. By and large, however, the rules are the same for both. In this Chapter, we will examine three of the most commonly studied topics concerning the importance of possession: (1) possession of owned and unowned personal property, (2) gifts, and (3) adverse possession.

I. POSSESSION OF UNOWNED AND OWNED PERSONAL PROPERTY

A. UNOWNED PERSONAL PROPERTY

Possessors' claims depend on whether the property has a legal owner. If the property is unowned (e.g.

wild animals, undiscovered minerals, and abandoned goods), the taking of possession may enable the possessor to claim ownership of the asset. At the very least, no other owner can assert rights against the possessor.

Illustration: Paul captures a whale on the high seas. While governments or conservation groups may challenge Paul's right to capture the whale, no person can say "That whale is mine."

1. Rights of Possessors

Unless a person is legally prohibited from taking unowned assets (e.g. no killing of endangered species or taking rocks from a national preserve), the possessor of an unowned asset is its "owner" and is entitled to all the rights owners have over goods they have purchased or inherited.

Illustration: Paul catches a fish in the ocean, and Sue purchases a fish in the grocery store. Paul's and Sue's rights with regard to their fish are the same.

2. Rival Possessors

The law gives priority to the person who first takes possession of an object. "First in time is first in right." However, this rule will not apply if the circumstances make it unfair.

Illustration: Paul spots a diamond lying on the ground. As he is about to pick it up, Sue hits him from behind and takes it for herself. A court may not award the diamond to Sue as the first possessor.

3.   What Constitutes Possession

Possession requires both physical control over the item and an intent to control it or to exclude others from it. But these generalizations function more as guidelines than as direct determinants of possession issues. Possession is a blurred question of law and fact. The following Illustrations show some of the more common and troublesome situations.

Illustration—Killing: Paul was pursuing a fox on horseback when Sue took her gun and shot it. Pursuit of a wild animal alone does not constitute taking it into possession. However, if Paul had shot and killed the fox before Sue got to it, Paul would have been the prior possessor. If Sue's shot merely had wounded the fox, rather than killed it, Paul might have prevailed if he got to it first. The result is the same whether the quarry being pursued is a wild animal (i.e. *in ferae naturae*) or previously had been captured by another and then escaped back into the wild (demonstrated an *animus revertendi*) and thereby had become unowned again. State hunting statutes could alter these outcomes.

Illustration—Trapping: Paul had thrown a net around a school of fish, but then Sue caught some of them. If the net was closed so that the fish could not escape, Paul had possession, but he did not have possession if the fish had a means of escape. Conservationists often attack outcomes such as this as leading to the premature depletion of scarce resources.

Illustration—Spotting: Paul finds an ancient Greek treasure ship at the bottom of the ocean and leaves a marker on the ship. However, before he can return with the necessary equipment to raise it, Sue finds the ship and brings it to the surface. The outcome depends on whether leaving a marker on a sunken ship is a sufficient act of possession to qualify Paul as the first possessor.

Illustration—Unconscious Possession: Paul is standing on a $100 bill without realizing it. Sue asks him to lift his foot, picks up the money, and pockets it. Or Paul finds and removes a box lying in a trash can, but Sue opens it first and discovers a $100 bill in it. It can be argued on one hand that Paul lacked possession in these cases because he had no intent to appropriate or to exclude since he was unaware of the asset. On the other hand, Paul had possession of the money, albeit unconscious, in light of his undisputed physical control over it.

Illustration—Landowner's Possession: Paul finds money in Olga's house. Courts often say that a landowner has "constructive possession" of whatever is on her property, whether she knows it is there. Therefore, Olga is the prior possessor. When this issue comes up in the case of previously owned goods, additional considerations apply. See p. 9–11.

B. OWNED GOODS

When someone takes possession of property that is owned by another, he has an obligation to return it to the owner. A borrower, renter, finder, and thief all are obligated to return the property to its owner on demand or according to the terms of their agreement. Each also has some duty of care in handling the property.

Illustration: Olga loses a camera, and Ann finds it. Ann loans it to Bob, and Cathy steals it from him. Cathy has a duty to return it to Bob, who has a duty to return it to Ann, who has a duty to return it to Olga. Any person's failure to do so creates liability for recovery of the camera or for damages. Additionally, each may be liable to the one with the prior claim for negligent handling of the camera.

1. Types of Possessors

A possessor's duties to an owner frequently depend on the nature of the possession. (1) Persons who take possession of goods with the owner's consent, such as borrowers, coat checkers, and auto mechanics, usually are referred to as bailees under a bailment transaction. (2) Persons who take possession of goods without the owner's consent, such as finders and thieves, sometimes are referred to as involuntary or constructive bailees. (3) Persons who do not take possession of goods that are stored in a space that they control, such as unattended parking lots and wet umbrella stands in store entrances, are not bailees. The space owner's duties are determined by rules other than those for bailments, such as by landlord-tenant law. (4) Courts sometimes distinguish between possessors and custodians who hold goods subject to the owner's direction and control, such as a friend or customer examining a book shown to him by the owner. The old criminal law distinctions between larceny and embezzlement depended on this characterization. (5) A person asked to take possession of a container does not necessarily possess its contents if they are unknown to him. For example, a person holding another's purse, briefcase, coat, or car may not have possession of its contents.

2. Duty to Return

A true bailee has an absolute duty to return goods to their owner. He is liable if he fails to do so, even if the goods were stolen from him or were destroyed without his fault. An involuntary bailee may be liable for nonreturn only if it results from his negligence. A space owner has no duty to return goods that were never in his possession unless he agreed to do so or in special cases, such as when a parking lot ticket states that no bailment exists, but car owners believe that their cars are being watched by guards and by attendants who are visibly present.

3. Duty of Care

A possessor has some duty of care toward the item during his possession. Traditionally, the duty's extent depended on the nature of the possession. (1) When the bailment is for the bailor's benefit, such as when the bailee is doing a favor for the owner by holding her goods, the bailee's duty of care is only slight. He is liable only for gross negligence. Finders generally have no duty of care for goods they see but do not pick up. But if a finder takes possession, he may come under the slight care standard. (2) When the bailment is for the bailee's benefit, such as when the owner is doing the bailee a favor by loaning him the item, the bailee's duty of care is extreme. However, he does not have an absolute duty of protection. For example, he is not liable for damage from an earthquake. (3) When the bailment is for the bailor and bailee's mutual benefit, the bailee is liable for ordinary negligence. This standard applies when both parties benefit from the transaction, such as when an owner pays a shipper to transport goods. (4) If no bailment is created, the owner of the space may have no duty of care for the goods placed there by the owner. For example, a parking lot owner sometimes has no duty of care for cars parked in the lot.

4. Exculpatory and Limitation of Liability Clauses

Many courts limit a possessor's ability to disclaim liability for nonreturn of goods. Such issues are not unique to property law. They apply in contract and tort law as well.

5. Possessors' Rights Against Others

A possessor's obligation to return goods to their owner is not a duty owed to anyone else, because the possessor has a better claim to the goods than they do. Therefore, the possessor does not have to give the goods to any third person (a "stranger to the title") who demands them from her, and the possessor may demand that any such third person who takes the goods from her return them to her.

Illustration—Borrowing and Renting: Ann borrowed or rented a car for a week and then loaned or rented it to Bob for the day. At the end of the day, Bob must return the car to Ann, and Ann is entitled to demand the car from Bob.

Illustration—Finding and Stealing: Ann picked up a camera she found lying on the ground, but Bob stole it from her. Ann may recover the camera from Bob, even though she does not own it and will have to give it to the owner if he is ever identified. Just as the owner did not lose his rights to the camera when he lost it, Ann does not lose the rights she acquired on finding the camera just because Bob steals it. However, finding situations may be subject to statutory modifications.

A hierarchy of claims exists by virtue of the possessor's ability to demand that a third person return the goods on one hand, but the possessor's duty to return them to the owner on the other hand. In the last

Illustration, the finder's rights are below the owner's but above the thief's. The common saying that possession is nine points of the law expresses this notion, since there is usually only one owner above the possessor and many other persons who neither own nor have the right to possess the item. When more than one person claims the right to possess the same asset, the conflict is resolved by determining who has the better claim to it as between the two claimants. This standard may require a court to determine whether the first claimant's acts constituted possession, such as whether seeing or picking up a lost wallet constitutes possession. Considerations other than time of possession are irrelevant. Success does not depend on which claimant is needier, will make better use of the asset, or has a morally superior claim.

One party need not have a perfect claim (i.e. be the owner), so long as her claim is better than the rival claimant's. Therefore, a person cannot take or withhold goods from another merely because they are owned by a third person. The person from whom they were taken still may have a better claim than the person who took them. In the previous Illustration, the thief cannot defend his wrongful retention by arguing that the finder does not own the goods.

Illustration—Finder v. Finder: Ann finds a camera but loses it. Bob then finds it. As between Ann and Bob, Ann has the better claim because she possessed it first. Except as against Olga, the owner, she has the same right to recover what she loses as does an owner. She can recover "her" lost camera from the finder, Bob.

Illustration—Thief v. Thief: Ann steals a camera, and Bob steals it from her. Ann has a better claim to the camera than Bob, even though she acquired possession by theft. She is a wrongful possessor as far as Olga and the penal system are concerned, but she is the prior possessor against Bob and is higher in the hierarchy. Although Ann possibly should be sent to jail, strangers are not entitled to confiscate her goods.

Illustration—Thief v. Finder: Ann steals a camera but loses it, and Bob finds it. The outcome is the same as in the previous Illustration. The guilty possessor prevails over the innocent possessor because she possessed first. Commentators often attack this outcome, but property rules sometimes lack the reasonableness or fairness involved in a torts analysis. For instance, Ann need not share possession of her property with Bob even though she has more than enough of everything and Bob has nothing. "Property rights" is not necessarily a "reasonable" concept, and the rules protecting possessors do not purport to eradicate many of the world's ills.

6. Landowner's Claims

Since goods often are found on property that belongs to or is possessed by someone else, conflicts often arise between the finder and the person on whose land it was found. This straightforward issue has not led to straightforward outcomes. Instead, courts employ a number of somewhat conflicting distinctions.

a. *Status of the Finder*

The finder's claim to the found goods is weaker if he (1) is a trespasser on the property, (2) is on the property for a limited purpose, such as to repair the sink or to deliver the mail, (3) is on the property as an employee of the landowner, or (4) agreed to give any found goods to the landowner, as often occurs in agreements between hotels and their housekeeping crews.

b. Status of the Premises

The finder's claim is weaker if the goods were found in a private, rather than public, place. For example, a person who finds a lost item in another's private home is less likely to prevail against the landowner than one who finds the item in a supermarket.

c. Status of the Land Based Claim

The strength of a land based claim may be affected by whether the claimant is a landowner who has not yet moved in, a landlord who has never resided on the premises, a long-term tenant, or a weekend guest.

d. Where the Goods are Found

Goods found under the soil, rather than lying on it, generally are awarded to the landowner, rather than to the finder. However, if the goods were buried intentionally, they may be characterized as treasure trove. In that case, the outcome may change, or they may belong to the state.

e. How the Goods came to be There

When goods are found in a public place, the finder is entitled to possession if the goods were lost or abandoned. The landowner is entitled to possession if they were mislaid (i.e. intentionally set down by the owner who forgot to pick them up later). The assumption is that the owner of mislaid goods will return to retrieve them, which will be facilitated if the landowner, rather than the finder, has the goods. Statutes regarding findings sometimes abolish these distinctions, but some courts have held that statutes that refer only to "lost" goods do not apply to mislaid goods.

7. Modern Status

Many issues in this area now are resolved by tort or contract concepts or by statutory rules, rather than by the more primitive distinctions of possession and bailment. Many states have estray statutes that regulate how individuals should deal with found goods. These statutes are helpful but are not essential knowledge in this part of the Property Law course, because finding is studied as a method for acquiring possession.

II. GIFTS

A gift is a voluntary transfer of property by the owner for no consideration. The donor (the person making the gift) may make an inter vivos gift or a gift causa mortis to a donee (the gift recipient). A gift is inter vivos if it is between a living donor and donee and if the donor intends the gift to take effect immediately, irrevocably, and unconditionally. A gift is causa mortis if the donor makes it in anticipation of her imminent death. A third type of gift is a testamentary gift. A testamentary gift becomes effective only at the donor's death. It generally must be made by will, which is subject to statutory requirements. Because testamentary gifts are the subject of an upper-class course on Wills, we will not consider them further here.

A. INTER VIVOS GIFTS

The three necessary elements for an inter vivos gift are (1) intent, (2) delivery, and (3) acceptance.

1. Intent

The donor must intend to make a present, irrevocable transfer of a property interest. The gift can be of a presently possessory interest or of a future interest. However, if the donor intends the transfer to take effect only in the future, rather than immediately, the transfer is a mere promise to make a gift in the future, which is unenforceable for lack of consideration.

a. *Effect of Conditions on the Transfer*

When a gift is subject to a condition, you must determine whether the condition is precedent or subsequent. If it is precedent, the condition must occur before the gift becomes effective. Therefore, the attempted gift is invalid because it is not a present transfer. If the condition is subsequent, a present transfer of the property occurs, but the gift will be revoked if the condition subsequently occurs. Because a gift subject to a condition subsequent is a present transfer, it is a valid gift. Determining whether a particular condition is precedent or subsequent requires an analysis of the donor's verbal and written statements.

Illustration: Daniel says to his friend: "If you get an A in Property Law, I will give you a new car." The language Daniel used indicates that he was promising to make a gift in the future if the condition of getting an A occurred. He said, "I *will* give," rather than "I give." Therefore, the gift was subject to a condition precedent and is unenforceable.

Illustration: Daniel says to a friend: "Here are the keys to my car. It is yours. But, if you don't get an A in Property, you must return the car to me." Daniel's language and actions reflect an intent to make a present gift, even though the gift might be revoked in the future. Therefore, the gift is subject to a condition subsequent and is enforceable.

Illustration: Dora owns a painting. She writes a letter to her son that says: "In honor of your birthday today, I give you my painting. However, I am going to keep possession of it until my death." Her use of the present verb tense—"I give"—shows an intent to make a present transfer. Because her son is not entitled to immediate possession of the painting, it is a present transfer of a future interest in the painting.

b. Circumstances Surrounding the Gift

To determine the donor's intent, courts also consider the surrounding circumstances, including the parties' relationship, the gift's size in relation to previous gifts from the donor to the donee, and the donor's conduct after the transfer. For instance, in the preceding Illustration, the intent to make a present transfer is supported by the facts that the transfer was made on the donee's birthday and that the letter expressly referred to the birthday.

c. Effect of Donor's Retention of Rights

Although a gift need not be of all rights in the property, the donor's retention of certain rights may invalidate the gift. For example, if the alleged donor retains control of the property, reserves a right to revoke the gift, or continues to treat the property as her own, the transfer probably is not a gift.

A special issue arises when one person deposits money into a joint bank account and retains the right to make withdrawals. The issue is whether the depositor intended to make a gift to the other party named on the signature card or merely created the joint account as a convenience for himself. A majority of jurisdictions use gift theory in this situation and apply the usual legal requirements of intent, delivery, and acceptance. The creation of the account provides prima facie evidence of a gift. But the prima facie evidence is rebutted if the alleged donor maintained control over the account and did not intend to give up control.

Illustration: Owen transfers the entire balance of his bank account to an account in the name of his two minor children. Owen retains possession of the passbook and makes withdrawals from the account to purchase items for his personal needs. Because Owen retained control over the account and treated it as his own, he does not have the necessary intent to make an irrevocable gift to the children.

A minority of courts apply contract theory and hold that the contract with the bank gives the donee a right to the money in the account.

2. Delivery

To satisfy the delivery requirement, the donor generally must give actual possession of the gift and must surrender all dominion and control over it. The delivery requirement serves three purposes. First, it protects the donor by impressing upon her the significance of the act done. Second, it makes the donor's act unequivocal to witnesses. Finally, it gives the donee prima facie evidence that a gift was made.

a. Types of Delivery

What constitutes a valid delivery depends on the circumstances.

(1) Actual Delivery

Actual delivery consists of giving possession of the gift to the donee or to the donee's agent. It is a formal, immediate transfer of property, and it is always an accepted means of effectuating a gift.

Illustration: Father told Son he could have two of Father's colts and that Father would advance money so that Son could buy hay for the horses. Father retained possession of the colts until his death one year later. The horses were not given hay until three or four days before Father's death. Because there was no actual delivery of the colts, there was no gift.

(2) Constructive and Symbolic Delivery

If actual delivery has not occurred, a court may uphold the gift on the basis of constructive delivery. "Constructive" delivery refers to those situations in which a court determines that delivery has occurred even though it literally has not. Symbolic delivery is one type of constructive delivery in which a written instrument or some item is delivered that generally is accepted as a symbol of the gift or as providing access to it. Constructive and symbolic delivery normally are sufficient only if the gift cannot reasonably be delivered manually or if other circumstances prevent actual delivery. Courts examine factors such as the property's proximity and size and the state of the donor's health.

Illustration: Father wanted to make a gift of stock and cash to Son and Daughter. The stock already was in Son's possession in a vault 3,000 miles from Father when he made the gift. Father directed his bookkeeper to change his books to reflect the transfer of the property to Son and Daughter. Because Son already had possession of the stock, Father did not have to manually deliver the stock again, and the bookkeeper's change in the records was sufficient to satisfy the delivery requirement. However, because no entry was made on the books to support the gift of cash, the attempted gift of cash did not satisfy the delivery requirement.

Illustration: On Wife's birthday, Husband gave her a written instrument that said he was giving her stock for her birthday. At the time, the stock was in a safe deposit box in another state, which prevented Husband from manually delivering the stock. The instrument was a legally sufficient symbolic delivery.

Illustration: Mae manifested a present intent to give securities contained in a safe deposit box to Everett. She gave him the key to the safe deposit box. This constituted sufficient delivery.

b. Delivery to Third Parties

A gift is valid if delivered to someone other than the donee only if the donor intended the gift to be irrevocable upon transfer to the third party and the third party is the donee's agent. If the evidence clearly demonstrates the donor's intent to make an irrevocable gift, delivery to a third party on behalf of the donee does not defeat the gift.

Illustration: Father wanted to make a gift of stock to Son and Daughter. The stock already was in Son's possession. Father directed Son to deliver to Daughter her share of the stock. Even though Son had not manually delivered the stock to Daughter before Father's death, delivery to Son was sufficient to satisfy the delivery requirement with respect to Daughter.

In contrast, if the third party is the donor's agent, the delivery requirement probably has not been satisfied because the donor could revoke the gift by directing the agent to return it to him. However, if the property was delivered to donee's agent, the delivery requirement is satisfied.

Illustration: When he was in failing health, Grandfather signed a document assigning twenty shares of stock to Granddaughter. Grandfather handed the document to Grandmother. Grandmother thereby became Granddaughter's agent, and the delivery requirement was satisfied.

Illustration: When Father was ill, he signed documents that assigned an interest in a bond and mortgage to Son. Father delivered the documents to his lawyer and instructed him to deliver the documents to Son if Father died during surgery. The delivery requirement was satisfied because the lawyer held the documents as Son's agent.

To uphold a gift that is otherwise invalid for lack of delivery, a court may hold that the donor held the property in trust for the donee. As beneficiary of the trust, the donee is entitled to the benefit of the property. To create a trust, there must be a settlor, a beneficiary, a trustee, and a res, and the settlor clearly must have intended to create a trust. The settlor is the person who creates the trust (the donor in this case). The beneficiary is the person who is entitled to the benefits of the property held in trust (the intended donee in this case). The trustee is the person who holds the legal title to the trust property and administers it for the beneficiary's benefit. The trustee may be the settlor or a third party. The res is the property that is placed in trust. In this context, the res is the property that was the object of the imperfect gift.

Illustration: Xavier purchased bonds for Nephew and told his father that he had put the bonds aside for Nephew. After Xavier's death, the bonds were found in an envelope, which said that Xavier had held them for Nephew. This created a valid trust with Xavier acting as trustee for Nephew.

3. Acceptance

If an intended donee refuses to accept a gift, title to the property will not pass to the donee. When a gift is beneficial to the donee, acceptance is usually presumed. The presumption of acceptance is rebutted if the intended donee's actions indicate a refusal to accept or if other facts demonstrate that the gift would not be beneficial. Acceptance need not be contemporaneous with delivery of the gift.

B. GIFTS CAUSA MORTIS

A gift causa mortis is made in anticipation of the donor's imminent death. It is intended to give a person who is near death one last opportunity to dispose of her property. The substantial possibility for false claims to the decedent's property generally has caused courts to strictly apply the requirements for a gift causa mortis.

1. Elements

a. *Intent, Delivery, and Acceptance*

A gift causa mortis requires the same elements as an inter vivos gift–intent, delivery, and acceptance. In determining whether these elements have been satisfied, courts tend to be more exacting than for an inter vivos gift because of the greater potential for fraud inherent in a claim made against the estate of a deceased donor.

b. *Donor Anticipates Imminent Death*

For a gift causa mortis to be valid, it must be made when the donor is suffering from a life-threatening illness or injury. A generalized fear of death, such as a fear of flying or of nuclear war, is insufficient.

Illustration: Dan indorsed a check and laid it on a table with a note stating that it was for Elizabeth. Dan then committed suicide. Suicide can satisfy the requirement that the donor is stricken with a disorder that makes death imminent.

c. *Death as Anticipated*

The donor must die from the illness or injury that prompted the gift, rather than from an intervening cause.

Illustration: A car accident victim is put in an ambulance after making a gift causa mortis. If the ambulance is struck by a train and the injured person dies from the injuries suffered in the train crash, the older view is that the gift is invalid because the injured person died from an intervening cause. The modern view is more liberal and treats the entire chain of events as one connected occurrence. Therefore, the gift would be valid despite the intervening train crash.

d. *Donor does not Recover*

If the donor recovers from the illness or injury that prompted the gift, the gift automatically is revoked by operation of law.

e. *Absence of Revocation by Donor*

Unlike an inter vivos gift, a donor can revoke a gift causa mortis.

f. *Donee Survives Donor*

Because a gift causa mortis is a gift to a particular individual, the gift is revoked by operation of law if the donee predeceases the donor. Otherwise, the donee's heirs or legatees, rather than the donee, would receive the benefit of the gift.

g. *Condition Precedent or Subsequent*

Some courts will invalidate the gift if the donor uses language of condition precedent, indicating that the gift is to take effect only at the donor's death. These courts reason that the donor did not intend to make an immediately effective gift causa mortis, but only a testamentary transfer. Because the gift did not satisfy the legal requirements for a valid will, the attempted gift is invalid. The better opinions, however, look to the donor's intent and to the surrounding circumstances, because a donor who is about to die is unlikely to think about the legal requirements for a gift causa mortis or to articulate his wishes precisely. By definition, such gifts are emergency measures.

III. POSSESSION OF LAND APART FROM OWNERSHIP

While it is often the case that a person in possession of land is the owner of it or is in possession by virtue of the owner's consent (e.g. a tenant), it also may happen that a possessor of land is there without either being the owner or having the owner's consent.

Illustration: Paul received a deed to Lot 1 but mistakenly moved onto Lot 2 instead. Here, Paul owns Lot 1 but possesses (without owning or having the consent of the owner) Lot 2.

Illustration: Paul received a deed to Lot 1 and took possession of Lot 1, but the deed to Paul was defectively executed (or, alternatively, an earlier deed in the chain of title was defectively executed) so that he is not the owner of Lot 1, although he is in possession of it.

Illustration: Paul received a valid deed to Lot 1 and took possession of Lot 1. However, by mistake, Paul built a fence that encroached five feet onto Lot 2 and then built his house up to the fence line. Paul possesses but does not own the five foot strip.

Illustration: Paul is a squatter on Lot 1. He knows that he does not own Lot 1 but hopes that the real owner will not do anything about it. He intends to stay until evicted. Paul possesses but does not own Lot 1.

A. CONSEQUENCES OF POSSESSION UNCONNECTED TO OWNERSHIP

Possession has always been an important concept in our legal system. The old doctrine of seisin had more to do with possession than with ownership. (On seisin, see Chapter 2, p. 50) A possessor has a legal status in the common law even when he or she is not an owner. Both rights and liabilities attach to possession.

1. Liabilities of a Possessor—Ejectment

If a possessor is not the owner and does not have the owner's permission to possess the property, the owner may bring an ejectment action to recover both possession and damages against the possessor. Ejectment is an action designed to restore possession to the person entitled to it. Not only must the plaintiff establish a right to possession in himself, he also must show that the defendant is in wrongful possession, i.e. dispossessing the plaintiff. If the defendant has not possessed the property but has only occasionally trespassed on it, an action for trespass (damages) may lie, but not for ejectment.

2. Rights of a Possessor

Even though a possessor does not own the property and is subject to ejectment by the owner, as against the rest of the world the possessor is entitled to maintain that possession ("Possession is nine points of the law."). If a stranger appears and dispossesses him, he may bring ejectment against the stranger to be restored to possession. It is no defense for the stranger to show that the former possessor was not in fact the owner (unless the stranger can also show that he owns the property or claims through the owner).

Illustration: Paul entered Lot 1 under a deed he believed to be valid. Paul then was ousted from possession by Rachel and brought ejectment against her. At the trial, Paul discovers that his deed is defective and that it did not in fact convey title to Lot 1 to him. Nevertheless, he may prevail against Rachel by virtue of having been in peaceable possession of the lot before her entry. Paul prevails, because he is a prior possessor as against Rachel, though he is a wrongful possessor as against Olga.

3. Possession as Both Rightful and Wrongful

Since a nonowning possessor may defend that possession against all the world (except the owner) and yet is subject to ejectment by the owner, such possession is both "rightful" and "wrongful." To the extent that ownership usually is taken as the ability to exclude others, the possessor is in a sense a 99% owner because he or she can exclude everyone else in the world from the property except the owner.

B. DURATION OF POSSESSION

A plaintiff in ejectment need not show any particular duration of possession to claim as a prior possessor. Time is relevant only in that the plaintiff must have possessed first, but it does not matter how long he was there beforehand (so long as he was still there at the time of the defendant's entry). But time is relevant with regard to the statute of limitations. A cause of action in ejectment arises in favor of the owner or a prior possessor the moment someone else wrongfully takes possession of the property. And, like all causes of action, it expires after a certain lapse of time, except when the government owns the property. Thus, if a person has been in possession long enough, others who previously were entitled to eject him lose their rights to do so.

Illustration: Paul possessed Lot 1 but was dispossessed by Rachel eleven years ago. The statute of limitations on eject-ment actions is ten years. Paul no longer can recover in ejectment against Rachel, even if Paul's prior possession had continued for fifteen years.

Illustration: Paul possessed Lot 1 for two years before Rachel dispossessed him five years ago. The statute of limi-tations for ejectment actions is ten years. Paul still may bring ejectment against Rachel, even though she possessed the property longer than he did.

Illustration: Paul has possessed Lot 1 for eleven years. The statute of limitations in ejectment is ten years. Olga, the owner, no longer can eject Paul.

C. ADVERSE POSSESSION

1. Duration and Adverse Possession

It already has been said that a nonowning possessor of property may protect that possession against every-one but the owner. The last illustration shows that, if such possession lasts long enough, the possessor is protected even from the owner's claims. The posses-sor's 99% rights have become 100%. If no one in the world can eject him and if he can eject anyone in the world who intrudes, then for all practical purposes he now owns the property. He might as well be said to have title to the property, since he now has all the rights that title gives to its owner. The possessor is now a successful adverse possessor. Adverse possession does not transfer the former owner's title to the possessor; rather, by eliminating the one defect that previously existed in the possessory title, it creates a new and complete title in the possessor.

a. How Long Possession Must Continue

Statutes dealing with adverse possession vary from an upper limit of twenty years in some states to a lower one of five years in other states, with more extreme time periods covering certain special cases. There may be different periods of time within a single state, depending on whether the adverse possessor has "color of title" or has paid the property taxes. (Color of title is described at p. 35). In some cases, a longer possession is required against an owner that is a public entity than against a private individual. (In all the following illustrations, assume that a ten-year statute is in effect.)

b. Tacking

Even if the possessor has not personally possessed the property for the requisite time period, he may be able to "tack" (add) on time that his predecessors possessed the property so as to accumulate enough years to satisfy the statute.

Illustration: Paul possessed the property from 1980 to 1986 and then gave a deed to the property to Rachel who possessed it from 1986 to 1991. Under a ten-year statute of limitations, Rachel prevails against Olga, because Rachel can tack Paul's six years to her own five years and claim eleven years of possession.

(1) Privity

Tacking will not be allowed unless privity exists between the possessor and his or her predecessor. This means that the possessor must be connected with the predecessor in such a way that the two possessions may be viewed as related by virtue of a conveyance from the predecessor.

Illustration: Paul possessed the property for six years and then died leaving Rachel as his heir. Rachel then possessed the property for five years. The two periods may be tacked together because there is privity between ancestor and heir.

Illustration: Paul possessed for six years and sold the property to Rachel who possessed for five years. Privity exists between a grantor and grantee and so the periods may be tacked together. Although Paul had no "title" to convey to Rachel, he had a transferable possessory interest, which Rachel purchased from him.

Illustration: Paul possessed for six years and then was ousted by Rachel, who possessed for five years. Tacking is not permitted here because Rachel's possession is not related to Paul's earlier possession. Rachel will not gain title by adverse possession until she has possessed for at least five more years. Theoretically, on Paul's ouster, Olga's constructive possession was reinstated momentarily, so that Olga acquired a whole new cause of action against Rachel which would be good for ten years from the date of the ouster.

(2) Tacking Without Color of Title

If the claimed privity comes from a deed between the possessor and his predecessor, but the deed does not cover the property in question so that it does not create color of title, the more common view is that privity exists anyway, if both the possessor and predecessor actually possessed the property. (Color of title is described at p. 35).

Illustration: For six years, Paul possessed Lot 1 based on a deed describing (and perhaps actually conveying to him) Lot 2. Paul then executed a deed to Rachel using the same description, and Rachel entered Lot 1 and possessed it for five more years. Rachel should be allowed to tack on Paul's prior possession of Lot 1, even though Rachel and Paul are connected by a deed referring to Lot 2. They were still in privity as to the possession of Lot 1. The same tacking will be allowed where Paul possessed Lot 1 and a part of Lot 2 under a deed that described only Lot 1 and then executed a deed to Rachel containing the same description. Rachel will acquire good title to Lot 1 and can tack Paul's possession of Lot 2 to her own.

2. Acts of Possession Required—Standards

Under some state statutes, a person can qualify as an adverse possessor only by performing certain acts during the running of the statute of limitations, such as cultivating, enclosing, or residing on the property. However, in most states, no such requirement exists, and any acts of possession, if they have the correct quality, will support a finding of adverse possession. Any acts by the possessor during the statutory period that establish that, in fact, he or she possessed the property for the requisite period of time will suffice.

No set rules exist concerning the types of activities that constitute possession. A standard sometimes applied is whether the possessor's activities were of such a character as to support an action of ejectment by the owner. For example, occasional trespasses would justify an action in trespass, but not ejectment. Therefore, the occurrence of only those acts during the statutory period would not make the trespasser an adverse possessor. However, most courts prefer a less circular requirement and use phrases such as "acts which publicly indicate a control consistent with the character of the land" or "acts such as an average owner of similar property would undertake."

a. Payment of Taxes

Under some state statutes, a person cannot become an adverse possessor unless he or she pays taxes on the property being possessed. In other states, the time required for adverse possession may be shortened by the payment of taxes (usually when coupled with color of title in the possessor). One justification offered for this requirement is that, by checking the tax records, an owner can discover any potential adverse possession. Possibly the requirement is based on the belief that squatters should not be able to acquire land by adverse possession and that nonsquatting possessors who really believe themselves to be owners will pay the taxes. In this light, payment of taxes is just another appropriate act of possession.

(1) When Both Parties Pay Taxes

When payment of taxes is required, it is a requirement that the adverse possessor must meet; it is not a requirement for an owner who wants to eliminate threats of adverse possession. As long as the adverse possessor is paying taxes, this test usually is satisfied, even if the owner also is paying the taxes at the same time. However, in some states, the issue turns on who paid the taxes first.

(2) Boundary Disputes

The tax requirement can cause particular trouble in boundary line cases when the disputed strip has not been separately taxed and both neighbors have been paying all the taxes billed to them by the assessor. Probably no one involved, including the assessor, knows to which party the disputed strip has been assessed. Some courts strictly apply the tax payment requirement, but, in boundary line cases, the most sensible result is to ignore that requirement entirely.

3. The Required Qualities of Possession

Although rarely provided in statutes, every court requires that the possession be "open, visible, notorious, actual, adverse, exclusive, continuous, uninterrupted, hostile, and under claim of right," or at least some of these elements, as common law requirements for adverse possession. The burden of proof is usually placed on the alleged adverse possessor to establish that the possession has complied with all the necessary elements. From a strictly technical point of view, any possession that subjected the possessor to liability in ejectment during the limitations period should perhaps lead to a holding of adverse possession at the end of the period. Under that analysis, none of the elements mentioned should be required except as a means of requiring that the possession be real (i.e. actionable) or at least that the possession be such that it would have supported a claim of prior possession in an ejectment action by the possessor against subsequent intruders. In fact, in most cases, that is all that many of the elements do.

a.   *Open or Visible*

Usually, the requirement of open or visible possession is just another way of saying that there has to be real possession by a person in order to become an adverse possessor. The furtive possessor is really not a possessor at all. It is doubtful whether one could ever sustain a claim to have been a prior possessor in an ejectment action brought against a subsequent intruder by proof of nothing more than previous clandestine entries upon the land. A real possessor generally treats the property as a true owner would and leaves physical evidence of his possession. Thus, some cases state that the possession must be "appropriate" or that there must be permanent signs of the possession, such as a building or a fence.

b.   *Notorious*

"Notorious" is rarely mentioned separately from open, but it may serve a slightly different function.

There is no requirement that the owner actually know of the adverse possession, and the owner's ignorance does not extend the limitations period. The absence of such a requirement can be justified by the existence of notoriety as an element of adverse possession. If a possessor is using the property in a manner that all who are interested will know about it, the possessor has done all that can be expected. Often, the possessor mistakenly believes that he owns the property he is possessing. In that case, he can hardly be expected to notify an owner of whom he has never heard. Instead, the owner is obliged to check the property periodically.

Illustration: Paul lives in a house on Lot 1, which he believes he owns. However, Olga actually owns Lot 1. Everyone in the neighborhood knows that Paul lives on Lot 1, but Olga resides elsewhere and does not know. Paul will own the property after the statutory period has run, because Olga should have checked on her property. Paul had no duty to inform her of his possession.

Illustration: Paul's house encroaches onto Olga's property, but Olga does not realize it. Paul can acquire title to the encroachment area even though Olga does not have the property surveyed until the limitations period has expired.

(1) Subjacent Possession

A person may adversely possess property underneath another's land (i.e. below the surface or subsurface) even though the owner cannot see it. The possession is open and notorious where it is occurring. Although the owner does not know that the adverse possession is taking place below the surface of his or her land, this is basically no different from the situation in which an owner does not realize that a neighbor's building is encroaching over the lot line.

Illustration: Paul operates a cave (or a coal mine) that tunnels under Olga's property. Paul makes no secret about his activities. The fact that Olga does not realize that the tunnel runs under her property is irrelevant, and Paul may gain title to the cave under Olga's property by adverse possession.

c. Actual and Constructive Possession

"Actual" possession as a requirement of adverse possession means no more than real possession. Its main function is as a counterpoint to constructive possession. Constructive possession is the absence of real possession. By itself, constructive possession never ripens into title by adverse possession. Ejectment lies only against real possessors.

Illustration: For twenty years, Paul has claimed that he owns Olga's lot, but he has never actually set foot on it. No statute of limitations will run against Olga because she never had a cause of action against Paul for ejectment. She can bring ejectment only if Paul actually takes possession of her land. Claiming land is not the same as possessing it. Although Olga might have a quiet title action against Paul's claim, that is not a possessory action.

(1) Constructive Possession and Color of Title

An adverse possessor can acquire title to more property than was actually adversely possessed if (1) she actually adversely possessed part of that property, (2) she entered onto that part based on a deed giving color of title to a larger parcel, and (3) the larger parcel included the property actually possessed.

Illustration: Paul has a deed to a five acre parcel. However, the deed was defective and did not actually convey title to him. Paul enters onto the parcel and lives on one acre but does not use the other four acres. At the end of ten years, Paul will acquire title by adverse possession to all five acres. The boundaries in Paul's deed effectively serve as a substitute for a fence built by Paul, which probably would have made Paul an actual possessor of the five acres. Some states require that Paul have a good faith belief in his deed's validity for this doctrine to operate. Other states require that the deed be recorded in the public land records before it constitutes color of title.

(2) Constructive Possession and Prior Possession

The same enlargement of area conferred by color of title protects a prior possessor from subsequent intruders. Thus, a person actually possesses only one acre under color of title to five acres should be able to eject subsequent intruders from any of the five acres.

(3) Limitations on Constructive Possession

The doctrine does not apply when (1) the portion of the property that is only constructively possessed is separately owned, (2) the part actually possessed is not being adversely possessed, or (3) the color of title does not describe the property in dispute.

Illustration: Paul has a void deed to Lots 1 and 2, which are in fact owned by Olga and Owen respectively. Paul enters and occupies only Lot 1. Paul will never acquire title to Lot 2 by adverse possession, because Owen has never had a cause of action in ejectment against Paul.

Illustration: Paul has a deed to Lots 1 and 2. The deed is valid to convey title to Lot 1 but not to Lot 2 because Paul's grantor owned only Lot 1. Paul actually possessed only Lot 1. Paul cannot claim title to Lot 2 by adverse possession because he has not adversely possessed it. His possession of Lot 1 was not adverse, because he really owned it, and he never possessed Lot 2.

Illustration: Paul has a deed to Lot 1 but mistakenly entered onto Lot 2 and possessed only part of it. Paul cannot claim constructive possession of any other part of Lot 2. Because his deed describes only Lot 1, it affords no color of title to Lot 2. Paul can acquire title by adverse possession only to that part of Lot 2 that he actually occupied. Whether the deed is valid or invalid as to Lot 1 is irrelevant, because Lot 2 is in question. The same result occurs for cases in which Paul claims strips of land outside the boundaries of the parcel described in his deed.

(4) Conflicting Constructive Possessions

Real title also provides constructive possession without the need for any actual possession. Thus, an absentee owner can eject wrongful possessors because his or her title provides constructive possession, which has been breached by the trespassers. Sometimes the constructive possession claims of various parties may conflict. The resolutions of these conflicts are demonstrated in the following illustrations.

Illustration: Olga is absent from her forty acre parcel. Paul enters under a color of title to all forty acres, but he actually possesses only one acre. Paul will acquire all forty acres by adverse possession because his constructive possession of thirty-nine acres, coupled with his actual possession of the one acre, prevails over Olga's constructive possession.

Illustration: Olga is actually occupying only one of her forty acres. Paul enters under a color of title to the forty acres but actually possesses only one acre. The acre he actually possesses is different than the acre Olga possesses. Paul will acquire title by adverse possession to only one acre because his claim of constructive possession to the other thirty-nine acres is defeated by Olga's constructive possession of thirty-eight of them plus her actual possession of one acre. Olga's claim of constructive possession, supported by both title and some actual possession, is superior to Paul's claim, which is supported only by some actual possession.

Illustration: Olga is absent from her forty acres. Paul enters under a color of title to all forty acres but actually possesses only one acre. Subsequently, Rachel enters the same forty acres under a color of title to all forty acres but actually possesses only one different acre. Paul now can acquire title by adverse possession to only thirty-nine acres (the one acre he actually possesses and the thirty-eight acres no one else actually possesses). He cannot acquire title to the acre Rachel actually possesses, because her actual possession defeats his claim to constructive possession of it. If Rachel remains long enough, she can acquire title by adverse possession to the one acre she actually possesses, but she cannot claim constructive possession of the rest because Paul's claim of constructive possession, being prior in time, is superior to hers.

d. *Color of Title*

In the context of adverse possession, "color of title" refers to a document that purports to convey actual title but fails to do so. A typical example is a void deed. If the deed is valid, the grantee acquires real title and may claim rights as the owner. Because the adverse possessor is always someone who does not own the property, any deed by which he or she claims title is by definition void. Possession of a void deed, however, may have important consequences, discussed in the following sections.

(1) Color of Title as an Absolute Requirement of Adverse Possession

In a few states, title cannot be acquired by adverse possession except under color of title. An adverse possessor of property who has no document supporting the possession gets nothing.

(2) Color of Title as Affecting the Acts Required

In a few states, color of title enables an ordinary use of the property to qualify as an adverse possession, whereas more significant possessory acts, such as fencing or cultivating, are necessary if there is no color of title.

(3) Color of Title as Affecting the Time Period

In a few states, a possessor with color of title needs fewer years of possession to become an adverse possessor than does a possessor without color of title.

(4) Color of Title and Hostility

In some states, a possessor with color of title is presumed to be hostile to the owner, whereas independent proof of hostility is otherwise needed.

e. *Continuous and Uninterrupted*

In the context of adverse possession, these words have no constant meaning, are often used interchangeably, and are sometimes entirely devoid of content, signifying no more than real possession. "Continuous" does not mean constant. There is no requirement that the possessor possess every minute of the day. Many successful adverse possessors have merely made a seasonal use of the land, such as grazing or hunting. In these situations, "continuous" means only that the activity is carried on regularly (i.e. the grazer must graze every year during the grazing season). If the acts are too irregular, they will be viewed as a series of unconnected trespasses not amounting to a dispossession of the owner. Also, a possessor who abandoned the property (i.e. with no intent to return) and then returned did not continuously possess the property, and the statute of limitations starts anew from his reentry.

The most common meaning of "uninterrupted" is that no one other than the possessor has possessed the land during the statutory period without the possessor's consent.

Illustration: Rachel intruded onto Paul's possession after he had been on the land for nine years, and she remained for a year. Paul cannot claim adverse possession under a ten-year statute because his possession was interrupted after nine years. This result also can be explained by saying that Paul's possession was not exclusive for ten years or by saying that Paul was not in actual possession for ten years.

Illustration: Paul possessed for five years and then was ousted by Rachel. As the prior possessor, Paul brought a successful ejectment action against Rachel and was restored to possession one year after his initial dispossession. He has been in possession the second time for three years. Most authorities agree that Paul should not have to start all over again, which would mean seven more years under a ten-year statute. However, they do not agree whether Paul can include the time Rachel was in possession. If Paul can include Rachel's year, he needs to possess for only one more year. If he cannot, he needs two more years. The result depends on whether Olga's cause of action against Paul is viewed as continuing to run during the year that Rachel had possession.

(1) Interruptions by the Owner

A successful ejectment action, followed by an execution of the judgment, interrupts an adverse possession by revesting possession in the owner. A successful judgment relates back to the date of filing the complaint, so that the action need merely be filed in time. But a complaint that is not followed up in court will not interrupt an adverse possession.

Any act by the owner that constitutes a resumption of possession is an interruption. But a furtive entry, an accidental entry, or an entry based on the possessor's consent does not constitute an interruption because it is not a possessory act. To interrupt another's possession, the owner actually must become a posses-

sor by committing acts that would entitle the possessor to bring ejectment if the acts were committed by
someone other than the owner.

Illustration: Paul's deed conveyed Lot 1, but he mistakenly possessed Lot 2. Olga, who owns Lot 2, possessed Lot 3
under a similar mistake. During the statutory time period,
Olga frequently visited Paul on Lot 2 and even slept over
occasionally. None of these acts by Olga interrupted Paul's
possession, because they all occurred with and as a result of
Paul's permission.

f. Exclusive

"Exclusive" does not mean that no one other than
the possessor is ever on the property. This term generally means that no one else is on the property without
the possessor's consent. It derives from the notion
that possession usually includes an intent to exclude
others. Consequently, an adverse possession which
fails for want of exclusivity is probably lacking other
requirements as well.

Illustration: During Paul's ten years on the property,
others frequently intruded and were not ousted by Paul.
Paul will not acquire title by adverse possession because his
possession was not exclusive. This result also can be explained by saying that Paul was not in actual possession,
because a "real" possessor does not tolerate intruders.

Illustration: During the past ten years, Paul has sometimes possessed the property exclusively. However, at other
times, he has brought friends with him or has leased the
property to third persons. Paul is an adverse possessor; the
other activities were all done with Paul's permission, which
enables Paul to count them as his own possessory acts.

g. *Hostile, Claim of Right, and Adverse*

Although these terms are used in almost every jurisdiction, a great deal of disagreement exists concerning
their meaning and significance. All courts agree that a
person who is possessing property with the owner's
permission is not adversely possessing. Under an objective view of adverse possession, lack of permission is
all that is required. Under a subjective view, however,
more is required.

(1) *The Subjective Standard*

An adverse possessor is someone who does not in
fact own the land he is possessing. Generally, he either
knows or does not know this fact. The subjective view
requires a person both to possess the property and to
have a certain state of mind throughout the time of
his possession. The courts requiring a mental element
do not agree as to which state of mind is the "correct"
one.

(a) *The Mentality of Thievery*

If the possessor knows that he does not own the
property, some jurisdictions hold that he cannot become an adverse possessor. In effect, he has a "claim
of wrong," rather than a "claim of right," or he is not
in "good faith" as some courts require an adverse
possessor to be. If he intends to stay only until he is
evicted by the owner, he lacks true hostility. This rule
is designed to keep squatters from acquiring title to
land.

(b) The Mentality of Mistake

On the other hand, if the possessor believes that he is the owner, some other states hold he cannot become an adverse possessor. The rationale is that one must "claim" the property. If the possessor testifies that he only intended to claim what he owned and would not have claimed the property if he had known the truth, his actual nonownership of it means that he did not claim it. In these states, only a "thief" can become an adverse possessor.

(2) The Objective Standard

Most states now hold that the possessor's state of mind is irrelevant. "Hostility" can defeat the claim only of a possessor who publicly disclaims during the time of possession any intent to acquire title by adverse possession. This result also could be based on the doctrine of estoppel.

(3) Permissive Possession

A tenant under a lease is not adverse to the landlord, because the lease voluntarily has transferred the possessory right from the landlord to the tenant. Nor is the possession of a cotenant adverse to the other cotenants, because each has a right to possess the entire property. Therefore, no cotenant is entitled to demand that the other not possess the property. In each of these cases, the possession is permissive; it does not give rise to a cause of action in ejectment.

Consequently, such possession never ripens into title by adverse possession, no matter how long continued.

(a) Ouster

A permissive possessor can become adverse to the owner if he repudiates the owner's title, asserts his own independent possessory right, and makes this claim known to the owner or is otherwise appropriately notorious about it. This constitutes an ouster of the owner, and generates a cause of action that will expire when the statute of limitations has run.

Illustration: Paul has been in possession for three years as a tenant under a lease from Olga. He has now told Olga that he will no longer pay rent to her, because he has learned that she is not the owner. Paul is wrong; Olga is in fact the owner. If Paul stops paying rent, he will be an adverse possessor. However, in computing his period of adverse possession, he cannot include his first three years, because those were years of permissive possession. Many states, however, have a special statute dealing with adverse possession by tenants.

Illustration: Paul and Olga are joint tenants, but Paul has been in sole possession for the past three years. Paul has now told Olga that he no longer will allow her to share in the ownership, profits, or possession of the property. Paul's possession will ripen into a full title after the limitations period expires, but the first three years cannot be counted.

(b) What Constitutes an Ouster

Any act that gives notice to the owner that the possessor no longer recognizes the owner's title to the property should serve as an ouster. In the case of cotenants, a refusal to permit the other cotenant to enter, a refusal to account for the profits, or sometimes merely a statement that the possessor regards himself as the sole owner can be sufficient. In the landlord-tenant context, a refusal to pay rent constitutes the clearest kind of ouster.

(4) Other Cases of Permissive Possession

A mortgagor's possession is not hostile to the mortgagee and does not become so until the mortgagor repudiates the mortgage or retains possession after his rights have been cut off by a foreclosure. A mortgagee in possession is not hostile to the mortgagor until the mortgagee refuses to account for the profits from the land.

A grantor under a valid deed who retains possession is usually not considered hostile to the grantee unless the deed is repudiated. But a grantee taking possession under a void deed is considered hostile to the grantor.

In general, possession by a family member is not deemed to be hostile to the rest of the family.

4. External Factors that Prolong the Statute of Limitations

a. Disabilities

Generally, the statute of limitations is tolled if a plaintiff is under some legal disability, such as infancy, mental impairment, imprisonment, or military service when the cause of action arises. This is also true in adverse possession cases. Either the entire statutory period or some shorter period is allotted to the owner for suit after the disability ends. Further refinements of this principle are shown in the following illustrations, all of which assume a ten-year statute of limitations that is entirely suspended during the disability.

Illustration: Paul wrongfully took possession in 1980, while Olga was mentally impaired. Olga recovered her mental health in 1983. Paul did not gain title by adverse possession until 1993, ten years after Olga's disability ended.

Illustration: Paul wrongfully took possession in 1980, when Olga was twelve years old and mentally impaired. The age of majority is eighteen. Olga recovered her mental health in 1983. However, Paul could not acquire title by adverse possession until 1996, which is ten years after Olga reached majority. If Olga remained mentally impaired until she was twenty years old (1988), Paul would have to wait until 1998. Whenever two disabilities exist when the adverse possession begins, both must be eliminated before the limitations period begins to run.

Illustration: Paul wrongfully took possession in 1980, and Olga was imprisoned in 1983. Paul acquired title in 1990, because subsequently occurring disabilities generally have no effect on the running of the statute.

Illustration: Paul wrongfully took possession in 1980, and Olga died in 1983, leaving a fifteen-year old daughter, Diana, as her heir. Paul acquired title in 1990. Diana's infancy was not a disability of the person who had the cause of action when it first accrued. However, some statutes refer to the time when "the adverse possession commences or the title first descends." These statutes can be interpreted as giving Diana up to ten years after she reaches majority (1996). But even in states with this type of statute, courts often reach a contrary result by disregarding the daughter's disability.

b. Future Interests

Generally, the holder of a future interest in property is not entitled to bring ejectment against a wrongful possessor because the future interest gives no present possessory right. Therefore, it is also generally held that the statute of limitations does not begin to run against the future interest holder until that interest becomes possessory.

Illustration: In 1979, Olga died, leaving land to her husband for life and thereafter to her daughter. In 1980, Paul entered. In 1990, assuming Olga's husband was still alive, Paul gained only a life estate from his adverse possession (measured by the husband's life). Paul does not acquire the entire fee by adverse possession until he is there for at least ten years after the death of Olga's husband, which is when her daughter acquires her own cause of action against him.

Illustration: Olga rented her property to Tom for a twenty year term, ending in 2000. Paul entered in 1985. In 1995, Paul became a successful adverse possessor against Tom, but that only gave Paul the balance of Tom's term. For Paul to become a successful adverse possessor against Olga, he must possess for ten years after her reversion becomes possessory at the lease's termination.

Illustration: Paul entered Olga's property in 1985. In 1990, Olga leased the property to Tom for fifteen years. In 1995, Paul gained the fee title by adverse possession. Because the adverse possession began before the lease, Olga could lease only adversely possessed land. The same would be true if Olga had conveyed the property to Tom after Paul had entered. She is only transferring to Tom her cause of action against Paul, and the time Paul needs to perfect his title by adverse possession is not thereby extended.

c. *Effect of Adverse Possession on Nonpossessory Interests*

Easements and restrictive covenants held by third parties are not automatically extinguished by adverse possession of the property. Those claims are not dependent on the owner's title and, therefore, do not fail merely because that title fails. They also are not necessarily affected by the acts of adverse possession on the property. But, if during the period of possession, the possessor has interfered with the rights of the easement and covenant holders, thereby creating causes of action for them, their interests also will be extinguished based on the running of the statute of limitations on their independent claims.

Illustration: Paul adversely possesses Olga's property by, among other acts, fencing it off. One effect of this fence is to block off a right of way that Olga formerly had granted to Sam. If Sam fails to sue Paul to recover access, he will lose his easement over the property. But if Paul's possessory acts do not interfere with Sam's easement, the title Paul acquires by adverse possession will be subject to Sam's easement.

Illustration: Olga owns property subject to a restrictive covenant that limits any building to two stories. Paul adversely possesses the land but never builds a building over two stories. At the end of the limitations period, Paul will have title by adverse possession, but it will be subject to the covenant because the beneficiaries of the covenant have never had a cause of action against Paul for breach.

5. Consequences of Having Been an Adverse Possessor

When all the requirements for adverse possession are met, two significant changes occur in the adverse possessor's status. On one hand, he is no longer liable in ejectment or trespass for his former possession; the statute of limitations eliminates yesterday's, as well as last year's, liability. On the other hand, he acquires an original title to the property by virtue of no longer being subject to ejectment by the former owner.

Thereafter, whether he knows it or not, the adverse possessor has title. From then on, he is freed not only from liability for his previous possession, but also from the earlier requirements of adverse possession, such as exclusive and continuous possession. The property is his, and he may do with it as he pleases. He may find it necessary to obtain a quiet title decree to have a marketable title (i.e. one that he can force a contract purchaser to accept), but the decree itself only confirms the title he already has acquired. That title arose at the moment that the former owner lost the right to bring ejectment.

Illustration: Paul possessed for the requisite number of years. Thereafter, Paul failed to pay the property taxes. Even if payment of taxes is a requirement of adverse possession in the jurisdiction, Paul will prevail against Olga. Possession plus taxes during the limitations period made Paul the owner, and failure to pay them thereafter does not transfer title back to Olga.

CHAPTER TWO

COMMON LAW ESTATES
I. PRESENT (POSSESSORY) ESTATES IN LAND

A. KINDS OF ESTATES

Under the common law system, a person is regarded as holding or owning an estate in land, rather than land itself. Such estates are classified according to duration. The estates described in this Chapter are the only ones that are legally recognized in our common law system.

1. Fee Simple

This estate comprises the greatest ownership interest in property recognized by the law. Today, we would call it absolute ownership. The owner can dispose of the land as he or she pleases, and it will descend to the owner's heir at death or according to the terms of the owner's will.

2. Fee Tail

This estate passes from generation to generation of the family line and does not end until the family line ends. It passes only to each holder's children and cannot be inherited by collateral heirs, such as the holder's siblings. By statute in most states, this estate has been abolished or substantially modified.

3. Life Estate

This estate's duration is measured by the length of a specified person(s)'s life. It lasts as long as the measuring life continues.

4. Estate for Years (also known as Tenancy for a Term)

This estate lasts for a specified period, from 999 years or more down to a single day. Technically, it is not inheritable, but upon the death of the owner of the estate, it passes by will or by intestate succession.

5. Periodic Estate (also known as Tenancy from Period to Period)

This estate lasts for a certain term, and, unless seasonably terminated before the end of the term, repeats for another like term. The term may be for any length of time, such as a year, a month, or a week or less.

6. Tenancy at Will and Tenancy at Sufferance

The tenancy at will and the tenancy at sufferance are also sometimes called estates in land, but their significance is so slight that they will not be discussed here; they are covered, along with the other tenancies, in the Landlord and Tenant Chapter (Chapter 4, p. 133 & 134).

B. FREEHOLD v. NONFREEHOLD ESTATES—SEISIN

The fee simple, fee tail, and life estate are called freehold estates; the tenancy for years and the periodic tenancy are nonfreehold estates. The time for termination of freehold estates cannot be precisely determined in advance because death (with or without heirs) is always the terminating event. In contrast, nonfreehold estates terminate on or before an ascertainable date.

The need for distinguishing between freehold and nonfreehold estates derived from the common law concept of seisin. The holder of a freehold estate had seisin (i.e. was seised of the land), whereas the holder of a nonfreehold estate had possession but not seisin. In England, all land titles came from the monarch, either directly to the possessor or by way of intermediate lords. The holder of a freehold estate owed certain services to the overlord, somewhat equivalent to modern rent or property taxes.

C. CREATION OF ESTATES (CREATING WORDS)

1. Fee Simple—"To Bob and his Heirs"

At common law, the only language that could create a fee simple was a grant to the transferee "and his heirs." "And his heirs" was the grantor's way of indicating that the estate was inheritable by the grantee's heirs. However, this language does not directly give anything to the heirs. They do not share the estate with the transferee and have no interest of their own from this conveyance. The words "and his heirs" are "words of limitation," which designate the estate as being inheritable, rather than "words of purchase," which designate the taker. Today, the requirement of such special words of limitation to create fee simple has been abolished in virtually every jurisdiction and has been replaced by a statutory presumption in favor of the fee simple estate.

2. Fee Tail—"To Bob and the Heirs of his Body"

Like the fee simple, the fee tail is inheritable because of the words of limitation "and the heirs of his body." However, it is inheritable only by lineal descendants and not by collateral heirs. To create a fee tail, the conveyance must use words of indefinite succession, such as "heirs of the body" or "issue of the body." Any limitation on these technical terms of art causes them to become words of definite succession. Therefore, a conveyance "to Bob and the heirs of his body who are alive when he dies" cannot create a fee tail because the words "who are alive when he dies" limit the technical term "heirs of his body." Similarly, courts normally construe "and the heirs of his body share and share alike" as language of definite succession. Therefore, this language cannot create a fee tail.

a. Special Forms of Fee Tail

The fee tail may be a fee tail general, as described above, or it may be a fee tail special: "To Al and the heirs of his body and the body of his wife Jane." The fee tail special is limited to the lineal descendants of a specific man and woman. There may also be a fee tail male: "To Al and the male heirs of his body" or a fee tail female. It is also possible to convey a fee tail special male or female.

b. The Earlier Fee Simple Conditional

Before 1285, a conveyance to a person and the heirs of his body created a fee simple conditional. The fee simple conditional would become a fee simple as soon as the transferee had a child who was born alive. Since this result did not conform to what grantors intended, the Statute De Donis Conditionalibus (1285) declared that a conveyance to a person and the heirs of his body created an estate descendible only to his issue and that the birth of a child did not enlarge the estate into a fee simple. This became the fee tail. If the grantee conveyed this estate to another, then upon his death either his issue (if there were issue) or the original grantor (if there were no issue) could recover the estate. Today, three states still characterize a conveyance to a person and the heirs of his body as creating a fee simple conditional.

c. Disentailing Conveyances—The Common Recovery and the Fine

At early common law, certain collusive lawsuits, known as common recovery and fine, made it possible for the holder of a fee tail estate to enlarge it into a fee simple despite the Statute De Donis. Today, most states either do not recognize the fee tail estate, preserve it for one generation only, or provide a means by which its holder can convert it into fee simple.

3. Life Estate—"To Bob for his Life"

At early common law, a conveyance of a freehold estate that did not include the words "and heirs" or "and heirs of the body" was deemed to convey only a life estate. Today, one or two states still may follow this rule of construction. In virtually every jurisdiction today, though, an intent to convey only a life estate must be clear in order to overcome the modern presumption in favor of the fee simple. Therefore, a life estate is created by words such as "to Bob for his life." However, a life estate also is created if the estate necessarily will terminate when the measuring life dies. Therefore, "to Bob for so long as he farms the land" also creates a type of life estate (it is a defeasible life estate, as described on p. 56). A voluntarily created life estate is a "conventional" life estate, as distinguished from a legal life estate.

a. Life Estate Pur Autre Vie—"To Bob for the life of Cathy"

The life estate pur autre vie is measured by the life of someone other than the life estate holder. It can be created by its express terms ("to Bob for the life of Cathy") or when a life tenant who is the measuring life conveys the life estate to someone else. At early common law, when the holder of a life estate pur autre vie died before the person who is the measuring life, no person was eligible to hold the estate; the estate was not inheritable by the holder's heirs, and the future interest holder had to wait until the measuring life died. Therefore, the land was open to the first person who occupied it, known as a general occupant. Today, a life estate pur autre vie can be conveyed at death by will or by intestate succession.

b.   *Legal Life Estate*

In contrast to a conventional life estate, a legal life estate is created by operation of law.

(1) *Fee Tail Special with Possibility of Issue Extinct*

The language "to Bob and the heirs of his body and the body of his wife Jane" gives Bob a life estate once Jane dies without issue, because no possibility exists that this estate will continue after Bob's death.

(2) *Marital Estates*

The spouse of the person seised of an interest in land may have dower or curtesy in the estate upon the death of the other. See p. 104–108. Dower and curtesy could create a life estate in the surviving spouse by operation of law.

4.   Estate for Years—"To Bob for Ten Years"

There is no need to add "heirs" to the grant of an estate for years because it is a nonfreehold estate. It merely must specify beginning and ending dates. The estate for years passes at the death of its owner by will or by intestate succession.

5. Estate from Period to Period—"To Bob from Month to Month" or "To Bob for $10 per Month"

To create an estate from period to period (also known as a periodic estate), the conveyance either can state that the term is periodic or can state a periodic rent without specifying a termination date. The length of the period is usually the period for which rent is stated. Therefore, the language "to Bob for $10 per month" will create a term from month to month. Other forms of periodic estates are covered in the Landlord and Tenant Chapter. See Chapter 4.

D. THE QUALITY OF ESTATES—ABSOLUTE OR UNQUALIFIED

All the estates described so far differ "quantitatively," i.e. according to their duration and the events that lead to their natural termination. A fee title can last indefinitely, the life estate naturally ends when the measuring life expires, and the nonfreehold estates end when the designated time interval passes. However, all these estates can expire sooner if the grant specifies that they are subject to some other condition or limitation. When and if that condition occurs, the estate will terminate even though the condition occurs before the event that would cause the estate to terminate naturally. An estate that is subject to a condition is called a "qualified," "base," or "defeasible" estate, while an estate that is not subject to a condition (other than the condition that naturally terminates it based on the nature of the estate) is called an "absolute," "unqualified," or "indefeasible" estate. If an estate is a qualified estate, it is "determinable," "subject to a condition subsequent," or "subject to executory limitation." To distinguish among them, focus on two features: (1) When the qualified estate was created, did the grantor retain the future interest following it or convey it to someone else? and (2) What words are used to connect the condition to the words conveying the estate?

1. Determinable Estate (also called the Estate Subject to Special Limitation)

The determinable estate can be created only when the grantor retains the future interest. It uses words of time, such as "so long as," "until," and "during," to attach the condition to the grant. This estate lasts only as long as the condition described in it continues to exist. Once the condition occurs, the estate automatically ends.

Illustration: "To Bob and his heirs so long as the land is farmed." This creates a fee simple determinable. The moment the land is no longer farmed, the estate ends.

Illustration: "To Barb and the heirs of her body so long as the land is farmed." This creates a fee tail determinable. The estate ends when the land is no longer farmed or when there are no lineal heirs, whichever occurs first.

Illustration: "To Bob for life so long as the land is farmed." Bob has a determinable life estate, which will end when he dies or stops farming, whichever occurs first.

Illustration: "To Barb for ten years so long as the land is farmed." Barb's determinable term for years will end in ten years unless Barb stops farming before then.

2. Estate Subject to Condition Subsequent

The estate subject to condition subsequent can be created only when the grantor retains the future interest. It uses words of condition, such as "upon condition that," "provided that," and "but if," to attach the condition to the grant. Like determinable estates, these estates can end when the condition occurs. However, termination is not automatic but is at the election of the owner of the future interest. For this reason, ambiguous language is construed as an estate subject to condition subsequent, rather than as a determinable estate.

Illustration: "To Bob and his heirs, but if the land is used for a farm, then the grantor may re-enter and repossess." This creates a fee simple subject to a condition subsequent.

Illustration: "To Barb and the heirs of her body, but if the land is used for a farm, then the grantor may re-enter and repossess." This creates a fee tail subject to a condition subsequent.

Illustration: "To Bob for life, but if the land is used for a farm, then the grantor may re-enter and repossess." This creates a life estate subject to condition subsequent.

Illustration: "To Barb for ten years, but if the land is used for a farm, then the grantor may re-enter and repossess." This creates a term for years subject to condition subsequent.

Illustration: "To Bob and his heirs, for so long as the land is used for a farm, but if he violates this condition, the grantor can re-enter and repossess." This grant uses both the language for a determinable fee simple and for a fee simple subject to condition subsequent. To reduce the possibility that Bob will lose his title to the land, a court will construe it as the latter.

II. FUTURE INTERESTS

Every estate in land is either present (entitling its owner to immediate possession of the land) or future (potentially entitling its owner to possession in the future). There are five future interests: (1) reversion, (2) possibility of reverter, (3) power of termination (also known as right of re-entry), (4) remainder, and (5) executory interest. To begin the process of distinguishing among them, look to the document that created the future interest. If the grantor retained the future interest, it must be a reversion, possibility of reverter, or power of termination. If the document that created the future interest conveys it to a grantee, it must be a remainder or executory interest.

A. REVERSION

If the owner of land grants a present estate (or estates) legally smaller than the estate he had, i.e. one which will not endure as long as his own estate, he has a reversion to make up the difference.

Illustration: Ann, holding in fee simple, conveyed "to Bob and the heirs of his body." The fee tail conveyed to Bob is legally smaller than the fee simple Ann had. Therefore, Ann now has a reversion in fee simple. When there is a failure of lineal descendants in Bob's line, the land will return to Ann or her heirs or devisees and will be held by them in fee simple.

Illustration: Ann, holding in fee simple, conveyed "to Bob for life." Ann has a reversion in fee simple, which will give her or her heirs or devisees the land when Bob dies and his life estate ends.

Illustration: Ann, holding a fee tail, conveyed "to Bob for life." Ann has a reversion in fee tail. When Bob dies, the land will revert to Ann, but Ann will hold only a fee tail because that is all she ever held. Someone else holds the future interest following Ann's fee tail to make up the rest of the fee simple.

Illustration: Ann, holding a life estate for her own life, conveyed "to Bob for Bob's life." Bob's life estate will end when either Ann or he dies because Ann cannot grant an estate greater than for her own life. Bob's estate is smaller than Ann's because either one of two deaths will end Bob's estate, whereas Ann's estate is affected only by her death. Therefore, Ann has a reversion in a life estate that will allow her to recover her original life estate when Bob dies, if Bob dies first. Ann's reversion will last only for the rest of her life, however. Someone else holds the future interest following Ann's life estate.

Illustration: Ann, holding a fee or a life estate, conveyed "to Bob for ten years." Today, it is generally said that Ann has a reversion (either in fee or for life) after Bob's term of years. However, it was earlier said that Ann held a fee (or life estate) subject to a term of years. Ann's interest was not characterized as reversionary because, as the owner of a nonfreehold estate, seisin had not passed to Bob.

1. Creating Words

No words are necessary to create a reversion in the grantor. He has a reversion simply because he has not given away his entire estate, but only an estate smaller than what he had.

Illustration: Ann, holding in fee simple, conveyed to "Bob for life, then to Cathy for life, then to Don and the heirs of his body." Ann has a reversion, because the two life estates and the fee tail do not add up to a fee simple (no number of lesser estates ever add up to a fee simple).

2. Reversion as an Interest only in the Grantor

A reversion is always an interest left in the grantor. If such an interest is created in someone else, it will have a different name. However, if the grantor conveys the reversion to someone else, it still is called a reversion.

Illustration: Ann, holding in fee simple, conveyed "to Bob for life." When Ann died, her will left all her real property to Cathy. While Bob is alive, Cathy's future interest in the land is a reversion.

3. Other Future Interests in the Grantor that are not Reversions

The reversion arises when the grantor creates in the grantee estates which are legally smaller than his own original estate. Determinable estates and estates subject to condition subsequent are not "smaller" than absolute estates of the same rank, and so there is no reversion in the grantor. Rather he has a different sort of future interest depending on what sort of qualified estate he has given away.

B. POSSIBILITY OF REVERTER AND POWER OF TERMINATION

If the grantor conveys a determinable estate, he retains a possibility of reverter, i.e. a possibility that the estate will come back to him or to his heirs or devisees if the limitation occurs. The determinable estate and the possibility of reverter always travel together. A possibility of reverter always follows a determinable estate, and a determinable estate is always followed by a possibility of reverter.

Illustration: Ann, holding in fee simple, conveyed "to Bob and his heirs so long as the land is used as a farm." Bob has a fee simple determinable, and Ann has a possibility of reverter. Ann or her heirs or devisees will get the land back automatically if and when the land is no longer used as a farm.

Illustration: Ann, holding in fee simple, conveyed "to Bob for life so long as the land is used as a farm." Bob has a determinable life estate. Ann has both a reversion because her fee simple is larger than Bob's life estate and a possibility of reverter because the land may revert to her before Bob dies.

If a grantor conveys an estate subject to condition subsequent, he retains a power of termination, which is the power to declare that the grantee's estate is forfeited because of the breach of condition. The estate subject to condition subsequent and the power of termination always travel together. You can't have one without the other.

Illustration: Ann, holding in fee simple, conveyed "to Bob and his heirs, but if liquor is ever sold on the land, the grantor may re-enter and repossess." Bob has a fee simple subject to condition subsequent, and Ann has a power of termination.

Illustration: Ann, holding in fee simple, conveyed "to Bob for life, but if liquor is ever sold on the land, the grantor may re-enter and repossess." Bob has a life estate subject to condition subsequent. Ann has both a reversion and a power of termination.

The possibility of reverter automatically gives the grantor or his heirs or devisees the estate when the limitation ends (or occurs), whereas the power of termination merely gives the option to terminate the previous estate. The holder of a power of termination may elect not to exercise it when entitled to and thereby waive it. Until the power of termination is exercised, the grantee continues with his estate.

A grantor may have either a possibility of reverter or a power of termination after a nonfreehold, as well as a freehold, estate. Therefore, a conveyance "to Bob for ten years so long as he farms the land" creates a determinable term for years. Similarly, a conveyance "to Bob for ten years, but if he sells liquor on the land, the grantor may re-enter and repossess" creates a term for years subject to condition subsequent.

C. REMAINDER

When the deed or other conveyance creates a future interest and conveys it to someone other than the grantor, the future interest must be either a remainder or an executory interest. Remainders are discussed in this section of the book. Executory interests are discussed beginning at p. 85.

Whenever the grantor would have retained a reversion because he conveyed a smaller estate than he owned, he may create a future interest in another person, comparable in size to or smaller than his reversion. Such a future interest in the third person is called a remainder. It can be a remainder in fee simple, in fee tail, or in a life estate, depending on what the grantor had and what he conveyed. There are four types of remainder: (1) contingent remainder, (2) vested remainder subject to total divestment (also known as a vested remainder subject to condition subsequent), (3) vested remainder subject to partial divestment (also known as a vested remainder subject to open), and (4) indefeasibly vested remainder.

In the following illustrations, assume that Ann, the grantor, began with a fee simple.

Illustration: "To Bob and the heirs of his body, and then to Cathy and her heirs." Without the gift to Cathy, Ann would have a reversion in fee simple after Bob's legally smaller fee tail. When instead she creates this future interest in Cathy, Cathy has a remainder in fee simple.

Illustration: "To Bob for life, and then to Cathy and her heirs." Bob has a life estate, and Cathy has a remainder in fee simple.

Illustration: "To Bob for life, and then to Cathy and the heirs of her body." Bob has a life estate. Cathy has a remainder in fee tail. Ann has a reversion in fee simple, because the combined interests of Bob and Cathy do not equal the fee simple that Ann originally had.

Illustration: "To Bob for life, and then to Cathy and the heirs of her body, and then to Don and his heirs." Bob has a life estate, Cathy has a remainder in fee tail, and Don has a remainder in fee simple. Ann has no reversion, because there is nothing left—the entire fee simple has been given.

Illustration: "To Bob for life, and then to Cathy for life, and then to Don and his heirs." Bob has a life estate, Cathy has a remainder in a life estate, and Don has a remainder in fee simple. Ann has nothing left.

Illustration: "To Bob for ten years and then to Cathy and her heirs." Bob has a term for years, and Cathy has a remainder in fee simple after a term for years. Alternatively, it could be said that Cathy has fee simple absolute subject to a term of years, because seisin is in Cathy, rather than in Bob.

1. What is not a Remainder

A remainder exists only where the same interest would have been a reversion if the grantor had not created it in someone else. Thus, there is no remainder after a determinable estate or after an estate subject to condition subsequent. In these cases, the grantor would not have a reversion, but would have a possibility of reverter or a power of termination, respectively.

Illustration: "To Bob and his heirs so long as the land is used for a farm, and then to Cathy and her heirs." Cathy does not have a remainder, because the equivalent interest in the grantor would be a possibility of reverter, not a reversion. Because Cathy's interest is not a remainder, it must be an executory interest because that is the only other type of future interest that is originally held by someone other than the grantor.

Illustration: "To Bob and his heirs, but if liquor is ever sold on the land, then Cathy and her heirs may enter and repossess the land." Cathy does not have a remainder, because this would be a power of termination in the grantor, rather than a reversion. Therefore, Cathy has an executory interest.

2. Remainder v. Power of Termination

Like a reversion, a remainder does not become possessory until the prior estate naturally ends, such as by the death of the life tenant or the failure of the line of tenants in tail. Because the remainder does not become possessory before the prior estate naturally ends, it is unlike the power of termination.

D. CONTINGENT REMAINDER

A remainder is contingent when: (1) the remainder holder (the person holding the remainder) is either unborn or unascertained, (2) some condition precedent (other than the termination of the prior estate) must occur before the remainder holder is entitled to take an interest in the land, or (3) both.

Illustration: "To Bob for life, remainder to those of his children who survive him." Bob's children have a contingent remainder because it is unknown which of them will survive him. Therefore, the remainder holders are unascertained. Survival also may be viewed as a condition precedent to the child acquiring an interest in the land.

Illustration: "To Bob for life, remainder to Cathy's heirs." No living person has heirs. Thus, so long as Cathy is alive, the remainder is contingent because her heirs are unascertainable. A gift to the widow or widower of a living person is similarly contingent.

Illustration: "To Bob for life, and then to Cathy and her heirs if she has reached the age of 21 before Bob dies." Cathy's remainder is contingent by virtue of this condition precedent of her reaching 21 before Bob dies. Once she reaches 21 before Bob's death, she will have satisfied the condition. Therefore, her future interest will no longer be a contingent remainder.

Illustration: "To Bob for life, remainder to Cathy and her heirs if she is 21 when Bob dies, and if not then to Don and his heirs." Cathy has a contingent remainder and so does Don. The condition precedent for Don is Cathy's not becoming 21 before Bob dies. These are "alternative" contingent remainders because the same condition applies to both.

Illustration: "To Bob for life, and then to Cathy for life." Cathy's remainder is not contingent, because there is no condition precedent except the natural termination of Bob's estate. Of course, Cathy will never take possession if she dies first, but throughout her life she will have had this remainder, which merely ended with her death in the same way that Bob's estate ended with his death. Surviving long enough to take possession of a life estate is an inherent feature of a life estate, rather than a separate condition on the estate.

Illustration: "To Bob for life, remainder to Cathy for life if she is 21 when Bob dies, remainder to Don and his heirs." Cathy has a contingent remainder in a life estate. It is contingent because of the condition precedent that she become 21 in time. Don's remainder in fee simple is not contingent because it is not subject to any condition.

E. VESTED REMAINDER

If a remainder is not conveyed to an unborn or unascertained person and if there is no condition precedent on the interest, other than termination of the prior estates, it is a vested remainder. As described above, there are three different types of vested remainders.

Illustration: "To Bob for life, then to Cathy and her heirs." If Cathy is alive, she has a vested remainder. She is ascertained, and the interest is not subject to a condition precedent.

Illustration: "To Bob for life, then to Cathy for life." As stated before, this remainder is not contingent. Survival is not a condition precedent for it. It is merely another way of referring to termination of the prior estate. Cathy's vested remainder in a life estate ends at her death, the same as a possessory life estate ends at the life tenant's death. The remainder is vested in interest even though it may never become vested in possession.

Illustration: "To Bob and the heirs of his body, and then to Cathy and her heirs." Cathy has a vested remainder in fee simple. It is uncertain whether or when Bob's line will run out, but the remainder is still vested because this condition is merely the termination of the prior estate.

1. Vested Remainder Subject to Total Divestment (also known as Subject to Condition Subsequent)

The fact that a remainder is vested does not mean that it can never be lost. It can be subject to divestment by operation of a condition subsequent. Normally, a condition subsequent is included in a separate clause following the words conveying the interest to the grantee. In contrast, a condition precedent (contingent remainder) is normally in the same clause as the language of conveyance or in a separate clause preceding it.

Illustration: "To Bob for life, remainder to Cathy and her heirs, but if Cathy ever sells liquor on the land, then Ann may re-enter and repossess." Cathy has a vested remainder in fee simple subject to divestment, i.e. subject to a condition subsequent, and Ann has a power of termination.

2. Vested Remainder Subject to Partial Divestment (also known as Subject to Open)

Partial divestment occurs when the holder of an estate is compelled to share it with others. Usually, this type of interest is created when a conveyance is to a class of people, rather than to a specifically identified person or persons.

Illustration: "To Bob for life, remainder to his children." Bob has one daughter. Since the child is ascertained and there is no condition precedent, she has a vested remainder in fee simple. But when and if other children are born to Bob, they will share the remainder in fee simple with her, thereby reducing her share. She has a vested remainder in fee simple subject to *partial* divestment.

3. Indefeasibly Vested Remainder

If a vested remainder is not subject to a condition and is not held by a class that might expand, it is indefeasibly vested.

4. "Divestible" Contingent Remainders

Contingent remainders can be made subject to conditions that may subsequently defeat or dilute them in the same manner as occurs for vested remainders.

F. REVERSION FOLLOWING REMAINDER

If the last estate granted is a contingent remainder, the grantor retains a reversion in case the contingency fails. If a contingent remainder subsequently vests, the reversion is then divested. In a sense, the condition precedent for the contingent remainder is a condition subsequent for the reversion.

Illustration: "To Bob for life and then to Cathy if she is 21 when Bob dies." Bob has a life estate, Cathy has a contingent remainder if she is not yet 21, and the grantor has a reversion. If Cathy turns 21 while Bob is alive, her remainder vests, and the grantor's reversion is thereby divested.

III. TRANSFER OF ESTATES
A. METHODS OF TRANSFER

Because the holder of a freehold must be seised, seisin must have passed to him or her from the previously seised freehold owner. The ancient ceremony by which seisin passed—livery of seisin—involved the grantor and grantee going on or near the land and the grantor (feoffor) symbolically handing over some soil or other part of the land to the grantee (feoffee), thereby making livery of seisin to the grantee. This ceremony was called a feoffment, and it operated immediately to transfer seisin to the feoffee. No writing was needed.

When seisin was not involved, as in the case of an estate for years or other nonfreehold estate, a feoffment was not required. Therefore, a nonfreehold estate could be transferred without going on the land. Similarly, the transfer of a nonpossessory future interest was accomplished by grant or deed rather than by feoffment. Today, all interests usually are transferred by a deed or other written document.

Illustration: Bob, who has a remainder in fee simple, wishes to convey it to Cathy. He gives Cathy a deed of grant. Cathy now owns the remainder.

Illustration: Ann, who has a reversion in fee simple, wishes to convey it to Cathy. Ann gives Cathy a deed of grant. Cathy now has the reversion. This reversion does not become a remainder, because a remainder must be created originally in a third person. In this illustration, the future interest was created in the grantor and merely has been transferred to a third person.

1. Release Deeds

The word to describe the conveyance of a future interest by the person holding that interest to the person holding the prior possessory estate is "release." Thus, a reversioner or remainder holder "releases" the future interest to the holder of the presently possessory freehold estate.

2. Surrender Deeds

If the conveyance goes in the opposite direction, it is called a "surrender." For example, a life tenant "surrenders" the tenancy to the reversioner or remainder holder, as the case may be.

B. TRANSFERABILITY OF INTERESTS

Vested interests were generally transferable at common law. The holder of a possessory estate, a vested remainder, or a reversion could convey or devise it to whom he pleased. When a future interest was conveyed, the consent of the holder of the present possessory estate often was required (attornment). Partly because of their similarity to choses in action, nonvested future interests were initially not transferable or otherwise alienable at common law except to the owner of the possessory estate or to a vested remainder holder. Thus, a contingent remainder or power of termination could not be conveyed or devised. In the case of the power of termination, an attempted conveyance was not only ineffective, but also actually destroyed the power. Some states also prohibit a conveyance of a possibility of reverter.

C. INHERITABILITY OF INTERESTS

Any estate greater than a life estate was inheritable, even though it was contingent, unless the terms of the contingency made inheritability impossible (as where the contingency involved a timely marriage by that particular remainder holder). In the following illustrations, assume that Ann, the grantor, held in fee simple absolute.

Illustration: Ann conveyed "to Bob for life." Ann died, and then Bob died. On Bob's death, the estate reverts to Ann's heir or devisee. Ann's reversion descended to her heir or devisee. That person held it until it was ready to vest in possession and then took the possessory estate when Bob died.

Illustration: Ann conveyed "to Bob for life, remainder to Cathy and her heirs." Cathy died, and then Bob died. The estate now goes to Cathy's heir or devisee. The vested remainder passed to Cathy's heir or devisee at her death, and that person now takes possession of the fee simple estate because Bob's life estate has terminated.

Illustration: Ann conveyed "to Bob and the heirs of his body, then to Cathy and her heirs." Cathy died before Bob's line ran out. The estate will go to Cathy's heir or devisee whenever Bob's line ends, no matter how many generations are involved.

IV. RULES REGULATING COMMON LAW ESTATES

Note that the rules described in this section of the book are primarily of historical interest. However, even in jurisdictions where these rules have been invalidated, you need to know them when examining property records, such as deeds, that predate the invalidation.

A. SEISIN CAN NEVER BE IN ABEYANCE

Someone always must be seised of the land.

B. SEISIN PASSES OUT OF THE GRANTOR ONLY BY LIVERY

Seisin can sometimes go from one grantee (purchaser) to another without livery, but for it to come out of the grantor, livery of seisin is necessary.

C. NO SPRINGING INTERESTS (NO FREEHOLD TO COMMENCE IN THE FUTURE)

Because seisin can pass from a grantor to a grantee only by a livery, a grantor cannot give a grantee a freehold estate to begin at some future time unless it is supported by some present estate in a third person. Either the grantee gets the seisin by livery now, in which event he has a present rather than a future estate, or he must get seisin from the grantor at a later time, in which case the livery of seisin will have to be made then. Nothing can be done now in its stead.

Illustration: Ann conveys "to Bob and his heirs one year from now." Bob has nothing. Ann must have the seisin for this year or else it would be in abeyance. Bob can get seisin only if Ann makes a livery next year. If Bob did have an interest now, it would be because an estate were somehow allowed to "spring" out of Ann's estate next year. Thus, this rule preventing that result is called the rule against springing interests.

1. A Remainder Cannot Spring

Illustration: Ann conveys "to myself for life, and then to Bob and his heirs." The gift to Bob is invalid. As a remainder, it would have to spring, which is not allowed. For Bob to take, Ann must make livery of seisin to Bob, which cannot be done now because Ann wants a presently possessory life estate. Ann cannot make livery when her life estate terminates because she will be dead.

Illustration: Ann conveyed "to Bob for life, and one year later to Cathy and her heirs." The gift to Cathy fails. Bob received seisin, but upon his death it would revert to Ann because Cathy is not to be seised until a year later and seisin cannot be in abeyance. Seisin in Ann, the grantor, can be transferred to Cathy only by a livery, which clearly cannot be done now. If Cathy's remainder became possessory, it would have to spring out of Ann's reversion without a livery. But a remainder cannot spring, and so Cathy gets nothing.

2. A Remainder must be Created in the Same Document as the Estate Supporting It

The holder of a possessory estate is deemed to accept seisin for both herself and for any remainder holder. Therefore, when the first estate terminates, seisin goes directly to the remainder holder without reverting back to the grantor in between. However, for this theory to work, the remainder holder must be designated in the same instrument as the prior possessory estate.

Illustration: Ann conveyed "to Bob for life and then to Cathy and her heirs." Cathy's vested remainder in fee simple is valid. Seisin passed immediately from Ann to Bob, who holds it both for himself and for Cathy. When Bob dies, seisin will pass to Cathy from him. Because the grantor is no longer involved, seisin may pass at a later time without livery. The rule barring transfers of seisin without a livery refers only to transfers from the grantor. Bob is not a grantor in relation to Cathy.

Illustration: Ann conveyed "to Bob for life" in one document and "to Cathy and her heirs when Bob dies" in another document. Cathy's interest is invalid, because it would be a springing remainder. Bob cannot be said to hold seisin for Cathy, because she was not mentioned in the conveyance to Bob. So Cathy must get seisin from Ann, if from anyone. But that would involve a transfer of seisin from the grantor in the future without livery, which is impossible. To avoid this problem, Ann could have transferred her reversion to Cathy by deed of grant, which would make Cathy a reversioner, rather than a remainder holder.

a. Application to Nonfreeholds

The same principle applies to nonfreeholds.

Illustration: Ann conveys "to Bob for ten years, and then to Cathy and her heirs." Cathy has a valid estate. Livery of seisin can be made presently either directly to Cathy, because as a nonfreeholder Bob does not have seisin, or to Bob as Cathy's agent. In this case, characterizing Cathy's estate as a remainder in fee simple after Bob's term is permissible, but it was more descriptive and accurate at common law to say that Cathy had fee simple subject to Bob's term, thereby indicating that Cathy has seisin.

3. No Contingent Remainder after a Term of Years

Illustration: Ann conveys "to Bob for ten years, and then to Cathy's heirs." If Cathy is alive when the conveyance is made, the gift to her heirs fails because it is a gift of a contingent remainder (unascertained takers). An unascertained taker cannot be seised. Thus, seisin cannot be in Cathy's heirs. Nor can Bob hold seisin as agent for the heirs because they cannot hold seisin themselves. Bob also is unable to hold seisin for himself because he has a nonfreehold estate. Therefore, seisin remains in Ann. For Cathy's heirs to take, they would have to receive seisin from Ann even if they can be ascertained before Bob's death. The heirs would take by a springing remainder if they took. Therefore, "no contingent remainder can be supported by a term of years" is another way of saying "no springing remainders."

D. NO SHIFTING INTERESTS—NO CONDITION IN A STRANGER

Illustration: Ann conveyed "to Bob and his heirs, but if Bob ever sells liquor on the land, then to Cathy and her heirs." At early common law, Cathy's estate would fail, because she cannot get seisin. Bob cannot hold seisin for Cathy, because Cathy does not have a remainder. The holder of a present estate can accept seisin for himself and for his remainder holders because a remainder does not become possessory until the prior estate naturally terminates by the current holder's death. But in this case, Cathy's interest will cut off or cut short Bob's interest. Therefore, seisin cannot pass from Bob to Cathy. When Bob's estate ends, seisin therefore must revert to Ann. Were it then to go automatically to Cathy, it would be an impermissible springing interest. Thus, there can be "no condition in a stranger."

E. DESTRUCTIBILITY OF CONTINGENT REMAINDERS

At common law, a contingent remainder was destroyed if it did not vest on or before the time it becomes possessory.

Illustration: Ann conveyed "to Bob for life, remainder to Cathy's heirs." Bob dies before Cathy. The contingent remainder to Cathy's heirs is now destroyed because it could not vest when the prior estate terminated. This rule is a corollary of the rule against springing remainders. In this example, Bob had seisin during his life. If Cathy's heirs are ascertained before Bob's death (i.e. if their remainder becomes vested), then seisin can pass from Bob to Cathy's heirs upon Bob's death. But if no ascertained heir exists when Bob dies, seisin must return to Ann, because it cannot be in abeyance. To permit the seisin to then go from Ann to Cathy's heirs when Cathy died would permit a springing remainder, because it would spring out of Ann's reversion without livery from her.

Illustration: Ann conveyed "to Bob for life, then to Cathy and her heirs, if Cathy is then 21." If Bob dies before Cathy becomes 21, Cathy's contingent remainder is destroyed. Seisin goes back to Ann and will not later spring out to Cathy when she turns 21.

Illustration: Ann conveyed "to Bob for life, then to Cathy for life, then to Don and his heirs if Don is 21." Bob dies before Don is 21. Don's contingent remainder is still good, because it need not vest until it is ready to become possessory, i.e. when both Bob and Cathy have died. The same result would obtain if Cathy died before Don became 21, but Bob were still alive.

1. Reversions are not Subject to the Rule

Because reversions are vested interests, they are not destructible. In fact, a reversion following a contingent remainder always becomes possessory when the prior contingent remainder is destroyed.

Illustration: Ann conveyed "to Bob for life and then to Cathy and her heirs if Cathy is 21." Bob dies before Cathy is 21. Cathy's contingent remainder fails, and the property now goes to Ann by virtue of her reversion. Had Cathy been 21 before Bob died, she would have taken the fee simple estate, which would have had the effect of divesting (but not "destroying") Ann's reversion.

2. How Prior Estates Terminate

Contingent remainders are destroyed if they have not become vested remainders before the prior estates terminate whether those prior estates terminate naturally or prematurely.

3. Premature Termination of Estates—Merger

A life tenant may terminate his estate before his death by renunciation or by tortious conveyance (attempting to convey more than he has). Any contingent remainders that are not ready to vest at that time are destroyed.

Illustration: Ann conveyed "to Bob for life and then to Cathy and her heirs if Cathy is 21 before Bob dies, or to Don and his heirs if Cathy is not 21 before Bob dies." Cathy and Don have alternative contingent remainders in fee simple. But if Bob renounces his estate before he dies and before Cathy is 21, neither remainder will become possessory. Cathy cannot take because she is not 21, and Don cannot take because it is not certain that Cathy will not be 21 before Bob dies. Thus, both contingent remainders are destroyed, and the estate vests in Ann by virtue of her reversion. A reversion always follows alternative contingent remainders in fee simple.

A life estate also is destroyed when it merges into the next vested estate. Whenever the same person holds two consecutive vested estates, the lesser is "merged" into the greater and is destroyed.

4. Effect of Merger on Contingent Remainders

Because merger destroys the lesser present estate, any contingent remainders supported by that estate also will be destroyed unless they have previously vested.

Illustration: Ann conveyed "to Bob for life, remainder to his eldest child who survives him for life, then to Cathy and her heirs." Cathy transfers her remainder to Bob. This destroys the intervening contingent remainder in Bob's child. Cathy's transfer to Bob means that Bob has a life estate and the vested remainder in fee simple following it. These interests merge to form fee simple absolute, thereby destroying Bob's lesser life estate. Because the contingent remainder cannot vest until Bob dies, it is destroyed because it does not vest before the life estate was terminated by merger. Therefore, Bob has the fee simple absolute.

5. Exception to the Doctrine of Merger

Merger will not destroy contingent remainders when the two next vested estates are conveyed to the same person in the same instrument.

Illustration: Ann conveyed "to Bob for life, remainder to Bob's children who survive him for their lives, remainder to Bob and his heirs." Bob has a life estate and a vested remainder in fee simple. His children have a contingent remainder. But the contingent remainder is not destroyed by merger because Bob acquired both of his interests in the same instrument.

Illustration: Ann conveyed "to Bob for life, remainder to Bob and his heirs." Bob has fee simple absolute. Although both estates were given to him in the same instrument, there are no intervening contingent remainders. Therefore, merger applies.

6. Exception to the Exception

Although merger is barred by the simultaneous creation of the estates in a grantee, merger later can occur if the grantee conveys both estates to a third person, even if the grantee conveys both in the same instrument. This exception is important when the Rule in Shelley's Case applies (See p. 94–98).

V. EQUITABLE INTERESTS IN LAND—USES

Because seisin passed only by livery at common law, livery had to be made directly to the grantee or his agent or he would have no legally recognized interest in the land. But the court of equity recognized certain situations where a person owned the land even though seisin had never been transferred to him by livery.

A. EQUITABLE CONVEYANCES

Certain forms of conveyancing permitted courts of equity to treat a person as having a *use* (an equity) of the land, even though seisin was in someone else.

1. Conveyance for Use

Illustration: Ann conveyed by livery "to Bob and his heirs for the use of Cathy and her heirs." Bob is seised, but equity would regard Cathy as having the use of the land in fee simple, even though she does not have legal title. That is to say equity would compel Bob to put the land to Cathy's use. Today, this document would be construed as a conveyance to Bob in trust for Cathy.

2. Covenant to Stand Seised

Illustration: Ann covenanted "to stand seised to the use of my brother Bob and his heirs." Without livery, Bob does not have seisin. However, equity would give Bob the use in fee simple because a covenant was made and because Bob, the cestui que use (i.e. the beneficiary), is a relative.

3. Bargain and Sale Deed

Illustration: Ann gave a bargain and sale deed to Bob and his heirs. The deed recited a valuable consideration, which creates conclusive presumption. Without livery, Bob does not have seisin. But since consideration was given, Bob is the equitable owner and has a use in fee simple.

4. Resulting Use

Illustration: Ann conveyed by livery to Bob, but Bob gave no consideration. Bob has seisin, but equity creates a resulting use for Ann because of the absence of consideration.

B. USES COMPARED TO COMMON LAW ESTATES

Uses can be possessory or nonpossessory (future interests). They can be life estates, fee tails, fee simples, reversions, or vested or contingent remainders. All the legal rules relating to remainders apply to equitable remainders.

Illustration: Ann conveyed "to Bob and his heirs for the use of Cathy for life, and then for the use of Don and his heirs if Don survives Cathy, or if Don does not survive Cathy, then to the use of Eve and her heirs." Bob has the legal fee simple. Cathy has an equitable life estate. Don has an equitable contingent remainder in fee simple. Eve has an alternative equitable contingent remainder in fee simple. Because no vested remainder in fee simple has been given, Ann has an equitable reversion in fee simple and may take possession if both contingent remainders are destroyed. This is exactly the way the estate would look at common law without the uses.

C.   NEW EQUITABLE ESTATES (EXECUTORY INTERESTS)

Considerations of seisin prevented remainders from springing or shifting as a matter of law. But because seisin is in someone else when a use is involved, no reason exists in equity to bar springing and shifting uses. Therefore, equity recognized these interests, which were called executory interests (also known as executory limitations).

1.   Springing Use

A springing use springs out of the grantor's estate in the future.

Illustration: Ann bargains and sells "to Bob for life and one year after Bob's death to Cathy and her heirs." Cathy has a springing executory interest or springing use. This could not be a remainder, because a remainder is incapable of springing; it must take immediately upon termination of the prior estate. The interest here springs out of the reversion in the grantor. Therefore, Bob has a life estate, and Ann has a reversion in fee simple subject to Cathy's springing use. All these estates are equitable, because Ann has legal title.

Illustration: Ann bargains and sells "to Bob for ten years and then to Cathy's heirs." Cathy is alive. The gift to her heirs is an executory interest. It cannot be a remainder, because it would be a contingent remainder, which cannot be supported by a term of years (see p. 65–66). Therefore, Bob has a term for years, and Ann has fee simple subject to Bob's term and subject to a springing use in fee simple in Cathy's heirs. All these estates are equitable. Ann has legal title.

2. Shifting Use

A shifting use shifts ownership of an interest from one grantee to the grantee who holds the executory interest. When the shift occurs, the executory interest holder has "divested" the previous grantee.

Illustration: Ann bargains and sells "to Bob and his heirs, but if liquor is ever sold on the land, then to Cathy and her heirs." Cathy has a shifting executory interest because the use shifts the fee simple from one grantee, Bob, to another grantee, Cathy. Cathy's interest cannot be a remainder because it divests Bob's prior fee estate by cutting it short. Therefore, Bob has fee simple subject to shifting executory interest (sometimes called a fee simple subject to an executory limitation), and Cathy has a shifting executory interest in fee simple. Both estates are equitable. Ann has legal title.

Illustration: Ann bargains and sells "to Bob and his heirs so long as liquor is never sold on the land, then to Cathy and her heirs." Technically, Cathy's interest does not divest Bob's, but rather waits for it to terminate naturally. Nevertheless, it is an executory interest because a remainder cannot follow a fee simple estate.

Illustration: Ann bargains and sells "to Bob for life and then to Cathy and her heirs." Cathy has a remainder and not an executory interest. An executory interest exists only when a remainder cannot be created. A remainder always takes immediately after the natural termination of the prior estate and not sooner or later. In contrast, an executory interest always takes either before the prior estate naturally would terminate (shifting interest) or remotely after it terminates (springing interest). In this illustration, Cathy's interest becomes possessory immediately upon the natural termination of Bob's life estate, so it is a remainder, just as it would be if there had been a common law livery to Bob. Because there was no livery, however, it is an equitable remainder.

D. INDESTRUCTIBILITY OF USES

The doctrine of destructibility of contingent remainders was a corollary of the rule against springing remainders. But because uses can spring, executory interests are indestructible.

Illustration: Ann bargains and sells "to Bob for ten years and then to Cathy's heirs." The executory interest in Cathy's heirs is indestructible. Therefore, it will continue in existence even if Bob predeceases Cathy. Therefore, Bob has a term for years, Ann has a reversion in fee simple subject to springing use, and Cathy's heirs have a springing use. All these interests are equitable. Whenever Cathy dies, her heirs will get the equitable fee simple. If Cathy predeceases Bob, her heirs have fee simple subject to Bob's term. If Bob predeceases Cathy, Ann's reversion becomes possessory until Cathy dies.

Illustration: Ann bargains and sells "to Bob for life, and then to Cathy and her heirs if Cathy is 21." Bob dies before Cathy is 21. Cathy has nothing. The gift was an equitable contingent remainder and not an executory interest. Contingent remainders are destructible even in equity. This remainder was destroyed by its failure to vest in time. (Note that the great majority of jurisdictions have abolished the doctrine of destructibility of contingent remainders.)

E. STATUTE OF USES (1536)

The Statute of Uses provided in part: "Where any person be seised of lands to the use or trust of any other person, [then] such person that shall have the use or trust in fee simple, fee-tail, for term or life or for years, shall from henceforth be deemed in lawful seisin and possession in such like estates as [he] had in use [or] trust." In other words, the Statute "executed" uses by transferring seisin from the trustee to the cestui (beneficiary).

Illustration: Ann made livery "to Bob and his heirs for the use of Cathy and her heirs." By its terms, this conveyance gave seisin to Bob for the use of Cathy. Despite this language, the Statute executes the use and gives seisin to Cathy. Instead of Bob having legal fee simple and Cathy having equitable fee simple, Cathy has legal fee simple.

Illustration: Ann bargains and sells "to Bob and his heirs." Before the Statute, Ann retained the legal fee simple, and Bob had the equitable fee simple. Now, Bob has legal fee simple.

Illustration: Ann made livery "to Bob and his heirs for the use of Cathy for ten years." Cathy's equitable use for a term becomes a legal term for years. The Statute does not require that the cestui have a freehold. Ann has a resulting use for the "reversion" following the term unless Bob gave consideration. If Ann had a resulting use, the Statute would execute it and give her the legal fee simple subject to Cathy's term.

Illustration: Ann conveys "to Bob for ten years for the use of Cathy for ten years." The Statute does not apply because Bob is not seised to the use of Cathy. The trustee must have a freehold estate, even though the cestui need not.

1. Effect of the Statute on Future Interests

a. *Executory Interests*

After the Statute of Uses, springing and shifting uses became valid legal interests. However, the springing and shifting executory interests became legally valid only when they would have been a valid equitable use before the Statute.

Illustration: Ann bargains and sells "to Bob for life and, after one year, to Cathy and her heirs." As a result of the Statute, Bob has a legal life estate, Ann has a legal reversion subject to a springing executory interest, and Cathy has a springing executory interest in fee simple.

Illustration: Ann bargains and sells "to Bob and his heirs but if liquor is ever sold on the land, then to Cathy and her heirs." After the Statute, Bob has legal fee simple subject to shifting executory interest, and Cathy has a shifting executory interest in fee simple. Ann has nothing.

Illustration: Ann made livery "to Bob for life and, after one year, to Cathy and her heirs." Cathy's interest fails even after the Statute of Uses because it would have been a springing remainder at common law. This arrangement would work if done by a bargain and sale deed because the deed would create a valid equitable use, which the Statute then could execute into a valid legal executory interest. But here the livery created no equitable use, so there is nothing to execute, and the Statute has no effect. If an equitable conveyance created a valid use before the Statute, then after the Statute the same conveyance will create a valid legal interest. But if a legal conveyance was unable to create a valid future interest before the Statute, the same legal conveyance after the Statute is still ineffective.

b. *Contingent Remainders*

Contingent remainders are unaffected by the Statute. Therefore, they are still destructible in jurisdictions that apply the doctrine of destructibility.

Illustration: Ann bargains and sells "to Bob for life, and then to Cathy and her heirs if Cathy is 21." Bob dies before Cathy is 21. Cathy has nothing. Her equitable contingent remainder is executed by the Statute into a legal contingent remainder. But the Statute does not make it indestructible, because it is still a remainder and must abide by the rules of remainders.

c. Remainder or Executory Interest?

An executory interest exists only where a remainder is impossible. Therefore, whenever an interest is limited so that it can take effect as a remainder, it is a remainder, even though it also could take effect as an executory interest. This is the rule of *Puerefoy v. Rogers.*

Illustration: Ann bargains and sells "to Bob for life, and then to Cathy and her heirs if Cathy is 21." If Cathy becomes 21 after Bob dies, Cathy would take by way of executory interest. But if Cathy becomes 21 before Bob dies, she would take by way of remainder. Because the interest can operate as a remainder or as an executory interest, it will be treated as a remainder and not as an executory interest. Thus, it is destructible. If Cathy is not 21 before Bob dies, her interest fails under the doctrine of destructibility.

Illustration: Ann bargains and sells "to Bob for life, and then to his first daughter who becomes 21." This future interest can take effect either as a remainder (for the first daughter who is over 21 when Bob dies) or as an executory interest (where no daughter becomes 21 until after Bob dies). Therefore, the interest will be treated as a remainder; unless Bob has a daughter over 21 when he dies, the remainder will fail.

Illustration: Ann bargains and sells "to Bob for life, remainder to his first son over 21 at Bob's death, or if there is no son over 21 at Bob's death, then to the first son who becomes 21 after Bob's death when he reaches that age." Rather than making a gift of one interest that can take effect either as a remainder or as an executory interest, the grantor has separated it into two different interests. There is a gift of a remainder to any adult son and a gift of an executory interest to any minor son. Because the executory interest in this case cannot possibly take by way of remainder (a gift to a minor that will become possessory only when he reaches majority must be a springing interest), it is indestructible.

F. UNEXECUTED USES

The Statute of Uses does not transform every use into a legal estate. Some uses remain uses.

1. Active Trust

Whenever the person seised to the use of some beneficiary (cestui que use) is given any active duties regarding the land, the use is not executed. The grantee retains the legal title, just as the modern trustee does.

2. Use on a Use

Before the Statute of Uses, a use on a use (e.g., a conveyance "to Bob for the use of Cathy for the use of Don") was void. The use to Don was void because it was repugnant to Cathy's use. However, shortly after the Statute, the use on a use was declared to be valid and was treated as an unexecuted use. The first use was executed, so that the first cestui got the legal title. But the second cestui kept the equitable title because a second execution did not occur.

Illustration: Ann made livery "to Bob for the use of Cathy for the use of Don." The Statute executes the use to Cathy and gives her legal title. But it does not execute the use to Don. Therefore, Don has equitable title, and Cathy has legal title.

Illustration: Ann bargains and sells "to Bob for the use of Cathy." The bargain and sale gives Bob only a use. But the Statute executes it and gives Bob legal title. No second execution occurs. Therefore, Bob has legal title for the use of Cathy.

Illustration: Ann made livery "to Bob to his own use to the use of Cathy." The first use to Bob is executed but not the second use to Cathy. This is a *Doe v. Passingham* use.

Illustration: Ann made livery "to Bob and his heirs, for the use of Cathy for life, and then for the use of Don and his heirs." Both Cathy's and Don's uses are executed, and both have legal estates. Don has a use after a use, but not a use on a use, because Cathy's use is not for the use of Don.

3. Uses and Seisin

Whether a use is executed is important when ascertaining whether a holder has seisin, as in the case of dower. A widow has dower only in estates of which her husband was seised. On dower, see p. 104–106.

Illustration: Ann made livery "to Bob for the use of Carl and his heirs." Because the Statute gives Carl a legal estate and, therefore, seisin, Carl's widow will have dower.

Illustration: Ann made livery "to Bob for the use of Carl for the use of Don." Because Don's use is not executed, Don does not have seisin, and Don's widow will not have dower.

VI. RULE AGAINST PERPETUITIES
(1682)

A. THE RULE

"No interest is good unless it must vest, if at all, not later than 21 years after some life in being at the creation of the interest." This was the common law version of the Rule. The Rule invalidates certain future interests that vest too remotely. The Rule is concerned only with the remoteness of vesting and not with the duration of the interests once vested or with their alienability. Interests which vest too remotely are void and are stricken from the conveyance.

B. MEASURING THE TIME PERIOD

An interest has to vest within 21 years, plus actual periods of gestation, after some life in being. If there is any possibility that the interest might vest at a later time, the interest is void.

Illustration: Ann conveyed "to Bob for life, then to Bob's children who reach 25." The gift to the children is void, because it could vest more than 21 years after the termination of all lives presently in being, i.e. the grantor, Bob, and Bob's children now living. However, if the doctrine of destructibility of contingent remainders still applies in the jurisdiction where this gift occurs, the gift is valid, because Bob's children must be 25 by his death to take, and the possibility of taking long after his death no longer exists.

Illustration: Ann created an inter vivos trust "to my grandchildren when they reach 21." The gift is invalid. Ann may have additional children, and they cannot be used as measuring lives because they are not now lives in being. And those unborn children may have children of their own (Ann's grandchildren) who will not become 21 until more than 21 years after the settlor and all her presently existing children are dead.

C. INTERESTS THAT ARE SUBJECT TO THE RULE

1. Contingent Remainders are Subject to the Rule

Contingent remainders must vest within the perpetuities period or they are invalidated.

Illustration: Ann conveyed "to Bob for life, remainder to his children for their lives, and upon the death of the last of them, remainder to their children who are living at the time of Bob's death and their heirs." The gift to the grandchildren is a contingent remainder. It may not vest in possession within the perpetuities period, because Bob may have children in the future, whose grandchildren may be unable to take until more than 21 years after the death of all Bob's presently living children. However, the remainder will vest in interest within the perpetuities period. The contingent remainder will become a vested remainder when Bob dies, because the gift is limited to those who are living when Bob dies. The gift is valid.

Illustration: Ann conveyed "to Bob for life, remainder to his children for their lives, and upon the death of the last of them, remainder to their children and their heirs." The gift to Bob's grandchildren is invalid. The contingent remainder will not vest in interest until the last of Bob's children dies, which may be more than 21 years after the death of all lives in being now since Bob may have more children. It does not matter that Bob may now be eighty years old. The law conclusively presumes him to be capable of having more children (the "fertile octogenarian").

2. Executory Interests are Subject to the Rule

Executory interests are nonvested until they vest in possession. There is no such thing as a vested executory interest. If an executory interest divests a prior interest before it becomes possessory, it is no longer an executory interest but becomes the interest it divested.

Illustration: Ann conveyed "to Bob and his heirs, but if liquor is ever sold on the land, then to Cathy and her heirs." The gift to Cathy fails. This shifting executory interest may not become possessory until more than 21 years after the lives of Bob and Cathy.

Illustration: Ann conveyed "to Bob and his heirs once my will is probated." This springing executory interest to Bob fails, for it is possible (though unlikely) that it will take more than 21 years after the measuring lives to probate the will.

3. Vested Remainders Generally are not Subject to the Rule

Generally, the Rule does not apply to vested remainders because they are already vested. But a gift to a class of people is treated differently. Courts hold that the gift must vest in every member of the class in time.

Illustration: Ann conveyed "to Bob for life and then to all his children when they reach the age of 25." Bob has a son who is presently 25. The remainder is vested subject to open because that son already is able to take. But because Bob could have more children in the future who could reach 25 more than 21 years after the deaths of Bob and his living son, the entire gift fails as to all Bob's children.

4. Reversions are not Subject to the Rule

Reversions are always vested estates and, therefore, are not subject to the Rule. A reversion may not always become possessory, such as when it follows a contingent remainder and the contingency occurs in time. But it is a vested interest from the moment it is created.

5. Powers of Termination and Possibilities of Reverter are not Subject to the Rule

Powers of termination and possibilities of reverter are not subject to the Rule. Like a reversion, a power of termination is the portion of the estate remaining with the grantor after a conveyance of less than her entire interest in the land. Therefore, also like a reversion, it is vested from the moment of its creation.

In contrast, the power of termination is not a vested interest. However, because this interest was legally recognized for two centuries before the Rule was created, the Rule has not been extended to destroy powers of termination.

6. Other Interests Subject to the Rule

Options to purchase land and powers of appointment are subject to the Rule.

D. CONSEQUENCES OF VIOLATING THE RULE

If a gift violates the Rule, it is stricken, and the rest of the limitation stands as written, unless the grantor's intent is better served by reserving a future interest to her.

Illustration: Ann conveyed "to Bob and his heirs, but if liquor is ever sold on the land then to Cathy and her heirs." While the gift to Cathy fails, the gift to Bob remains valid. It is now a fee simple absolute, unless the grantor's intent was to keep the condition on the title even if the future interest for Cathy was invalidated. In that case, Bob would have a fee simple subject to condition subsequent, and Ann would have a power of termination.

E. MODERN REVISIONS TO THE RULE

Approximately half the jurisdictions have abandoned the common law version of the Rule and have replaced it with a less demanding version, either by statute or by court decision.

1. Wait and See

In some jurisdictions, the validity of a future interest is tested against the facts as they actually occur, rather than against the worst possible set of facts when the grant is made. In all the previous examples, the question in a wait and see jurisdiction is not whether the future interests described there *might* vest outside the measuring period, but whether they did under the actual facts of the case. Thus, the validity of an interest is determined later, rather than immediately.

Illustration: Ann conveyed "to Bob and his heirs, but if liquor is ever sold on the land then to Cathy and her heirs." If Bob sells liquor before he dies, Cathy's executory interest is valid. But if liquor is not sold until more than 21 years after both Bob and Cathy die, that executory interest (now held by Cathy's heirs or devisees) is invalidated.

2. Cy Pres

Another approach to modifying the Rule is to reform the grant to validate as much of it as possible to effectuate the grantor's intent to the greatest possible extent. This approach may be combined with the wait and see principle previously described.

Illustration: Using the same wording as in the prior illustration, a court may treat the grant as restricting liquor sales only during Bob's life, thereby saving much of the restriction.

VII. SPECIAL RULES FOR CONVEYANCES TO HEIRS

A. CONVEYANCES TO THE GRANTEE'S HEIRS—THE RULE IN SHELLEY'S CASE (1581)

If a freehold is given to a person and a remainder in fee simple or fee tail is given to the heirs of that person in the same document, the remainder to the heirs becomes a remainder to the ancestor. The rationale is that the word "heirs" in the document was intended to be a word of limitation rather than of purchase. (See p. 50–51 for the distinction between words of limitation and words of purchase.)

Illustration: Ann conveyed "to Bob for life, then to Bob's heirs." As written, this appears to give Bob a life estate and a remainder in fee simple to his heirs. But the Rule in

Shelley's Case dictates that both the life estate and the remainder are in Bob. The remainder is transferred from the heirs to the ancestor. So the gift becomes to Bob for life, remainder to Bob and his heirs.

Illustration: Ann conveyed "to Bob for life, then to Cathy for life, then to Bob's heirs." The Rule converts the remainder in the heirs into a remainder in the ancestor. The conveyance becomes "to Bob for life, remainder to Cathy for life, remainder to Bob and his heirs." The conveyance to the heirs need not follow directly after the conveyance to the ancestor; the conveyance can be "immediate" or "mediate."

Illustration: Ann conveyed "to Bob for life, remainder to Cathy's heirs." Bob then conveyed to Cathy. Cathy will have a life estate, and her heirs will have a remainder in fee simple. The Rule does not apply, because the conveyances to Cathy and to her heirs were in separate deeds, which destroys the presumption that the grantor intended "heirs" to be a word of limitation.

1. Consequences of the Rule

Once the Rule is applied to give the remainder to the ancestor instead of to the heir, other consequences usually follow.

a. *The Remainder Generally Becomes Vested Rather than Contingent*

A remainder to the heirs of a living person is contingent because the taker is unascertained. But once the remainder is put into the hands of the ancestor, who is ascertained, the remainder may be vested.

Illustration: Ann conveyed "to Bob for life, remainder to Bob's heirs." Before the Rule is applied, Bob has a life estate, and his heirs have a contingent remainder. Once the Rule gives the remainder to Bob, the remainder becomes a vested remainder because Bob is ascertained. Therefore, Bob now has a life estate and a vested remainder in fee simple.

Illustration: Ann conveyed "to Bob for life, and then if Bob marries Carol, to Bob's heirs." The Rule gives the remainder to Bob, but it remains a contingent remainder until Bob marries Carol, because their marriage is a condition precedent. Before the Rule was applied, the remainder was doubly contingent: it was given to unascertained persons and was dependent on a condition precedent. Switching it over to the ancestor only removed one contingency. Thus, Bob has a life estate and a contingent remainder in fee simple, and Ann has a reversion in fee simple.

b. Doctrine of Merger Applies

If the remainder becomes a vested remainder in the ancestor and no vested interests separate his two interests, they will merge.

Illustration: Ann conveyed "to Bob for life, remainder to Bob's heirs." The Rule transfers the remainder from Bob's heirs to Bob. Because Bob is ascertained and there is no condition precedent, it becomes a vested remainder. Because two consecutive vested estates are in one person, they merge. As a result, Bob has a present fee simple.

Illustration: Ann conveyed "to Bob for life, then to Cathy for life, then to Cathy's heirs." Bob has a present life estate. Cathy has a vested remainder in fee simple absolute. The Rule converts the contingent remainder in Cathy's heirs into a vested remainder in Cathy, and her two interests then merge. The ancestor's estate need not be possessory for the Rule in Shelley's Case or for merger to apply.

Illustration: Ann conveyed "to Bob for life, then to Cathy for life, then to Bob's heirs." Bob has a present life estate and a vested remainder in fee simple. Cathy's vested remainder in a life estate bars merger.

Illustration: Ann conveyed "to Bob for life, then if Cathy marries Don, to Cathy for life, then to Bob's heirs." Bob has a life estate, and the Rule gives him a vested remainder in fee simple. Since merger would destroy Cathy's contingent remainder, it does not apply, because the doctrine of destructibility of contingent remainders does not apply when the two estates to be merged are given simultaneously (the exact opposite of the requirement for the Rule in Shelley's Case to apply). See p. 76. But Bob can destroy Cathy's contingent remainder by conveying both his interests to a third person. See p. 79.

2.　Elements of the Rule

a.　*Both Estates Must be Legal or Both Equitable*

For the Rule to apply, both interests must be conveyed outright (legal) or both must be conveyed in trust (equitable).

Illustration: Ann conveyed "to Bob and his heirs in trust for Cathy for life, and then to Cathy's heirs upon her death." Cathy has an equitable life estate, and her heirs have a legal contingent remainder. The Rule in Shelley's Case does not apply because one estate is legal and the other is equitable.

b.　*The Rule is One of Law, Not of Construction*

Illustration: Ann conveyed "to Bob for life, remainder to his heirs. I intend by this to make a separate gift to the heirs." The Rule applies, giving the remainder to Bob, despite Ann's expressed intent.

c.　*The Grant Must use Words of Indefinite Succession*

The grant of the remainder must use a technical term, such as "heirs "or "heirs of the body," to refer to lineal descendants. Any words of limitation will cause the language to constitute words of definite succession.

Illustration: Ann conveyed "to Bob for life, remainder to his heirs if they have treated Bob, their father, kindly." The Rule does not apply. The grantor obviously meant children, rather than all lineal descendants, because of the reference to "father."

d. The Rule does not Apply to Executory Interests

Illustration: Ann conveyed by bargain and sale "to Bob, but if liquor is ever sold on the property, to Bob's heirs." The conveyance to the heirs is an executory interest. The Rule in Shelley's Case applies only to remainders.

Illustration: Ann conveyed by bargain and sale "to Bob for life and, one day after Bob's death, to his heirs." The heirs have a springing executory interest, so the Rule in Shelley's Case cannot apply. Bob has a life estate. Ann has a reversion in fee simple subject to a springing executory interest. Bob's heirs have an executory interest.

B. CONVEYANCES TO THE GRANTOR'S HEIRS—DOCTRINE OF WORTHIER TITLE

The Doctrine of Worthier Title invalidates a conveyance of a future interest to the grantor's heirs. This means that the grantor retains a reversionary interest of like size. The grantor's heirs will take (if at all) by descent, rather than by purchase, which gives them a "worthier title."

Illustration: Ann conveyed "to Bob for life, remainder to Ann's heirs." Bob has a life estate. By its terms, the conveyance appears to give a remainder to Ann's heirs. But the Doctrine of Worthier Title destroys the remainder and gives Ann a reversion in fee simple instead.

1. Elements of the Doctrine

a. *"Heirs" Must be Used in the Correct Sense*

Like the Rule in Shelley's Case, the Doctrine applies only when the reference to heirs is used in the technical sense of an indefinite line of succession, rather than to mean children or the first generation of takers.

b. *The Doctrine does not Apply to Accidental Heirs*

The Doctrine does not apply to a conveyance to a named individual who turns out to be the grantor's heir.

c. *The Doctrine is not Limited to Remainders*

Illustration: Ann conveyed "to Bob and his heirs so long as the land is used for a farm, and then to my heirs." The possibility of reverter remains in the grantor and is not given to the heirs. The Doctrine of Worthier Title differs in this respect from the Rule in Shelley's Case.

d. *The Doctrine Usually is a Rule of Construction*

At common law, the Doctrine was a rule of law. Today, however, it generally is treated as a rule of construction, unlike the Rule in Shelley's Case.

2. Companion Rule

A devise to a person of an interest of the same quantity as she would have taken by descent if the testator had died intestate is void, and the devisee takes by descent rather than by devise.

VIII. RESTRAINTS ON ALIENATION

Special rules deal with the validity of a provision that purports to limit the right of the holder of an estate to transfer it to other persons. The legal effectiveness of such a provision generally depends upon what type of restraint it is.

A. DISABLING RESTRAINTS

The terms of the grant expressly may deny the grantee the power to transfer the estate to anyone else or may declare that any attempted transfer is void. With the exception of spendthrift trusts (not covered in this book), such disabling provisions are always held to be void.

B. FORFEITURE RESTRAINTS

By its terms, the grant may be made determinable or subject to a condition subsequent and provide that any attempt to transfer title will terminate ownership. Courts often uphold this type of restraint if it is restricted as to duration or persons. Provisions giving the grantor the right to repurchase the property or to match a third person's offer before selling it (preemptive rights) are usually upheld.

Where an estate smaller than a fee simple is involved, a forfeiture restraint is more likely to be upheld. For example, a lease provision prohibiting the tenant from assigning or subletting the property without the landlord's consent is usually valid, as are similar restrictions on life estates, installment land contracts, and options.

C. PROMISSORY RESTRAINTS

The grant may include a covenant by the grantee not to alienate the property. Courts generally decide the validity of such promissory restraints according to the same principles as govern forfeiture restraints. Co-owners of property who covenant not to partition it often do so by way of mutual promises and may be entitled to have the covenants specifically enforced. However, judicial enforcement of racially restrictive covenants violates the Equal Protection Clause of the federal and state constitutions. Such clauses also violate federal, state, and local fair housing laws.

IX. WASTE

A. PARTIES

When title to land has been divided into a presently possessory interest and a future interest, the law of waste prevents the present possessor from causing undue harm to the property. The law of waste is designed to protect future interest holders against life tenants. It also protects landlords, nonpossessing co-owners, and, sometimes, mortgagees.

B. POLICY

The basic theory of waste law is that the future interest holder is entitled to receive the property in the same condition as when the future interest was created. Thus, waste is often defined as the commission of any act that alters the character of the property. Waste law may even prohibit "ameliorating" waste, i.e. changes that increase the land's value. More commonly today, however, waste is defined in terms of impairing the value of the future interest, on the assumption that the grantor intended to protect the future interest holder by limiting the present grantee's activities, rather than simply giving the future grantee only what is left after the present grantee's use.

Illustration: Owen leaves his house to his wife for life and then to his children and their heirs. Unless he explicitly indicated to the contrary, Owen's wife will be limited in her use of the property to ensure that the children receive the full economic benefit of the house. This means that Owen's wife may be prohibited from activities such as cutting and selling timber and removing minerals.

C. TYPES

1. Active Waste

This type of waste consists of affirmative acts done by the possessor that harm the property. It is also known as affirmative, voluntary, or commissive waste. *Per se* acts of waste at common law included cutting mature trees (except for cultivation, repairs, or fuel), changing the agricultural use of the land, opening new mines to remove minerals, and demolishing structures not erected by the occupant. These are all acts that destroy existing features of the property or exploit limited resources. Today, these acts usually are characterized as waste only when they cause economic harm. Where the acts are done willfully, they may constitute malicious or wanton waste, and liability may be trebled.

2. Passive Waste

This type of waste consists of the failure to make normal repairs to the property to prevent significant deterioration, such as keeping any building windtight and watertight. It is also known as permissive waste. It does not entail a duty to rebuild structures not destroyed by the occupant, although there may be a duty to protect them from further harm, such as boarding up a burned building. The failure to make hazard insurance, tax, or mortgage payments may be treated as a form of financial waste, because the consequences can be uncompensated damage to the property if uninsured or forfeiture of the title for nonpayment of taxes or the mortgage.

D. REMEDIES

Damages for waste equal the cost of restoration if the action is brought when the future interest holder takes possession or the reduction in the present market value of the future interest if brought before then. Equity may enjoin the commission of active waste or appoint a receiver to stop passive waste (a step also taken by tenant groups against landlords who will not make repairs).

X. COMMON LAW MARITAL ESTATES

Following a legally recognized marriage, each spouse may acquire a life estate in the lands of the other if certain further conditions are met. These are "legal" life estates, as distinguished from "conventional" life estates which are created by explicit deed or will language. The legal life estate is created by operation of law.

A. WIFE'S ESTATE—DOWER

Upon the death of her husband, a wife receives a life estate in one-third of certain lands owned by her husband during their marriage.

1. Conditions for Dower

a. Seisin

The husband must have been seised of the estate at some time during the marriage.

Illustration: Hubert is seised in fee simple of Blackacre. He conveys it to Xerxes and then marries Wilma. Wilma has no dower in Blackacre when Hubert dies because he was not seised during the marriage.

Illustration: Hubert is seised in fee simple of Blackacre and marries Wilma. He then conveys Blackacre to Xerxes. Wilma has dower in Blackacre because Hubert was seised during their marriage. Hubert need not be seised throughout the entire marriage or even at his death so long as he was seised sometime during the marriage.

Illustration: Hubert has a term for years in Blackacre and marries Wilma. He then conveys it to Xerxes. Wilma does not have dower because Hubert did not have seisin. A term for years is a nonfreehold estate.

Illustration: Hubert has a use in Blackacre, with title held by Xerxes. Wilma has no dower because an equitable owner is not seised, except when the Statute of Uses executes the use and gives seisin to the cestui que use. See p. 84.

Illustration: Hubert has a remainder in fee simple in Blackacre but dies before it becomes possessory. Wilma has no dower, because seisin was in the holder of the present possessory estate. It is irrelevant whether the remainder was vested or contingent.

Illustration: Hubert is trustee of a fee simple for the use of a cestui. Wilma has no dower, because Hubert has bare legal title only, which is not enough, even though he is seised.

b. Inheritability

The estate must be inheritable by the wife's issue in order for her to claim dower at her husband's death. The wife need not have issue in fact, so long as any such issue would qualify as heirs of the husband. Thus, an estate held in fee simple by the husband is subject to dower because any issue of the marriage would qualify as heirs of the husband, even if in fact the marriage produces no offspring.

An estate in fee tail is subject to dower even though death without issue would otherwise terminate the estate. In this case, the fee tail will not terminate until the widow dies, because her dower is viewed as an extension of the fee tail. If there are issue of the marriage, they do not take the wife's share until she dies, thereby terminating her dower interest. If the estate is fee tail special, excluding issue of the present wife, she cannot claim dower even though her husband dies with other issue capable of inheriting the estate.

There is no dower in a life estate measured by the husband's life, because this estate is not inheritable by her issue.

2. Extent of Dower

a. Before Husband's Death

Before her husband's death, a wife has no estate in his lands. At this point, her dower interest is called dower inchoate. This interest is protected by the courts against fraudulent transfers by her husband.

b. After Husband's Death

After her husband's death, dower gives the wife a life estate in one-third of the lands of which he was seised during their marriage. Usually, the husband's heir sets aside an appropriate share for her. If the wife is dissatisfied, she may go to court for judicial allocation.

B. HUSBAND'S ESTATE

Somewhat equivalent to the distinction between dower inchoate and dower, the nature of the husband's interest in his wife's estate depends on their stage of life.

1. Upon Marriage and Before the Birth of Issue—*Jure Uxoris*

At common law, a husband was given seisin in any land of which his wife was seised. His right was by *jure uxoris* (right of marriage). In effect, *jure uxoris* was a life estate measured by the husband's and wife's lives. It terminated upon the death of either unless it had been replaced by curtesy.

2.   Upon Birth of Issue Alive—Curtesy Initiate

Once a child was born alive (and if the wife did not die in childbirth), the husband's shared freehold (*jure uxoris*) was converted into a life estate in his own right in all his wife's freeholds. This life estate was measured only by his life. His previous smaller life estate (measured by the husband's and the wife's lives) merged into it. Curtesy initiate existed in all of the wife's freeholds that were inheritable by issue of the marriage. Unlike dower, curtesy initiate included the wife's equitable estates. Since a husband had a present life estate in his wife's lands, all that she could claim was a reversion, which would become possessory if she survived her husband.

3.   Upon the Wife's Death—Curtesy Consummate

Once his wife died, the husband's curtesy initiate became curtesy consummate. His right was not limited to one-third of her property as is true of dower. Instead, it applied to all property of which she was seised. Since he already was entitled to possession, there was no change in that regard. The issue born alive need not still be living at the wife's death.

C. MODERN STATUTORY
FORCED SHARE

Dower and curtesy have been replaced in virtually every jurisdiction by statutes that provide a share of the decedent's estate to the surviving spouse. The surviving spouse typically is given one-third or one-half of the decedent's estate even if the decedent intended to leave nothing to the survivor.

CHAPTER THREE

CONCURRENT OWNERSHIP
I. FORMS OF CONCURRENT OWNERSHIP

Although a life tenant and the future interest holder may be viewed as sharing ownership of the same property, their ownership is divided in time. At no one time do they share the same rights in the property. In contrast, concurrent owners own the same interests at the same time. There is no chronological separation in their ownership.

Our legal system recognizes only a limited number of ways in which two or more persons may share ownership of an interest in property. The basic forms of ownership now in use are joint tenancy, tenancy in common, and tenancy by the entirety. When you seen the word "cotenant," it may be referring generically to all three forms of concurrent ownership or just to a tenancy in common.

Coparcenary was an earlier form of concurrent ownership, which operated when female heirs took by descent, but it is today generally nonexistent. Tenancy in partnership is a form of concurrent ownership recognized by statute in some states, but it is generally covered in a Business Associations course, rather than in Property.

A. CHARACTERISTICS OF THE VARIOUS TYPES OF CONCURRENT TENANCIES

Joint tenancy and tenancy by the entirety require the existence of certain preconditions, called unities, only one of which is necessary to the existence of a tenancy in common.

1. Unity of Time

For two or more owners to be joint tenants or tenants by the entirety, each must have received its interest in the property at the same time. Tenancy in common does not require this unity of time.

Illustration: Owen conveyed to Ann and Bob. Depending on other factors, Ann and Bob may be joint tenants, tenants by the entirety, or tenants in common. There is unity of time, because Ann and Bob each became a grantee at the same time. This is not a requirement of tenancy in common, but its presence is not hostile to that estate.

Illustration: Owen conveyed an undivided half interest in Blackacre to Ann in 1971. In 1972, Owen conveyed the other undivided half interest to Bob. Ann and Bob can only be tenants in common. Since they took at different times, there is no unity of time.

Illustration: Ann conveys an undivided half interest in Blackacre to Bob, retaining the other half interest herself. Ann and Bob cannot be joint tenants or tenants by the entirety since there is no unity of time. Bob has acquired his interest only now, whereas Ann acquired her interest long ago.

2. Unity of Title

No joint tenancy or tenancy by the entirety can exist unless both owners receive title from the same source. Tenancy in common does not have this requirement.

Illustration: Ann conveyed an undivided half interest to Bob, retaining the other half herself. At common law, this could only be a tenancy in common. Not only is unity of time lacking, but also unity of title, because Bob's title came from Ann, and Ann's title came from her grantor. To avoid this result, Ann could convey her entire estate to a third person (a "dummy" or "straw person") who then conveys it back to Bob and her as joint tenants or as tenants by the entirety. In this way, the unities of time and title would be satisfied. Today, many jurisdictions permit an owner of property to convey to herself and another person as joint tenants without going through a third person.

Illustration: Owen conveyed undivided half interests to Ann and Bob in the same instrument. Bob conveyed his undivided half interest to Cathy. As between Ann and Cathy, only a tenancy in common is possible. Cathy's title came from Bob, while Ann's title came from Owen.

3. Unity of Interest

Joint tenancy and tenancy by the entirety require that each owner has an equal interest in the land. If one has a greater interest than another, only a tenancy in common exists.

Illustration: Owen conveyed an undivided one-third interest to Ann and an undivided two-thirds interest to Bob. Ann and Bob can only be tenants in common because there is no unity of interest.

4. Unity of Possession

Joint tenancy, tenancy by the entirety and tenancy in common all require that each tenant has an equal right to possess the whole of the property. This is the significance of the term "undivided ownership." If separate (divided) rights to geographic segments are given, there is separate ownership of different parts, rather than concurrent ownership. The parties are neighbors, not co-owners. If possession is given to one but postponed to others, there is a division of estates into possessory and future interests, rather than concurrent ownership, and again the rights are "divided."

Illustration: Owen conveyed to Xerxes for life and then in equal undivided shares to Ann and Bob. Ann and Bob may be tenants by the entirety, joint tenants, or tenants in common. Although neither has a present right to possess, their right to possess in the future is equal as between themselves. Xerxes is not a cotenant of any sort with Ann and Bob.

5. Unity of Person

The estate of tenancy by the entirety requires that the takers be legally married. There is unity of person between husband and wife at common law. Neither joint tenancy nor tenancy in common has this requirement.

B. PREFERENCES FOR ONE ESTATE OVER THE OTHER

At common law, a presumption existed in favor of the joint tenancy over the tenancy in common. This meant that if it were possible to construe a gift to two or more persons as a joint tenancy, rather than as a tenancy in common, it would be so construed. Today, the constructional preference is for tenancy in common over joint tenancy. To create a joint tenancy, it may be necessary for the deed to overcome this preference by stating "to * * * as joint tenants, and not as tenants in common, together with right of survivorship." (See the next paragraph for the right of survivorship). It also was the case at common law that an ambiguous gift to spouses was construed to create a tenancy by the entirety. Today, more than half the states have abolished this form of ownership. Where it still exists, some states have a constructional preference for it, whereas other states require a clear expression of intent to create it.

II. CONSEQUENCES OF DIFFERENT TYPES OF OWNERSHIP

A. SURVIVORSHIP

The chief and special aspect of joint tenancy and tenancy by the entirety is that of survivorship. When one cotenant dies, the surviving tenants acquire the decedent' s share as a matter of law. It is not a question of inheritance or descent because the surviving cotenants take the decedent's share even if they are not heirs of the decedent and even though decedent's heirs otherwise would take the entire estate. During the lives of the joint tenants or tenants by the entirety, each is viewed as owning the entire estate, subject only to the others' equal claims. When one cotenant dies, ownership is merely freed from one disability previously existing disability (the equal claim of the other). Thus, the survivors do not "inherit" the decedent's share, but merely continue their full ownership.

Tenants in common have separate, though undivided, interests in the property. Therefore, the interest of each is inheritable by his or her heirs or pass by the terms of any will. A surviving tenant in common takes the entire estate only when he or she qualifies as the heir of the deceased or is named in the will.

Illustration: Ann and Bob were joint tenants. Bob died. Wilma, his widow, was his only heir. However, Wilma takes no interest in the jointly owned property by descent. Ann takes all by survivorship. Any claim to dower by Wilma will be defeated, since this is not an estate inheritable by issue. See Chapter 2, p. 105–106. Ann is now the sole owner.

Illustration: Ann and Bob were joint tenants. Bob died. Wilma, his widow, was his only heir. Then Ann died without a will. Her son, Harry, was her only heir. Harry now owns the entire estate. Ann took all by survivorship, defeating any claims of Wilma. Upon Ann's death, Harry inherited her entire interest.

Illustration: Ann and Bob were joint tenants. Bob died, leaving a will that gave all his property to his wife, Wilma. Wilma does not take any interest in the jointly held property because Ann's right of survivorship prevails over Bob's will. If Bob had outlived Ann, Wilma would take the property pursuant to his will, because Bob would have become its sole owner when he survived Ann.

Illustration: Ann and Bob were tenants in common. Bob died. Wilma, his widow, was his only heir. On Bob's death, Wilma inherited his tenancy in common interest in the property and became a tenant in common with Ann. Ann's interest is unaffected by Bob's death. Because this is not joint tenancy, she does not take any part of Bob's interest by survivorship.

Illustration: Ann and Bob were tenants in common. Bob died, leaving a will giving all his property to his wife, Wilma. By virtue of the will, Bob's entire interest in the property passes to Wilma, making her a tenant in common with Ann.

Illustration: Ann, Bob, and Cathy were joint tenants. Cathy died, leaving a son, Jay, as her only heir. Jay takes nothing, because this is joint tenancy and the right of survivorship prevails over the rules of descent. Ann and Bob acquire Cathy's interest. Thus, the property becomes the joint tenancy property of Ann and Bob alone. They each hold an undivided one-half interest, rather than an undivided one-third interest in it.

B. SEVERANCE

A joint tenancy interest may be severed, which converts it into a tenancy in common interests. Severance occurs when a joint tenant conveys his or her interest to a third party, thereby eliminating the unity of time and title. The transferee holds an undivided interest in the property and concurrent ownership remains, but the parties become tenants in common with respect to the share that was severed.

Illustration: Ann and Bob were joint tenants. Bob conveyed his interest in the property to Cathy. Ann and Cathy are now tenants in common. There is no unity of time or title between them, since Cathy acquired her interest at a different time and from a different instrument than Ann. The joint tenancy has been severed, and a tenancy in common relationship now exists.

Illustration: Ann, Bob, and Cathy were joint tenants. Cathy conveyed her interest to Dora. The effect of the conveyance is to give Dora a one-third interest in the property as a tenant in common with Ann and Bob. But Ann and

Bob continue as joint tenants with regard to the two-thirds interest they still hold, although they stand as tenants in common to Dora. If Ann dies first, Bob will take her one-third interest by survivorship and Dora will be unaffected; Bob and Dora will then be tenants in common, with Bob owning two-thirds and Dora owning one-third. The same result will occur if Bob dies first, making Ann and Dora tenants in common. If Dora dies first, her heir will inherit her one-third, and Ann and Bob will be unaffected. When Ann or Bob dies, the survivor will then hold the two-thirds interest in common with the one-third interest held by Dora's heir.

1. Severance of Tenancy by the Entirety

A tenancy by the entirety is not severed by a conveyance by one of the tenants. No conveyance of such an estate is valid unless both spouses sign. A tenancy by the entirety ends when the cotenants divorce. In some states, the estate is converted into a joint tenancy; in others, it is converted into a tenancy in common.

2. Severance of Joint Tenancy

Any voluntary or involuntary conveyance by one joint tenant severs that tenant's interest from the joint tenancy. Generally, a contract to convey the property also severs by virtue of the doctrine of equitable conversion. (See Chapter 8, p. 281). In some states, a lease severs a joint tenancy. But in other states, the lease is not treated as severing the reversion. In states where a mortgage is viewed as conveying title to the mortgagee, the mortgage causes a severance. The same result is sometimes reached even in states where the mortgage gives the mortgagee only a lien on the property.

C. PARTITION

A partition is a physical division of the property, converting the former cotenants into neighbors. Instead of undivided ownership of the entire property, there is now divided ownership, with each cotenant owning a separate parcel. Thus, it differs from severance in that severance does not alter undivided ownership but merely eliminates the element of survivorship. The parties remain cotenants after a severance, whereas there is no cotenancy after a partition.

Partition may be physical, with each cotenant receiving a separate portion of the property (partition in kind). Partition in kind can occur by court action for partition, or by voluntary cross-conveyance among the cotenants. Where physical partition does not make sense or cannot be done equally, a court will order a sale of the entire parcel with a division of the sale proceeds between the parties (partition by sale).

Partition may be physical, with each cotenant receiving a separate portion of the property (partition in kind). Partition in kind can occur by court action for partition, or by voluntary cross-conveyance among the cotenants. Where physical partition does not make sense or cannot be done equally, a court will order a sale of the entire parcel with a division of the sale proceeds between the parties (partition by sale).

III. POSSESSION, PROFITS AND EXPENDITURES

The one unity shared by all forms of cotenancy is unity of possession. Each tenant has an equal right to possess the whole property, and none is entitled to exclude the others or to claim sole possession of any part. When one cotenant does "oust" the others, the excluded tenants may bring an action in ejectment to recover possession. If they don't assert their possessory rights, they risk losing title by adverse possession.

A. RENTS

1. Rents from the Possessing Cotenant

Since each cotenant is entitled to possess the whole property, the majority rule is that a tenant in sole possession is not liable to the nonpossessing cotenants for rent. The other cotenants, by staying out of possession, cannot compel the possessor to pay for what he or she has a right to do. The right of the nonpossessing cotenants is to share the possession, not to charge the other for his or her possession. However, if the possessor makes expenditures on the property and seeks contribution from the nonpossessors for them, the value of his possession may be allowed as an offset against the duty to contribute. Also a cotenant who ousts the other is liable for one-half the rental value in any ejectment action brought by the excluded cotenant to recover possession.

2. Rents and Profits from Third Parties

A cotenant is free to lease his or her possessory interest to strangers. A lease signed by one cotenant is as effective as a deed and conveys to the third person whatever possessory rights that cotenant has. There is no requirement that the other cotenant join in the execution of the lease. The lease entitles the tenant to take possession of the property, subject to the restriction that the other cotenant cannot be excluded from possession. For this reason, the common law originally provided that the leasing cotenant was entitled to retain all of the rent paid by the tenant. However, the Statute of Anne (1705) compels the possessing cotenant to share rents and profits received from a third person with the other cotenants. Not all states have followed this statute.

Illustration: Ann and Bob are tenants in common or joint tenants. Ann was in exclusive possession, farming the land herself, but recently she rented the farm to Cathy, for a rent of $1000 per year. Bob is entitled to $500 per year if the Statute of Anne is in force in the state. Otherwise, Ann is entitled to keep all the rent. Under the majority rule, Bob may not recover from Ann for the rental value of the property while she was in possession.

B. EXPENDITURES

1. Payment of the Purchase Price

Where the parties make unequal contributions toward the purchase price, a court may, on partition, award them correspondingly unequal shares of the property.

Illustration: Ann and Bob purchased property as tenants in common. Ann paid $20,000 of the price, and Bob paid $10,000. A court may determine that they intended that the property would be owned two-thirds by Ann and one-third by Bob.

Illustration: The same facts as above except that Ann and Bob took title as joint tenants. A court may now conclude that the taking of title in joint tenancy, with its attendant unity of interest, requires that the parties be treated as equal one-half owners. The excess contribution made by Ann would then be treated as a gift or loan to Bob.

2. Necessary Payments

Payments necessary for the preservation of the title, such as for property taxes and mortgage payments, are generally recoverable by the paying cotenant in an action for an accounting or in a partition suit. However, an action for contribution is available only if the nonpaying cotenant was personally liable for these expenses.

Illustration: Ann and Bob are cotenants and are both in possession of the property. Ann makes the entire payment of $500 for the annual property taxes. If the jurisdiction makes owners personally liable for property taxes, Ann can recover $250 from Bob by bringing an action for contribution. However, if the jurisdiction provides that the taxes are only a charge against the land and not against its owners, Ann does not have an action for contribution against Bob. However, in an action for an accounting for rents collected from the property or in a partition action, the court can offset the $250 from the amount that otherwise would be due to Bob. A court also may give Ann a lien on Bob's interest in the property if the action for contribution is unavailable to her.

Illustration: Ann and Bob are cotenants, but Ann is in sole possession. Ann makes the same property tax payment. In an action against Bob to recover half the payment, Bob may be permitted an offset for the value of Ann's sole possession.

3. Improvements

The cotenant who makes improvements to the property has an action for contribution against the other cotenants only if they agreed to be liable. There is no right of contribution for improvements, because the improver cannot force the cost of them onto an unwilling cotenant. For the same reason, the improver can claim them in an accounting for rents and profits collected from a third party only to the extent that they caused an increase in the rents. However, in a partition action, the improved part may be awarded to the improver or an increased share of the proceeds may be awarded to the improver to reflect the increase in the property's value that resulted from the improvement.

Illustration: On a two-acre tract that Ann and Bob own as cotenants, Ann built a house at her sole expense. In a partition by kind, Ann should be awarded the acre containing the house, and Bob should get the unimproved acre.

Illustration: Ann built a house at her sole expense, which added $20,000 to the value of the property. If the value of the land alone is $10,000, and there is a partition sale for $30,000, Ann should receive $25,000 of the proceeds, and Bob should receive $5,000.

4. Repairs

There is generally no right of contribution for repairs unless the nonrepairing cotenant agreed to be personally liable. It is considered to be too difficult to distinguish these from improvements. However, adjustments may be made in a partition or in an accounting action.

IV. COMMUNITY PROPERTY

Some jurisdictions have community property ownership, which is a form of co-ownership derived from the civil law system. In general, property may be held as community property only between parties who are legally married, although certain similar property rights may be held to exist between persons who believe themselves to be married, hold themselves out as married, or, sometimes, merely live together. "Marital" property is treated similarly under the Uniform Marital Property Act (1983), which has been adopted in at least one state. The Act treats all other property as "individual" property, which is the equivalent of "separate" property in community property jurisdictions.

Community property rights vary widely among the states that recognize them. Generally, however, "community property" includes everything the spouses acquire during their marriage. Wages earned by either spouse during the marriage are usually the most significant form of community income, together with income closely related to wages, such as pensions (saved wages) and personal injury awards (wage substitutes). Any asset acquired with such income also becomes a community asset.

"Separate property" includes property either spouse owned before the marriage, is not converted into community property by marriage. The income earned from separate assets, such as dividends from separately owned stock, is commonly treated as separate property, though not always.

Generally, gifts received by one spouse also are treated as his or her separate property. Property that the spouses acquire during the marriage but to which they take title as tenants in common or joint tenants is also separate property. However, some states have a presumption that family residences are presumed to be community property even if the title appears otherwise.

Separate property may be transmuted into community property, and vice versa, by agreement or gift between the spouses. Where parties have "commingled" separate and community funds, a court either will trace currently-held assets to their separate original sources or, if untraceable, will treat such assets as being entirely community property.

Illustration: Bob and Ann married and he moved into the house she owned. Thereafter, they both paid the mortgage from their salaries. The house was originally Ann's separate property and did not become community property because she married or because Bob moved in (unless it can be shown that she elected to make it a gift to Bob or to the community). But, after the marriage, community income (salary) was used to acquire the balance of the house. It does not matter whose salary was used, both salaries were community property. Therefore, the house is now either partly Ann's separate property (what she owned before the marriage) and partly community property or entirely community property if tracing cannot allocate the respective interests. Ann would have to show that Bob made a gift of all his interest in the community earnings to her to make the entire house her separate property. Bob would have to show that Ann made a gift of her separate interest in the house to him or to the community to claim a larger share of it.

Illustration: Before marrying Bob, Ann owned and managed an apartment building. After their marriage, she continued managing the building and used the rents from it to buy a car. The apartment building was and is Ann's separate property, and much of the rent it produced is therefore also her separate property. But to the degree the rental income is attributable to her management efforts, it is community income because it is earnings for her services. It also makes some part of the car community property, rather than her separate property.

Illustration: As a wedding present, Ann's parents purchased a house for Ann and Bob. If her parents had title placed in her name, it is probably her separate property notwithstanding the marriage because it was a gift. This would also be true if Bob paid for the house with money he inherited before the wedding and put title in Ann's name. However, if her parents put the title in both names, it would be community property unless the deed said "to Ann and Bob as joint tenants." In that case, both spouses would have separate property interests as joint tenants, unless residential joint tenancies are presumed by state law to be community property or the spouses had agreed it was community property notwithstanding the form of the title.

A. CHARACTERISTICS OF COMMUNITY OWNERSHIP

1. Management and Control

Originally, the husband had the sole power to manage and control the community property and could convey it without his wife's signature or consent. Today, however, spouses generally are given equal rights to management and control, and both may be required to join in the execution of any document affecting title.

Illustration: Ann and Bob, spouses, hold title to their house in joint tenancy. If this truly is a joint tenancy, either may convey his or her half interest without the knowledge or consent of the other. The grantee would be a tenant in common with the other spouse, because the joint tenancy is severed by the conveyance. But if the house is deemed to be community property, a deed executed by just one spouse cannot transfer any part of the title. The same may be true for mortgages executed b only one spouse.

2. Severance

Unlike joint tenancy property, community property cannot be severed, because neither spouse alone can convey any fractional interest in the property. Also unlike property held in joint tenancy or tenancy in common, community property cannot be partitioned by a court in an ordinary judicial proceeding. Instead, it is divided between the spouses in a marital dissolution proceeding. Depending on the jurisdiction's rule, distribution will be based either on fault (the old rule), "equitably," or equally.

3. Death Transfers

Each spouse has testamentary control over one-half the community property. If this power is not exercised, that half will pass to the surviving spouse. In this respect, community property resembles the right of survivorship in joint tenancy and tenancy be the entirety. But it resembles tenancy in common if a spouse dies testate, because the property will be distributed according to the terms of the will, rather than automatically going to the surviving spouse.

4. Liabilities

Community property cannot be seized to satisfy the separate debts of either spouse, such as debts incurred before the marriage. For those claims, a creditor must look solely to the separate property of the debtor spouse. Debts incurred by either spouse during the marriage may or may not entitle the creditor to reach community assets for satisfaction. The answer depends on whether the debt was a community debt, was acknowledged by both spouses, was for common necessaries, was based in contract or tort, and other factors relevant under local law.

V. CONDOMINIUMS

A condominium is not an ownership form different from those previously discussed, but it is a special combination of other forms. In a typical condominium project, for instance, each owner holds title in fee simple absolute to his or her individual "unit" and also holds title to the "common areas" of the project as a tenant in common with the other condominium owners. In a typical residential condominium, a unit is the equivalent of the apartment that its owner would occupy under a lease. The unit owned is generally the area encompassed by the interior walls. The walls themselves, the halls, plumbing, and other structural components of the building are common areas or elements owned by all unit owners as tenants in common.

If title to the common areas is held by a homeowners' or community association to which the individual owners belong, rather than in common by all the individual owners, the project is generally referred to as a "planned unit development" (PUD).

A. CONDOMINIUM OWNERSHIP

Condominium ownership gives exclusive right of possession over the unit owned and shared possessory rights to the common areas.

Illustration: Ann and Bob own different units in a condominium project. As the sole owner of Unit #101, Ann is entitled to exclusive possession of it, and she may exclude Bob from it or rent it to Tina. As co-owner of the hallway and the project swimming pool, Ann is entitled to use these facilities along with the other unit owners. She cannot exclude Bob from these areas. If the project includes a garage, both Ann and Bob may have exclusive easements for designated parking spaces.

B. CREATION OF A CONDOMINIUM PROJECT

No title starts out as a condominium. To create a condominium project, its owner must comply with the state's condominium enabling statute. This is generally done by recording: (1) a condominium declaration, which describes the units and the intended condominium arrangement; (2) a map of the entire project that includes vertical and horizontal dimensions; and (3) various supplementary documents regulating the operation of the condominium, such as the articles of incorporation and by-laws of the owners' association and the covenants, conditions, and restrictions applicable to the project. Thereafter, deeds are executed and delivered to purchasers who become owners of individual units, co-owners of the common areas, and members of the owners' association. The owners' titles are subject to the association rules and to the covenants and restrictions running with the land.

In most condominiums, management of the common areas is vested in a community or homeowners' association, composed of all unit owners in the project. The condominium documents generally address questions of membership and voting rights in the association, its rights and duties with respect to the common elements, and its power to levy assessments on individual units to maintain the common elements. These documents also often include restrictions on partition and provisions concerning partial and total destruction of the buildings.

C. TIME SHARING ARRANGEMENTS

Condominiums and other forms of co-ownership may be divided on a time-sharing basis, so that different parties have exclusive rights of possession at different times of the year. One method is to convey ownership to each purchaser during an annual recurring period for a term of years, together with an undivided fee in the remainder ("interval ownership"). Another method is to convey a tenancy in common interest to each purchaser, together with an exclusive right to possess the unit during a certain period of time each year ("time-span ownership").

Illustration: An interval ownership time-sharing deed would provide that the grantor conveys a designated unit and an interest in the common elements from January 1 to January 31, each year, until the year 2010, together with a remainder in fee simple absolute to the unit as a tenant in common with the other owners of the unit. A time-span deed would provide that the grantee takes an undivided interest in the entire project, together with the exclusive right to occupy a designated unit and the common areas during the specified use periods, and excepting from the grant the right to use at any other time of the year.

D. COOPERATIVES

In a cooperative, title to all the property is usually held by a corporation. An individual then purchases stock in the corporation and receives, along with the stock, a lease to an individual unit within the project, rather than fee title. In both a condominium and a cooperative, the members share the common expenses. Failure to make such payments may be treated as a form of financial waste, since the consequences can be uncompensated damage to the property (if uninsured) or forfeiture of the title (for nonpayment or taxes or the mortgage). Unlike condominium units, cooperatively held units often cannot be separately mortgaged and taxed because they are merely leased rather than owned outright.

CHAPTER FOUR

LANDLORD AND TENANT
I. TYPES AND CREATION OF TENANCIES

The owner of property may transfer an estate for a shorter time period to another person and retain the balance of the time for herself. In most commercial transactions, such a limited conveyance is done by lease, rather than by deed. The parties to the lease are the landlord and the tenant or the lessor and lessee. The tenant usually pays for his temporary right to possess the property in the form of "rent." In this section, "Lil" will be the landlord in the illustrations and will be referred to by feminine pronouns in the text. "Tom" will be the tenant and will be referred to with masculine pronouns in the text.

Illustration: Lil, who owns a building in fee simple, leases it to Tom for a period of five years. During the lease term, Tom has the exclusive right to possess the building and many of the other normal incidents of ownership. Unless the lease provides otherwise, he may decide what to do on the premises, such as whether to permit others to enter and whether to repair or improve it. At the end of the lease, possession and control of the building revert back to Lil. During the five year period, Lil has a reversion, or she may be regarded as having the fee title, subject to a five-year leasehold. In this case, Tom and Lil are not neighbors, as would result from a physical division of the building, nor cotenants, as would result from a division of present interests, nor dominant and servient tenants relating to an easement, as would result from a division of permitted uses on the property. The landlord-tenant relationship divides ownership differently than those other relationships.

Our legal system recognizes four different types of tenancies: (1) tenancy for a term, (2) periodic tenancy, (3) tenancy at will, and (4) tenancy at sufferance. The distinctions among them relate primarily to the methods of their creation and termination.

A. TENANCY FOR A TERM

A tenancy for a term (also known as a tenancy for years) is created when the landlord and tenant agree that the tenant will hold the property for a fixed period of time and for no longer. Despite its name, a tenancy for years can have a term of less than one year, such as one month. Whatever time period is specified, at the expiration of the lease term, the tenancy automatically terminates unless a new lease is executed. Depending on the jurisdiction, the Statute of Frauds may require any tenancy for a term to be in writing or only if the term exceeds a specified period, such as one year or three years.

B. PERIODIC TENANCY

The tenancy from period to period or periodic tenancy is created when the landlord and tenant agree that the tenant will pay a periodic rent, such as weekly, monthly, or annually, but do not specify a termination date for the tenancy. The tenancy automatically will renew for an additional period unless either party gives timely notice of an intent to terminate it. State law specifies how far in advance notice must be given. A periodic tenancy can be created expressly ("Lil and Tom hereby enter into a month to month tenancy.") or inadvertently.

1. Inadvertent Periodic Tenancies

Since a periodic tenancy requires only the payment of a regular rent without an agreement as to a termination date, this tenancy can be created by the parties' actions without an express agreement.

Illustration: Lil and Tom drafted a five-year lease that required annual rent payments. However, they did not sign the lease. Since the Statute of Frauds requires that such a lease be signed, it is invalid, and Tom does not have a fixed five-year term. But if Tom takes possession and pays Lil the annual rent, Tom has a periodic tenancy (from year to year).

Illustration: Lil and Tom executed a one-year lease that specified an annual rent. Tom took possession and paid the rent. He held over after the year ended and made another annual rent payment to Lil, which she accepted. Tom now may be a periodic tenant (from year to year) since there is a regular rent and no agreement as to a termination date. (On the nature of "holdover" tenancies, see p. 142–45).

2. Length of the Period

In most jurisdictions, the period is measured according to the interval for which rent is specified. Thus, a weekly rent creates a tenancy from week to week, a monthly rent creates a tenancy from month to month, and an annual rent creates a tenancy from year to year. The period can be based on how the rent is calculated (or estimated) rather than how it is paid. Thus, a stated rent of $1,200 per year, payable $100 per month, generally is held to create a tenancy from year to year, rather than month to month.

C. TENANCY AT WILL

This tenancy is created whenever a landowner permits another person to possess the property without any agreement between them as to a termination date or as to the payment of rent. In most states, as soon as the possessor begins to pay rent on a regular basis, the tenancy is converted into a periodic tenancy. However, a tenancy at will can be created expressly ("Lil grants Tom the right to possess at her will.").

1. Inadvertent Tenancies at Will

Since the essence of this estate is simply that the landlord has not objected to the tenant's possession, this estate may arise in a number of ways.

Illustration: Lil and Tom prepared a five-year lease but did not sign it, as required by the Statute of Frauds. If Tom takes possession, he is a tenant at will. As soon as he begins paying rent on a regular basis, the tenancy at will is converted to a periodic tenancy.

Illustration: Owen conveyed property to Ann by a void deed, and Ann took possession. Since the deed failed to transfer title, Owen still owns the property. Ann's possession under the void deed makes her a tenant at will.

Illustration: Lil and Tom entered into a valid tenancy for a term. At the end of the term, Tom asks Lil's permission to hold over for two additional days. If Lil consents, Tom is a tenant at will during those two days.

D.   TENANCY AT SUFFERANCE

A person becomes a tenant at sufferance by holding over after the expiration of the term without the landlord's consent. The tenancy at sufferance can arise after the termination of any of the other types of tenancy. Because the tenant does not have any legal right to remain in possession, he could be characterized as a trespasser. However, if he is a trespasser, the statute of limitations begins to run on the owner's action to recover possession. Her failure to bring suit within the limitations period could cause her to lose title to the property by the former tenant's adverse possession. To avoid this result, the former tenant is characterized as a tenant at sufferance, rather than as a trespasser.

Illustration: Tom's lease expired on January 1. On January 2, Tom is still in possession without Lil's consent. He is a tenant at sufferance.

Illustration: Tom was a month to month tenant. Lil gave proper notice of termination as of the following month. However, Tom is still there when the next month begins. He is a tenant at sufferance.

Illustration: Tom was a tenant at will, but Lil terminated the tenancy. If Tom does not leave, he is a tenant at sufferance.

II.   TERMINATION OF TENANCIES

A.   TERMINATION ACCORDING TO TYPE OF TENANCY

1.   Tenancy for a Term

Since the original lease agreement specifies a termination date, the tenancy for a term <u>automatically ends</u> on that date. No notice is required. The tenancy ends when the term ends.

2. Periodic Tenancy

This ten<u>ancy automatically renews u</u>ntil timely notice of termination is given by the landlord or tenant. Usually, such notice must be given at least one period in advance. Thus, a tenancy from week to week usually requires one week's notice of termination, and a tenancy from month to month usually requires one month's notice. The tenancy from year to year required only six months' notice of termination at common law. Some state statutes alter these common law notice periods.

The notice usually must coincide with the rental period, i.e. a tenancy from month to month commencing on the first day of each month can only be terminated by a notice effective on the first day of a month. Some states permit the parties to agree to a shorter notice period, such as seven days' notice for a month to month tenancy. On the other hand, some states require longer notice periods than the common law, such as one month's notice to terminate a weekly tenancy or sixty days' notice to terminate a monthly tenancy.

3. Tenancy at Will

This estate terminates when either party gives notice to that effect to the other. At common law, the notice could take effect immediately and was not required to be given in advance. Today, many states impose a waiting period, thereby making the tenancy at will very much like a periodic tenancy in this regard. Where the agreement gives one party the option to terminate early, the estate may be treated as a defeasible term rather than as a tenancy at will, such as a term for years subject to defeasance by the landlord or tenant at an earlier time. In other jurisdictions, courts will give both the landlord and the tenant the right to terminate despite a more restrictive lease provision.

4.   Tenancy at Sufferance

No notice should be required by the landlord to end this tenancy, since the original termination date has passed. However, if the holdover becomes a periodic tenant by virtue of the landlord's election, this estate must be terminated in the same manner as all other periodic tenancies.

B.   OTHER WAYS OF TERMINATING A TENANCY

1.   Destruction of the Premises

At common law, the destruction of the premises did not terminate the tenancy. The tenant still had a nonfreehold estate in land even if it could hardly be used. Today, many states provide by statute that destruction of all or a material part of the premises automatically terminates the tenancy or gives each party an option to terminate. Most leases also provide for this contingency.

2. Breach by the Tenant—Doctrine of Independent Covenants

At common law, the tenant's failure to perform covenants under the lease did not entitle the landlord to terminate the estate. Covenants in leases were independent, so that nonperformance by one did not excuse performance by the other. Thus, even though the tenant was not paying rent, the common law landlord remained obliged to let the tenant retain possession. The landlord's remedy was to enforce the particular covenant involved. For example, if the tenant did not pay rent, the landlord could sue to recover the rent or could bring the old remedy of distress and levy on the tenant's chattels.

Today, either by statute or by lease provision, a landlord can terminate the tenancy if the tenant defaults in the performance of any major covenant, particularly the obligation to pay rent. Most leases make the tenant's performance of all his lease covenants a condition for continuance of the estate. This has the effect of giving the landlord a power of termination (usually called a right of entry) incident to the reversion. After default by the tenant, the landlord usually is required to give a short notice that the tenant must correct the breach or quit the premises. If the tenant fails to do either, the landlord may commence summary proceedings to terminate the tenancy and to recover possession (unlawful detainer action).

3. Breach by the Landlord—Covenant of Quiet Enjoyment

As for the tenant, the landlord's lease covenants were independent. Therefore, the tenant was obligated to continue paying rent even if the landlord failed to perform her lease covenants. One exception was the covenant of quiet enjoyment, which is the landlord's promise that she will do nothing personally to disturb the tenant's possession of the premises. This covenant is implied into every lease. If the landlord breaches this covenant, the tenant is entitled to terminate the tenancy.

Eviction by the Landlord—Illustration: Tom has a tenancy for a term with six months remaining. However, Lil changed the locks on the door, thereby locking Tom out. Tom may now treat the tenancy as being terminated and may stop paying rent. Tom also may treat the lock out as a tort— either a trespass or a forcible entry—and may sue for damages. Finally, Tom can sue to recover possession.

Eviction by a Third Party—Illustration: Tom has a tenancy for a term with six months remaining. An intrusion by third parties makes it impossible for Tom to possess the premises any longer. Tom may not terminate his lease obligations, since there has been no breach by Lil. The landlord's covenant of quiet enjoyment applies only to acts of Lil or her agents. She does not insure Tom's possession against third parties. This reasoning also justified the common law rule that destruction of the premises did not terminate the tenant's lease obligation, unless the landlord caused the loss.

Eviction by Other Tenants—Illustration: Tom's possession is disturbed by other tenants in the building. In some jurisdictions, Tom may terminate under these circumstances. In many other states, however, the landlord is not responsible for the other tenants' actions, and Tom is not free to terminate. Sometimes the outcome depends on whether the tenants' disturbing acts violated their lease provisions. If so, Lil's power to prevent Tom's neighbors from violating their leases may entitle Tom to treat her as responsible for the disturbances they cause.

Eviction by Paramount Title—Illustration: Lil failed to pay her mortgage, and the mortgagee foreclosed and evicted Tom. This is an eviction by paramount title. Lil's covenant of quiet enjoyment protects against that contingency. Therefore, Tom may treat the lease as terminated.

a. Mortgages and Leases

If the landlord mortgages the property and then leases it, the tenant's interest is inferior to the mortgage. The mere existence or assertion of a mortgage or any other adverse claim does not of itself constitute a breach of the covenant of quiet enjoyment. There first must be an "eviction." If the mortgagee forecloses, the tenancy is destroyed because the leasehold, as well as the reversion, was subject to the mortgage. An eviction has now occurred, and the tenant may stop paying rent and quit the premises even if the mortgagee desires to preserve the tenancy. For mortgage foreclosures, see Chapter 12, p. 373–74.

If, instead, the landlord first leases the property and then mortgages it, the lease is paramount to the mortgage, and the mortgagee takes a mortgage only on the reversion. In this case, a foreclosure of the mortgage only gives the mortgagee the reversion and makes the mortgagee the new landlord of the tenant. The tenancy is not destroyed. Therefore, no eviction has occurred, and the covenant of quiet enjoyment is not breached.

Most mortgagees will not accept a mortgage that is subject to outstanding leases. Therefore, leases commonly provide that they will be subject to all mortgages whether executed before or after the lease.

b. Constructive Eviction

The landlord's failure to perform her lease covenants does not by itself entitle the tenant to terminate. At early common law, lease covenants were independent. Therefore, when the landlord defaulted, the tenant's remedy was for breach of covenant but not for lease termination. However, if the landlord's failure to perform a covenant materially impaired the tenant's ability to enjoy the premises, the landlord was in breach of the covenant of quiet enjoyment. When that covenant is breached by an actual eviction, the tenant always can terminate. By analogy, when the landlord has breached indirectly by a material failure to perform a covenant, a constructive eviction has occurred, and the tenant may terminate. Constructive eviction is examined in more detail at p. 169–71.

4. By Agreement—Surrender

The parties always can agree to terminate a tenancy before it would end naturally. Unlike a contract, however, this surrender is not accomplished by tearing up the lease (rescission). Since the lease conveyed an estate in property to the tenant, it is technically necessary for the tenant to reconvey that estate to the landlord by a surrender deed if the estate is large

enough to come under the Statute of Frauds. A conveyance of the landlord's reversion to the tenant is by
release deed. However, a surrender by operation of law
sometimes occurs when the tenant abandons the property and the landlord re-enters. Surrender by operation of law eliminates the need for a writing. See p.
147–48.

5. Eminent Domain

The government has the power to acquire private
property for public use. When leased property is taken,
the government acquires the tenant's, as well as the
landlord's, interest, which has the effect of terminating the lease.

The government is required to pay just compensation (i.e. the fair market value of the property), and
both the landlord and tenant may share in the condemnation award. If the value of the tenant's leasehold was equal to his rent burden, he has no claim to
any part of the award since his loss (future use of the
premises) is offset by an equivalent gain (future rent
liability). But if his leasehold had a value in excess of
his rent, some of the award belongs to him.

Illustration: Tom leased property for five years at $1,000
per month. Because neighborhood conditions have improved,
the fair rental value of the property is now $1,200 per month
(i.e. Tom could have sublet the premises for that amount). If
the government takes the property while Tom's lease has
one year to go, he should receive the lost bonus value of his
lease, which is $200 × 12 months, reduced to present value.
(Assume this equals $2,000 for purposes of this Illustration).

Since $2,000 of the award will go to Tom, Lil will
receive that much less. The government is liable only

for the land's fair market value and is not liable for more merely because the property is leased. And, in fact, Lil's interest is worth $2,000 less than otherwise because of the depressing effect of Tom's lease. If her property, unleased, would be worth $100,000, the fact that Tom pays $200 per month below the current market rent means that any buyer of the property would require that the purchase price be reduced to cover the shortfall in rent. Therefore, the buyer would pay only $98,000, rather than $100,000, because of Tom's lease.

When the government takes property only temporarily and for a shorter duration than the remainder of the tenancy, the lease is not terminated, and the award goes entirely to the tenant. However, the tenant must continue to pay rent to the landlord. When a physical part of the property is taken, most courts hold that the tenant's rent liability is unaffected. Therefore, the tenant is entitled to receive both the future rent owed for the part taken and its bonus value. The balance goes to the landlord.

C. LANDLORD'S REMEDIES AGAINST CONTINUED POSSESSION AFTER TERMINATION OF THE ESTATE— HOLDOVER TENANTS

The tenant's possession should end when the leasehold ends. If a tenant holds over after the term expires, the landlord has a choice of remedies.

1. Double Damages

Statutes in many states permit the landlord to recover two or three times the regular rent for the time that the tenant actually holds over. Sometimes this remedy is limited to willful or malicious holdovers.

2. Increased Rent

The lease may provide that any holding over past the term will be at some higher specified rent, or the landlord may notify the tenant before the end of the term of this same consequence. Generally, such a provision in a lease or in a notice sent later is upheld if not unreasonable. However, if the tenant already has begun holding over, the landlord may have special problems enforcing any subsequent rent increase notice. See p. 145.

3. Eviction and Damages

In every state, a landlord may evict a holdover tenant and recover damages for the fair rental value of the premises during the holding over period.

4. Self–Help

While a landlord may be entitled to evict a holdover tenant, the landlord may not enter the premises without a court order or use self-help to oust the tenant, such as by changing the locks. In many states, such acts make the landlord guilty of forcible entry or forcible detainer because the tenant is a peaceable, albeit wrongful, possessor. A landlord's right to evict is primarily the right to bring judicial summary dispossession proceedings against the tenant.

5. Compelling the Tenant to Stay

The landlord may elect to make a holdover tenant remain for another entire term, usually equal to the length of the original term, regardless of how long the tenant actually held over. In most states, the tenant then becomes a periodic tenant, but, in some others, the tenant becomes a tenant for a term.

Illustration: Tom had a one year lease and held over for five days after its expiration. Lil may elect to make Tom stay another period, either as a periodic tenant (majority rule) or as a tenant for a term (minority rule). Of those states where the holdover tenant becomes a periodic tenant, some treat him as a tenant from year to year (because the original term was a year), while others make him a tenant from month to month (if the rent was paid on a monthly basis).

Illustration: Tom was a tenant from month to month. Either Lil or Tom gave thirty days' notice of intent to terminate the tenancy effective the following month. However, Tom held over for three days after the termination date. As a result, Lil can hold Tom liable for the entire month, either as a tenant from month to month or as a tenant for a term (a month).

a. *Consequence of a Tenant for a Term Becoming a Periodic Tenant*

As stated, a tenant for a term who holds over may, at the landlord's election, be converted into a periodic tenant. Since periodic tenancies are terminated only by giving the necessary notice, that tenant may be required to stay for a third period, even though he did not hold over after the second period, if he did not give timely notice of intent to terminate during the second period.

Illustration: Tom held under a one year lease that commenced on January 1, 1997 and expired on December 31, 1997. Tom held over until January 5, 1998, and Lil elected to renew Tom's tenancy. Under the applicable state law, Tom became a tenant from year to year. On December 31, 1998, Tom vacated. However, Lil now can hold Tom liable for the next year (1999) since the tenancy from year to year that was created in 1998 automatically renewed in 1999 when neither party gave timely notice of termination.

b. Increasing the Rent

Most states require that a notice of rent increase be given as far in advance as notices of termination. Therefore, a landlord may be unable to increase the rent owed by a holdover tenant unless notice of the increase was given in a timely manner.

Illustration: Tom held over. Lil then notified him that, if he stayed, he would owe a higher rent. Unless she gave this notice sufficiently in advance of the date of the increase, the increase is invalid.

D. CONSEQUENCES OF A TENANT ATTEMPTING TO SURRENDER THE ESTATE BEFORE THE END OF THE TERM—ABANDONMENT AND SURRENDER

In the case of tenancies for a term and periodic tenancies, the tenant has an estate in the land that endures for a certain length of time. The duration of that estate is not dependent on the tenant being in possession of the land. The estate is possessory whether the tenant actually possesses. Consequently, even a nonpossessing tenant owes rent for the entire lease term.

1. Failure to Pay Rent

A tenant does not terminate the tenancy simply by failing to pay rent. Under the early common law doctrine that lease covenants are independent, the landlord could not terminate the estate merely because the tenant failed to perform the rent covenant. Today, however, a landlord generally may terminate the tenant's estate for nonpayment of rent. However, nonpayment of the rent does not automatically terminate the estate. Termination requires affirmative action by the landlord.

2. Failure to Retain Possession and to Pay Rent

If a tenant abandons the leased property and stops paying rent, the tenancy is not automatically terminated. The landlord can treat the lease as subsisting and can sue for the rent due each succeeding period.

Illustration: Tom is a tenant for a term of five years at a rent of $100 per month. After one year of possession, Tom abandoned the property and paid no more rent. Among her other alternatives, Lil can sue Tom for $100 each month thereafter, entirely ignoring Tom's abandonment. Lil also may wait three months and then sue for $300 in back rent or wait six months and then sue for $600. Only the statute of limitations dictates how long Lil may wait. Lil may sue for rent only when it becomes due. She cannot sue for the rent for the balance of the term immediately upon Tom's abandonment. Even if the lease has a rent acceleration clause, which makes all of the rent become due when Tom breaches, it is most unlikely that a court would grant Lil this extreme form of relief.

Illustration: Tom is a tenant from month to month. Tom paid January's rent, which was due on January 1. He abandoned the premises on January 20 and paid no rent thereafter. Lil filed suit on May 15. In this action, Lil can recover rent for the months of February through May. A periodic tenancy is terminated only by notice, and Tom gave no notice. Therefore, the tenancy is still alive, and rent for each month of its existence is owed. Although Tom's abandonment and rent default gave Lil the option of terminating the estate, she was not required to do so. She may continue to hold Tom liable for rent until he properly terminates the tenancy.

a. No Duty to Mitigate

The two previous illustrations assumed that a landlord is entitled to leave the premises vacant and hold the tenant liable for the rent. This has been the majority rule in the United States. However, a growing minority of jurisdictions compel the landlord (either through statute or judicial decision) to mitigate damages by looking for a new tenant. Even under the rule that a landlord must mitigate, the abandoning tenant is liable for the rent specified in his lease if the landlord is unable to find a new tenant.

b. Surrender by Operation of Law

If a tenant abandons the property and stops paying rent, the landlord may treat the tenant's conduct as an offer to surrender the leasehold estate. The landlord can accept this offer by re-entering the premises and retaking possession. Re-entry terminates the tenancy and the tenant's rent liability.

Illustration: Tom was a tenant for a term with eight months remaining on his lease. Tom stopped paying rent and abandoned the property. Lil immediately re-entered, remodeled, and began using the premises. These acts terminate the tenancy and Tom's liability for the remaining rent.

Since the original lease conveyed an estate in land to the tenant, the early common law provided that the estate could be terminated only by a reconveyance to the landlord by a surrender deed. To solve the practical problems posed by the tenant's abandonment, the courts created the fiction that the tenant's abandonment constituted an offer to surrender the leasehold estate and the landlord's re-entry was an acceptance of that offer. In this way, the tenant's estate was surrendered "by operation of law," rather than by surrender deed. Thus, the estate revested in the landlord without a writing.

3. Tenant's Failure to Pay Rent or to Perform Other Lease Covenants

Today, either by statute or by lease provision, the landlord usually can bring judicial proceedings to evict the tenant after a default. These proceedings usually operate not only to dispossess the tenant, but also to terminate the tenancy. Consequently, rent liability also is terminated.

Illustration: With six months remaining on the lease, Tom fails to pay rent, and Lil brings a summary dispossession action against him. In the action, Lil prays to have Tom's tenancy terminated. The suit will give Lil possession of the premises and will terminate Tom's liability for future rent.

a. Dispossession Without Termination

Some states permit a landlord to dispossess a defaulting tenant without terminating the leasehold estate. When this is permitted, the tenant is denied possession but remains liable for rent for the balance of the term. This fairly inequitable combination is rare.

4. Reletting for the Tenant's Account

When the tenant abandons the premises, the landlord may have a third remedy that is midway between the choices of terminating the tenancy and permitting the premises to stay vacant and suing for the rent. The landlord may re-enter and relet the premises as the tenant's agent or for the tenant's account, so that the tenant's liability is limited to the rent due before a new tenant was found, plus any rent differential if the new tenant pays a lower rent.

Illustration: Tom abandoned when his lease had one year remaining at a monthly rent of $1,000. Lil re-entered and, one month later, relet the premises for a monthly rent of $900. At the end of that year, Lil can sue Tom for $1,000 (for the month that the premises were vacant), plus $1,100 ($100 per month loss for the remaining eleven months).

In some states, this remedy is unavailable to the landlord unless the lease provides for it or the landlord notifies the tenant of her intent to pursue this remedy. However, the tenant's consent generally is not required.

Since re-entry and reletting are possessory acts, a danger exists that a court will treat them as a retaking of possession for the landlord's own account, thereby causing the lease to terminate. Generally, the landlord must make it plain throughout that she has taken these acts solely for the tenant's account. But some-

times the acts themselves may defeat contrary statements of intent, such as when the landlord entirely
reconstructs the premises to suit a new tenant who
agrees to rent the premises for a much longer period
than the balance of the original term. In such a case, a
court may hold that a surrender has occurred, despite
the landlord's assertion that she is acting solely as the
tenant's agent.

5. Difference Value Damages

When a tenant abandons, courts increasingly are
awarding the landlord damages that are measured by
the difference between the fair rental value of the
property and the rent reserved in the tenant's lease.
This measure of damages protects the tenant from
liability for the full rent and benefits the landlord by
allowing suit to be brought immediately after the
abandonment, rather than at the end of the term.
Where this measure applies, all alternative measures
of recovery often are prohibited.

Illustration: Tom had one year remaining on his lease
when he abandoned. The rent reserved under the lease is
$1,000 per month, but the fair rental value of the premises is
only $900. If permitted in the jurisdiction, Lil may sue
immediately for $1,200, which is the difference between
$900 and $1,000 for the remaining twelve months (12 ×
100). This may be the only remedy available to Lil.

Illustration: Tom had one year remaining on his lease
when he abandoned. The rent reserved under the lease is
$1,000 per month, but the fair rental value of the premises is
$1,100 per month. Lil can recover no damages, because
Tom's abandonment benefited her. Before Tom's abandonment, Lil was renting premises worth $1,100 per month for

only $1,000 and was "losing" $100 a month for every month that Tom stayed.

Illustration: Tom had one year remaining on his lease when he defaulted in his rent. Lil sued to terminate his estate. The rent reserved under the lease is $1,000 per month, but the fair rental value is $900. In addition to terminating Tom's interest in the land, Lil may recover $1,200 (the difference between $900 and $1,000 over twelve months), plus any unpaid back rent. It does not matter that the tenancy was terminated by Lil, rather than by Tom. Her damages are the same.

III. THE TENANT'S POSSESSORY INTEREST

The essence of a lease is the landlord's transfer of a temporary right of exclusive possession. The tenant has a nonfreehold possessory estate. This right to exclusive possession distinguishes a tenancy from an easement, because an easement merely gives its holder the right to use property for some limited use.

As the person with the exclusive right to possess, the tenant is entitled to exclude all others from the property. Even the landlord may be excluded unless the lease permits entry without the tenant's consent. The common law also recognized a limited right in the landlord to enter to "view waste."

A. TENANT'S REMEDIES FOR DISTURBANCE OF POSSESSION

1. Remedies Against Strangers

A tenant is entitled to protect his right to possession against all others. If trespassers intrude, the tenant, rather than the landlord, has standing to sue. The tenant may recover damages for trespass or may recover possession from the intruders in an ejectment action. Because the tenant, rather than the landlord, has the action for ejectment, the tenant is not excused from paying rent when he is dispossessed by strangers.

2.   Remedies for the Landlord's Interferences

The tenant may exclude the landlord from the premises the same as he may exclude everyone else. However, if the landlord dispossesses the tenant, the tenant may be allowed to terminate the tenancy.

Illustration: Lil entered and dispossessed Tom when he had one year remaining on his lease. Tom may either sue to recover possession or treat Lil's eviction as a breach of the implied covenant of quiet enjoyment and declare the leasehold terminated.

Illustration: Lil brought a summary dispossession proceeding against Tom for his failure to pay rent, and she recovered possession. Tom is probably excused from further rent liability. Although Lil was entitled to enter and is not liable in ejectment or tort or for breach of covenant, the condition on which Tom owed rent—possession—has been eliminated by Lil. Therefore, Tom's rent liability should cease.

3.   Eviction by Paramount Title

If the owner of a paramount title dispossesses a tenant, the tenant cannot recover possession. Instead, he can terminate the lease and can recover damages for the landlord's breach of the covenant of quiet enjoyment.

Illustration: Lil failed to pay the debt secured by a mortgage on property rented by Tom. The mortgagee foreclosed and took possession of the property. If the mortgage is superior to the lease because it was executed before the lease, Tom cannot resist the mortgagee's power to enter. But Tom is excused from further rent liability to Lil.

B. REMEDIES WHEN A HOLDOVER TENANT PREVENTS A NEW TENANT FROM TAKING POSSESSION

1. When the Landlord is at Fault

If the landlord is in possession of the leased premises and fails to leave when the tenancy begins, the tenant has the same remedies as if the landlord subsequently interfered with his possession. The tenant can sue to recover possession or to terminate the lease and can recover damages. When a third person is in possession with the landlord's consent, the tenant also can terminate the lease and recover damages from the landlord for breach of covenant. Whether the tenant can sue to recover possession from the third person depends on which of them has the superior right to possession. If the tenant's lease is superior, his right of possession is superior. But if the third person is in possession under a lease executed before the tenant's lease, the tenant probably cannot eject the third person.

Illustration: Tom signed a lease on January 1 that granted possession on February 1. On January 15, Lil signed another lease for the same property that gave Ann the immediate right to possess. On February 1, when Tom is unable to enter because of Ann, he may terminate his lease and sue Lil for damages, or he may bring an ejectment action against Ann.

Illustration: Tom signed a lease on January 15 that granted possession on February 15. On January 1, Lil had executed a lease for the same property with Ann, and Ann took possession on February 1. On February 15, when Tom is unable to enter, he may terminate his lease and sue Lil for damages, but he probably cannot eject Ann.

Illustration: Tom's tenancy is to begin on February 1. The lease of the former tenant, Ann, terminated on January 15, but she held over. On January 20, Lil elected to make Ann stay as a periodic tenant. Thus, Tom cannot enter on February 1. Tom may terminate the lease or may be able to recover possession from Ann.

2. When No One Is at Fault

The states are divided concerning a tenant's right to terminate his tenancy if he cannot take possession at the beginning of his lease term because of a third party's hostile possession without the landlord's consent.

a. The English Rule

Several states hold that the tenant may terminate the tenancy under such circumstances (the English rule). This rule imposes an obligation on the landlord to provide the tenant with actual possession at the beginning of the tenancy.

b. The American Rule

Under this rule, the landlord is obliged to deliver only "legal" possession (i.e. the right of possession) and not actual possession. This rule does not permit the tenant to terminate the lease. It limits him to relief against the wrongful possessor.

Illustration: Tom cannot take possession when his lease begins because Ann, the former tenant, failed to leave despite Lil's request for her to do so. Under the American rule, Tom still owes rent and has an ejectment action against Ann. Under the English rule, Tom may terminate his lease.

C. RIGHTS INCIDENTAL TO POSSESSION

In a multi-unit building, the tenant has the right to possess only that part of the building actually leased to him. However, the tenant also shares with the other tenants certain additional rights, such as the right to pass through the hallways, ride the elevators, and use the laundry room. In these "common areas," the tenant's right is for shared use, rather than for exclusive possession. These rights may be regarded as easements in the common areas that are incidental to the possessory right to the space actually leased.

D. LIABILITIES AS A POSSESSOR

As the person in possession of the leased premises, the tenant, rather than the landlord, usually is subject to the normal tort duties owed by occupiers of land to invitees, licensees, trespassers, and others.

IV. RENT

"Rent" refers to the periodic charge the tenant must pay for his use of the landlord's property. Usually, the lease specifies the amount of "rent reserved." However, if the lease does not specify an amount, a rent equal to the fair rental value of the property is implied unless a gift was intended.

A. PAYMENT

For common law agricultural tenancies, rent was a share of the crops harvested by the tenant. This practice was the origin of the term "rent," because it was something torn or "reserved" from the land. Today, the rent may include a share of the tenant's profits from the business he conducts on the premises ("percentage rent"). For other types of cash rent, payments usually are due at the beginning of each rental period.

The rent amount frequently stays the same over the lease term, but it may be increased periodically either by a fixed amount provided in the lease or by a cost of living ("escalator") clause in the lease. For periodic tenancies, a unilateral demand by the landlord for an increase often must be given at least one period in advance because, in essence, the landlord is terminating the tenancy at the former rent and is offering to enter into a new tenancy at the increased rent. The tenant need not agree to accept the new tenancy.

B. RENT CONTROL

By ordinance, many cities limit the amount by which residential landlords can increase their tenants' rents. Courts generally uphold rent control against attacks that it is preempted by state law, constitutes a "taking" of the landlord's property, denies landlords due process or equal protection, and violates the anti-trust laws. Common features of such ordinances are described below.

1. Premises and Persons Covered

Rent control rarely includes commercial premises. The rent control ordinance also may exclude certain forms of housing or tenants, such as boarders in single family homes, single family or two family dwellings, and luxury housing. The tenant may be required to show that the premises are his "primary residence" or that he is related to the originally protected tenant. The tenant also may be limited in the amount he can charge if he sublets the premises.

When the premises become vacant, some ordinances permit the landlord to increase rents without restriction ("vacancy decontrol"), while others continue the rent control. Ordinances that permit vacancy decontrol generally prohibit landlords from evicting tenants merely to increase rentals. Such "good cause eviction" restrictions limit tenancy termination to cases of tenant default or misbehavior or the landlord's personal need to occupy the premises.

2. Rates

To eliminate the incentive for landlords to raise rents when a rent control ordinance is about to be enacted, most ordinances "roll back" the allowable rent to the rent charged at some earlier date, such as one year before the ordinance was enacted or was first considered. Increases then may be made only pursuant to a formula applicable to all units, such as an annual increase equal to 50% of the consumer price index increase for that period. The rent control board may be given authority to permit an increase in an individual case after the landlord has demonstrated a special hardship, such as an increase in the cost of necessary services or an inability to make a fair return on investment otherwise.

3. Ancillary Restrictions

Landlords subject to rent controls may seek to convert their buildings to more profitable, unrestricted uses. To prevent depletions in the rental housing stock, rent control ordinances often are accompanied by restrictions on condominium conversions, conversions to nonresidential use, and demolition. Such restrictions may completely prohibit conversions and demolition or may provide a rationing system that permits, for example, 1,000 conversions a year. Landlords also may be required to pay compensation to existing tenants in the form of mandatory relocation services, reduced "insider" prices, or lifetime tenancies in newly converted condominiums.

V. PROBLEMS ARISING FROM DISREPAIR OF THE PREMISES

A. THE PARTIES' BASIC DUTIES

At early common law, the landlord had no legal responsibility for the condition of the premises. The doctrine of caveat emptor applied for defects that existed when the lease began, and leases were viewed as including no implied warranties. The landlord also had no duty to repair or correct defects that arose after the tenancy began. The landlord's only obligation was the same one imposed on everyone else in the world—not to harm the premises after the tenant had taken possession.

The tenant's only duty to the landlord for the condition of the premises was the duty not to commit waste. The tenant was prohibited from committing both active waste, i.e. harm caused by his acts, and passive waste, i.e. harm caused by a failure to make repairs. The landlord was entitled to receive the premises at the end of the lease term in the same condition as at the start, with the exception of reasonable wear and tear.

Illustration: Lil broke a fence on the premises before she rented them to Tom. Lil has no duty to repair the fence because she made no warranties to Tom concerning the condition of the premises. Tom also does not have a duty to repair the fence because he did not damage it, and its continued disrepair will not cause material harm to the reversion.

Illustration: Lil broke a fence on the premises during Tom's term. Tom may sue Lil for the damage, just as he could sue anyone else who broke the fence during his tenancy.

Illustration: Tom broke a fence on the premises during his term, which constitutes active waste. Tom owes Lil a duty to repair the fence.

Illustration: A third party broke a fence on the premises during Tom's term. Neither Lil nor Tom has any duty to the other to repair the fence. The third party is liable for the damage, and any damage award should either be used to repair the fence or apportioned between Lil and Tom according to their respective losses. Tom loses the use of the fence for his term; Lil loses the use of the fence thereafter.

Illustration: An unknown third party broke a window during Tom's term. If the window is not repaired, rain may get inside and cause the floors to warp. In this case, Tom has a duty to repair the window in order to avoid waste. This minor repair now will avoid major costs later. Therefore, the duty to repair is imposed on Tom as the possessor of the property.

1. Duties Owed to Third Persons

Even though neither party may owe a duty to the other to make a certain repair, either or both of them may owe duties to the public generally and may be held liable in tort for injuries to others due to the disrepair. See p. 173–82.

2. Modern Changes in the Basic Duties

Modern building and housing codes frequently change the common law rule by imposing a duty to repair. Some codes impose a duty to repair that is owed to the municipality. This duty indirectly may affect the duties owed to the other party to the lease. Other codes impose the duty of repair with a direct

right of enforcement vested in the landlord or the
tenant.

3. Duties Regarding Common Areas

The tenant's duties with respect to waste apply only
to those premises over which he receives exclusive
possession. As for the common areas, the landlord is
regarded as the possessor. Consequently, instead of a
landlord-tenant relationship in the hallways and other
common areas, there is a relationship of possessor-
invitee. Although the tenant has no duty regarding
waste, both the landlord and tenant may have duties
arising out of their possessor-invitee relationship.

Illustration: Tom damaged a step in the common stairway.
Tom is as liable as any third person would be.

Illustration: Lil cared for the common steps so negligently
that Tom was injured. Tom may recover for his injuries from
Lil the same as any outsider could recover from a possessor
of land for negligent care of the land.

B. ALTERING THE BASIC DUTIES
BY COVENANT

Unless prohibited by statute, either the landlord or
tenant can agree to undertake duties of repair not
otherwise existing. Either can agree to make general
or special repairs.

1. Enlarging the Scope of the Tenant's Duties
by a Tenant's Covenant to Repair

Absent a covenant, the tenant's duty to avoid waste
does not include extensive structural work or rebuild-

ing unless the tenant caused the injury. However, many states interpret a general covenant to repair made by the tenant as including the obligation to rebuild regardless of the cause of the destruction.

2. Diminishing the Scope of the Tenant's Duties by a Landlord's Covenant to Repair

When the landlord gives a covenant to repair, the tenant may be relieved of the repair obligations that the doctrine of waste imposes. However, the landlord's covenant to repair generally does not require her to repair damage caused by the tenant or to rebuild the premises if they are substantially destroyed.

C. RIGHT TO RECOVER THE COST OF REPAIRS

The availability of a particular remedy is not always resolved simply by demonstrating that the other party had a duty to repair that he did not perform. This section addresses the issue of when a party to a lease can sue the other for repair costs after the other party has refused to make the repair.

1. No Right to Recover when no Duty to Repair

If the nonrepairing party was not obligated to make the repair, the other party cannot recover the repair cost.

Illustration: Lil refuses to repair a fence that was broken by an unknown third party. Since a landlord has no general duty to make repairs, Tom cannot sue Lil for the cost if he makes the repair.

Illustration: Tom refuses to repair a fence that was broken when he took possession. Failure to repair a pre-existing defect that will not lead to greater loss later does not constitute waste. Therefore, Lil cannot sue Tom for costs if she repairs the fence.

2. Tenant's Right to Recover when the Landlord has a Duty to Repair

a. Duty Arising from a Building Code

Building codes generally impose duties on owners, including landlords. But, unless the code expressly provides that a tenant can enforce it, it does not give him the right to recover repair costs from the landlord.

Illustration: The local building code requires property owners to keep fences in good repair, but the fence is in disrepair. Tom cannot repair the fence and recover the cost from Lil. Lil's obligation under the code is to the local government and not to Tom. The local government can compel her to fix the fence, but Tom cannot.

b. Duty Arising from a Special Habitability Statute

An increasing number of states require landlords of residential premises to keep them in habitable condition throughout the term. These statutes sometimes permit tenants to make repairs and deduct the cost from their rent. Additional statutory provisions often provide how often this right can be exercised, a maximum amount, and whether the tenant can make the repair personally or must hire outside contractors. It is unsettled whether several tenants can cumulate their rights to make a single large repair.

c. Duty Arising from a Covenant

If the landlord violates her covenant to repair, the tenant generally is entitled to make the repair and recover the cost from the landlord. In fact, to mitigate damages, the tenant may be required to make the repair promptly to prevent further deterioration. Obviously, the resolution of most questions concerning rights and duties under a covenant to repair depends on the precise wording of the covenant.

d. Duty Arising in Common Areas

If the landlord fails to keep the common areas in good repair, the tenant probably cannot make the repairs and recover the cost. Although the landlord may be liable in tort to the tenant for injuries suffered as a result of the disrepair, normally the tenant cannot recover repair costs in this type of action.

3. Landlord's Right to Recover when the Tenant has a Duty to Repair

If the tenant has a duty to repair under the doctrine of waste or a covenant to repair, the landlord generally can recover repair costs from the tenant. The cost of repairs is the usual measure of damages when the landlord does not sue until the end of the term. If the landlord sues before that time, the measure of damages may be the diminution in the reversion's value instead.

Illustration: Tom breaks the fence with one year remaining on the lease term, and Lil sues immediately. It will cost $500 to repair the fence, but the value of Lil's reversion (i.e. the price for which she could sell her interest) is reduced by only $400. If Lil sues now, her recovery will be limited to

$400. To recover $500, she must wait to sue until the lease term expires.

a. Recovery when the Building Code Applies to the Tenant

Building and housing codes normally impose duties only on the landlord (as owner), rather than on the tenant. However, when a tenant's use of the property subjects it to special code requirements, this increased burden may be imposed on the tenant. But, just as a tenant generally cannot enforce the code against the landlord, the landlord probably cannot sue the tenant for the cost of code compliance.

b. Recovery Under Modern Statutes

Some recent residential statutes impose certain repair duties on the tenant. These statutes also provide that, if the tenant fails to perform his duties, the landlord can make the repair and add the cost to the rent.

c. Effect of Insurance

Both the landlord and tenant have insurable interests in the property. Each party who purchases insurance to protect herself against disrepair or destruction is entitled to any proceeds that are paid. This right to recover under the policy may be independent of any rights given under the lease.

Illustration: A fire destroyed the premises. Although Tom covenanted to repair, Lil had purchased her own casualty insurance policy. Tom's duty to repair is not eliminated because Lil receives an insurance award, and Lil's insurance company may be subrogated to her rights against Tom.

Illustration: A fire destroyed the premises. Tom has his own insurance policy and did not covenant to rebuild. The majority rule is that Lil is not entitled to share in Tom's insurance proceeds, and Tom may keep the proceeds even though he is not obligated to rebuild. Under the minority rule, Lil can compel Tom to use the proceeds to restore the premises.

D. RIGHT TO TERMINATE THE TENANCY

The question discussed in this section is that of either party's right to terminate the tenancy by virtue of the other's failure to correct a disrepair.

1. Landlord's Right to Terminate

Because the early common law treated lease covenants as independent, a landlord could not terminate the lease even if the tenant was liable for waste or breach of a covenant to repair. The landlord could only obtain damages or an injunction. Today, this doctrine generally has been modified by statute or lease provision so that the landlord may terminate the tenancy in these circumstances.

a. *No Right to Terminate if the Tenant has no Duty*

If the tenant did not cause the disrepair and does not have a duty to repair, the landlord cannot terminate the tenancy for the tenant's failure to repair.

b. *Right to Terminate After Destruction*

Many modern statutes and lease covenants permit either party to terminate if all or a substantial part of the premises are destroyed.

2. Tenant's Right to Terminate

Statutes or lease provisions often permit a tenant to terminate the tenancy if the premises are destroyed. Absent such a statute or provision, the common law rule applies, and destruction of the premises does not terminate the tenancy. See p. 136–37.

Illustration: The premises were destroyed by a fire of unknown origin, and neither a statute nor a lease provision addresses this situation. Neither party can terminate the tenancy. However, neither party can compel the other to rebuild. Tom is obligated to pay the rent but is not obligated to pay the cost of a new building. Lil also is not obligated to rebuild.

Illustration: The premises were destroyed by fire, and a statute or a lease provision permits termination in this situation. Tom or Lil now may terminate, and neither party is obligated to rebuild.

Illustration: The premises were destroyed by fire. No statute or lease provision permits termination, but Tom gave a covenant to repair. In this situation, Tom cannot terminate, and Lil can compel him to rebuild. If Tom fails to rebuild, Lil probably can terminate the lease for breach of covenant and can recover the cost of rebuilding.

Illustration: Tom caused the premises to be destroyed by fire. Although a statute permits termination after destruction, it probably is inapplicable to destruction caused by the party desiring to terminate. Thus, Tom cannot terminate. Based on the statute, Lil can terminate, and she can sue Tom for the cost of repairs because the destruction constitutes active waste.

Illustration: Lil caused the premises to be destroyed by fire. Tom had covenanted to rebuild, and a statute permits termination after destruction. Lil cannot terminate, since she caused the fire. But Tom can terminate, even without the statute, because Lil breached the covenant of quiet enjoyment. Alternatively, Tom may be able to stay and compel Lil to rebuild, or Tom may receive monetary compensation for the loss of the building. However, Tom cannot compel Lil to rebuild if Tom elects to terminate the tenancy.

If the building falls into disrepair, rather than being destroyed, the tenant may terminate only if the landlord has a duty to repair and fails to do so. See p. 176– 78.

a. When a Building Code Applies to the Landlord

Generally, the landlord's failure to comply with the building code does not entitle the tenant to terminate the lease. The landlord owes the duty of code compliance to the government and not to the tenant.

b. When a Special Statutory Duty Applies to the Landlord

In some jurisdictions, a statute requires landlords to maintain residential premises in habitable condition. The same statute often authorizes a tenant to terminate the tenancy if the landlord fails to do so. This termination remedy often is provided as an alternative to the tenant's remedy of making the repair and deducting its cost from the rent.

c. Failure to Repair Common Areas

The landlord's failure to maintain the common areas in good repair does not entitle the tenant to terminate the tenancy unless the condition seriously impairs the tenant's enjoyment of the demised premises.

d. Failure to Honor a Covenant to Repair—Constructive Eviction

If the landlord covenanted to make repairs but fails to do so, the tenant may be entitled to terminate the tenancy. Although the jurisdiction generally may treat lease covenants as being independent, the tenant's covenant to pay rent still is dependent on the landlord's covenant of quiet enjoyment. The covenant of quiet enjoyment clearly is breached when a landlord evicts the tenant. But it also is breached when the landlord's failure to perform lease obligations materially impairs the tenant's enjoyment of the premises.

Illustration: Lil covenanted to make repairs. A fence on the demised property is broken from external causes, but Lil refuses to repair it. Tom cannot terminate the tenancy merely because Lil has breached her covenant to repair. But if nonrepair of the fence materially impairs Tom's enjoyment of the premises, he is entitled to terminate the tenancy.

For a plea of constructive eviction to succeed, the tenant must show that (1) the landlord had an obligation imposed in the lease or by law, (2) the landlord failed to perform the obligation, (3) the failure materially impaired the tenant's enjoyment of the premises, and (4) the tenant promptly quit the premises thereafter.

Illustration: Tom's lease does not expressly provide that the landlord must provide heat to the leased premises. During the winter, Lil fails to provide any heat. At common law, Tom may not claim a constructive eviction, since Lil had no duty to furnish heat. She has breached no lease covenant and has not impaired Tom's quiet enjoyment of the premises. However, if these are residential premises, the landlord may be statutorily or judicially required to furnish heat in winter. In that event, Lil's failure breaches an implied obligation to Tom and entitles him to terminate the tenancy if the failure is sufficiently serious.

Illustration: Tom wants to convert the warehouse he leased from Lil into a movie theater. Under the building code, he must install an additional washroom on the premises if he wants to open the theater to the public. Because this requirement arises solely because of Tom's proposed special use of the premises, it is not imposed on Lil. Therefore, Tom cannot compel Lil to add a washroom or terminate the lease if she fails to do so.

When a landlord actually evicts a tenant, the tenant's obligation to pay rent is entirely suspended even if he has not been completely removed from the premises. Based on this doctrine of partial actual eviction, some tenants have argued for a doctrine of partial constructive eviction. They claim that the entire rent obligation should be suspended even though they have not entirely quit the premises. However, this argument has not persuaded any court. Therefore, a tenant must leave the premises completely to succeed on a claim of constructive eviction.

Illustration: Lil shuts off the air conditioning at 5:00 p.m. each day, which makes the premises unusable until the next morning. Tom does not move out, but he refuses to pay rent on the basis that he suffers a partial constructive eviction after 5:00 p.m. each day. Under traditional rules, the claim will fail. Tom's rent obligation is excused only if he moves out and terminates his lease. He cannot stay and refuse to pay rent.

Illustration: Lil fails to repair a leak and, as a result, the basement is continuously flooded and unusable. Tom continues using the rest of the house but refuses to pay rent on the basis that he has suffered a partial constructive eviction from the basement. Under traditional concepts of constructive eviction, Tom's only right is to leave the premises entirely if he wishes to terminate his rent liability.

Constructive eviction not only ends the tenant's rent liability, but also may provide a cause of action against the landlord for breach of covenant. The action is based on the covenant to repair, if the lease contains one, or on the covenant of quiet enjoyment. (See p. 176–78 & 138–39.)

A tenant who claims constructive eviction and leaves the property is still liable under the lease if a court subsequently holds that the claim was unfounded. In that case, the tenant has merely abandoned the premises and is subject to all the liability that an abandoning tenant incurs. (See p. 145–46.)

E. RIGHT TO A RENT REDUCTION (ABATEMENT)

In some jurisdictions, a tenant can reduce or withhold rent if the premises fall into disrepair.

1. Landlord's Covenant to Repair

If the landlord has given a covenant to repair and breaches it, the tenant generally is not entitled to withhold or reduce rent. If the tenant seeks a monetary remedy for the landlord's breach, it usually is limited to the cost of repairs, rather than the reduction of rental value.

2. Repair and Deduct Statute

Many statutes that require landlords of residential premises to keep the premises in habitable condition authorize the tenant to repair the premises and to deduct up to one month's rent. These statutes do not permit the tenant to pay a reduced rent based on the premise's reduced rental value.

3. Implied Warranty of Habitability

Since 1970, the great majority of states have created an implied warranty of habitability in residential leases. In some states, the implied warranty was judicially created. In other states, the warranty was statutorily created. Under the warranty, the landlord has the duty to maintain the premises in compliance with local codes. When a landlord violates the warranty, the tenant's rent is generally reduced by the decreased rental value resulting from the violation.

Litigation between a landlord and tenant under the implied warranty of habitability usually begins when the tenant withholds rent. When the landlord brings an action to dispossess the tenant for nonpayment, the tenant defends by arguing that the rent is not due because of the code violations. Because summary dispossession actions generally do not permit affirmative defenses, the tenant may be required to pay all or part of the rent into court each month while the case is pending as a condition to asserting this defense. At the conclusion of the hearing, the court allocates the escrowed rent between the landlord and tenant. You should note, however, that many jurisdictions do not permit rent withholding for breaches of the warranty of habitability.

4. Retaliatory Eviction

By statute or by judicial decision, many states prohibit landlords from evicting a tenant based on his assertion of rights under the warranty of habitability.

Illustration: Tom, a month to month tenant, withheld one month's rent to make a repair under a repair and deduct statute. Lil then gave the requisite notice to terminate the tenancy. If the termination is in retaliation for Tom's assertion of his statutory right, most states will not permit the termination. In some jurisdictions, termination by the landlord is prohibited for a specified period, such as six months or a year following the tenant's assertion of rights.

Illustration: Tom, a periodic tenant, made the same repair and deduction as in the last illustration. Lil then served notice that the rent would be tripled the following period. When Tom refused to pay the increase the next period, Lil brought an action to dispossess him. This also constitutes a retaliatory eviction.

Illustration: Tom notified the municipal health inspectors about code violations on the leased premises. As a result, Lil either terminated the tenancy or raised the rent. Either way, Lil has performed a retaliatory eviction, which is not permitted under most states' laws.

F. TORT LIABILITY FOR DISREPAIRS

1. Tenant's Relation to Visitors

A large body of tort law deals with the liability of an occupier or possessor of land, such as a tenant, to other persons on the land who are injured due to the premise's condition. Under the older view, liability depended in large part on the status of the injured person. Different duties of care were owed to licensees, invitees, and trespassers. Under the more modern view, the standard is one of due care under all the circumstances. The injured party's status is only one of many considerations. Therefore, in this section, all nonpossessing persons entering onto the premises are called "visitors" without regard to their common law status, and the phrase "negligent care of the premises" means that the possessor has not exercised its duties to visitors as defined by state law.

2. Landlord's Relation to Visitors

Since a lease transfers possession of the premises to the tenant, the landlord is no longer a possessor once the tenant enters. Thus, the duties and liabilities that apply to occupiers of land do not apply to the landlord, and a landlord does not owe any general duty of care to visitors.

3. Landlord and Tenant's Relation

a. *Tenant's Liability*

A landlord visiting the tenant's premises is as much a visitor as anyone else. As a general proposition, therefore, the tenant is liable for injuries suffered by the landlord caused by the tenant's negligent care of the premises.

b. *Landlord's Liability*

At early common law, the landlord owed no general duty of care to the tenant. However, the landlord is a "seller" of the premises to the tenant and may also be a former possessor. Therefore, doctrines somewhat analogous to products liability law may add a different dimension of liability for the landlord. Additionally, with regard to the common areas, the landlord is the possessor, and the tenant is a mere visitor. Therefore, the landlord owes the tenant a general duty of care in the common areas.

4. Liability for Common Areas

Common areas are those parts of the premises where a tenant cannot exclude others from use or enjoyment. Thus, entryways, common stairs, halls, shared laundry rooms, and shared bathrooms are all common areas. Service systems, such as the heating and plumbing, also are often regarded as common areas, and the exterior walls sometimes are characterized as common areas.

Because the landlord has possession of the common areas, she may be liable in tort for their negligent care. This responsibility includes injuries to visitors and to tenants. Because the tenants are mere users of these areas, rather than possessors, they generally are liable for disrepairs only when they have caused them. A landlord's duty of care for common areas has been expanded to include a duty to keep them safe from intruders who assault tenants or their visitors in the building.

Illustration: Lil negligently maintained the common hallway, and Tom was injured as a result. Tom may recover in tort from Lil.

Illustration: Lil negligently maintained the common hallway, and Tom's visitor was injured as a result. The visitor

may sue Lil in tort but probably has no cause of action
against Tom because he does not possess the hallway.

Illustration: Tom negligently damaged a step in the common stairway, and Lil failed to repair it. A visitor was
injured as a result. The visitor may sue Tom for creating a
dangerous condition and Lil for maintaining a dangerous
condition.

Illustration: Tom or his guest was robbed while entering
his apartment. If the assailant entered the building because
it had a faulty security system or faulty locks, Tom may be
able to recover from Lil.

a.   Tenant's Covenant to Repair Common Areas

If the tenant has agreed to maintain the common
areas, his covenant may affect the issue of tort liability, as shown in the following illustrations.

Illustration: Tom gave a covenant to repair a common area
and was injured by a disrepair that was his responsibility
under the covenant. He cannot recover from Lil.

Illustration: A visitor was injured because Tom breached
his covenant to repair a common area. The visitor can sue
Tom directly unless the jurisdiction requires privity of contract between the plaintiff and defendant. The visitor also
can sue Lil despite Tom's covenant, because Lil cannot
delegate her duty to another. However, Lil can cross-com-
plain against Tom for indemnity based on the covenant.

5.   Landlord's Covenant to Repair

If the tenant's injury is attributable to a disrepair
that the lease obliged the landlord to correct, the
modern view permits the tenant to recover if he re-
quested the repair and the landlord failed to make it.
An older common law rule limited the tenant's recovery to the cost of repairs or permitted him to termi-

nate the lease. The older rule regarded tort liability as being either outside the damages intended by the parties or subject to the defense that, once the tenant knew of the disrepair, he had a duty to avoid injury by repairing or by avoiding use of the damaged component. In guest injury cases, privity of contract constituted an additional defense.

For a landlord to be liable in tort for breach of a covenant to repair, generally the covenant itself must be enforceable. Thus, breach of a gratuitous covenant to repair will not create personal injury liability. However, even without a binding covenant to repair, a landlord is liable in tort if she voluntarily undertakes to repair and negligently performs it.

The covenant to repair generally is interpreted as a covenant to repair within a reasonable time after notice by the tenant. Courts do not treat the covenant as giving the landlord the duty or the right to enter the tenant's premises to inspect for disrepairs. Thus, the landlord is liable only after notice and a failure to repair within a reasonable time thereafter.

a.   *Rights of Visitors*

Occasionally, courts apply the old common law rule that the landlord's liability for failure to comply with the covenant to repair is limited to the tenant and possibly the tenant's family. Today, however, privity generally is not a defense, so that visitors as well as tenants can recover for personal injuries caused by disrepairs.

b. Tenant's Liability to Visitors

The landlord's covenant to repair does not excuse the tenant from liability for injuries to visitors resulting from the disrepair. The tenant is still the possessor of the demised premises and owes corresponding duties to his visitors. Thus, the visitor may have separate causes of action against both the landlord and tenant, but the tenant may seek indemnity from the landlord based on the covenant.

Illustration: Lil made a covenant to repair. A light switch in the leased premises is defective. Tom notified Lil about the defect, but Lil has not repaired it. Tom's visitor received a shock when he touched the light switch. The visitor may sue both Lil for breach of the covenant to repair and Tom for failing to warn him about the switch.

6. Liability for Code Violations

Where a statute imposes a duty on the landlord to keep residential premises tenantable but limits the tenant's remedies to terminating the lease or repairing and deducting, courts generally hold that the landlord has no tort liability if she fails to comply with the statute. However, courts in some states hold that the injured party may recover in tort from the landlord if the condition causing the injury violated a building, housing, or health code. The rationale is that the tenant or visitor is in the class intended to be protected by such safety statutes. Thus, tort recovery for injuries resulting from a code violation may be available even though the tenant could not directly enforce the code.

Illustration: Lil's failure to insulate the electric wires violates a municipal code. This violation does not authorize Tom to make the repair and charge Lil. But Tom may be able to recover from Lil in tort if he is injured as a result of the uninsulated wiring.

a. Rights of Visitors

A visitor also may be able to recover from the landlord for personal injuries resulting from a code violation, as well as from the tenant for negligent care of the premises.

Illustration: Tom's apartment has uninsulated wiring, which violates the code. A visitor is injured as a result of the wiring. The visitor can sue Lil based on the code violation and can sue Tom for failure to warn. As the possessor of the land, Tom owed a duty to keep the premises safe for visitors. His failure to warn the visitor, to protect him from the wire, or to insulate the wire makes Tom liable along with Lil.

b. Effect of the Tenant's Covenant to Repair

If the tenant covenants to keep the premises in repair and to comply with all codes, the landlord may assert the covenant as a defense if the tenant is injured. The tenant's covenant also may require the tenant to indemnify the landlord if a visitor is injured and recovers from the landlord. A tenant's covenant also might provide a cause of action by the visitor against the tenant directly.

7. Hidden Defects (Latent Defects)

A landlord has tort liability for injuries to the tenant that result from latent (hidden) defects in the premises about which the landlord knew but did not tell the tenant. This is a fraud theory of liability (fraud by omission), which means that the landlord need only make timely disclosure to eliminate the potential liability. The duty is to disclose and not to repair the defect.

Generally, the landlord must have actual knowledge of the defect before she is liable. But, in a few states, the landlord is liable even without actual knowledge if she should have known of the defect. This imposes a duty to inspect on the landlord and expands the doctrine beyond its original fraud foundation.

Lack of actual knowledge is all that should be required of the tenant to recover for his injuries. But, in some states, the landlord is not liable if the defect could have been discovered by a reasonable inspection. In those jurisdictions, the landlord's only duty is to disclose defects that the tenant could not reasonably discover. The landlord also should have a defense if the tenant actually discovered the defect or was informed of it before the injury even though the leasehold already had commenced. The landlord's failure to disclose at the beginning of the tenancy might permit the tenant to terminate (if caveat emptor does not apply) but would not permit him to recover for personal injuries if he did not terminate after discovery of the defect.

a. *Rights of Visitors*

Visitors usually can sue the landlord for her failure to inform the tenant of the defect that caused the visitor's injuries. A timely disclosure to the tenant should have caused him to correct the condition or to warn the visitor. Absent such disclosure, the tenant should be liable to the visitor only if the tenant was negligent in failing to discover the defect. However, if the tenant otherwise knew of the defect, he should be liable, rather than the landlord.

8. Landlord's Liability for Negligence

Just as the plaintiff's status is now irrelevant in many states, several states have now concluded that the distinction between the tenant/possessor and landlord/nonpossessor is not controlling in the area of tort law. Courts in these jurisdictions hold that a landlord is obligated to use due care in maintaining the premises. The landlord's nonpossession is just one factor courts consider in determining whether the landlord has exercised due care.

9. Exculpatory Clauses

The landlord's and tenant's tort liability to members of the public is not avoided by the use of exculpatory clauses in their lease. Although either may indemnify the other against such liability, they may not insulate themselves against it. Public policy also may invalidate a clause that attempts to exculpate a party against liability for his negligence toward the other.

Illustration: Tom's lease states that Lil is not liable for any negligent maintenance of the building. The clause is not a valid defense for Lil in a tort action brought by Tom's guest for injuries caused by Lil's negligent maintenance of the common hallway. The clause also may not protect Lil in a suit brought by Tom if he is injured as a result of Lil's negligent maintenance.

Illustration: Tom's lease states that he will hold Lil harmless against any liability imposed on her resulting from the condition of the premises (an indemnity clause). The clause is not a valid defense for Lil against a third party suing her in tort. But if the third party recovers a judgment against Lil, she may proceed against Tom based on the indemnity clause to recover the amount she was required to pay the third party.

VI.   TRANSFER OF THE TENANCY

A.   DISTINCTION BETWEEN ASSIGNING AND SUBLEASING

A lease assignment is an outright transfer of the entire remaining leasehold by the tenant (assignor) to another (assignee). In contrast, a sublease is a leasing of the tenant's estate by the tenant (sublessor) to another (subtenant or sublessee). Whether a transfer constitutes an assignment or a sublease is not determined by how the parties label the document. A court may declare that an assignment has occurred even though the parties have called it a sublease or vice versa. Under the original common law rule, the tenant must retain some part of the leasehold estate for the transfer to be a sublease. The original tenant's estate, measured in terms of time, serves as the yardstick. The more modern view makes the assignment/sublease distinction depend on the parties' intent, rather than on whether the tenant has transferred his entire estate or only some part of it.

Illustration: Tom has a term with five years left to run. He transfers to Sue the right to possess for the next four years. This is a sublease, since Tom has a reversion of one year after Sue's term expires.

Illustration: Tom has a term with five years left to run. Sue and he execute a document entitled "Sublease" that gives Sue the exclusive right to possess one room on the premises for the remaining five years. Under the traditional common law rule, this is not a sublease, but rather a partial assignment, because Tom has no reversion in that room. The length of the estate, rather than the size of the property, controls.

Illustration: Tom has a term with five years left to run. He transfers the entire balance of the term to Ann, who agrees to pay Tom $50 more per month than Tom owes to Lil. This is an assignment, despite the additional consideration, since Tom has no reversion. The court would characterize the additional $50 per month as deferred payment for the assignment.

Illustration: Tom has a term with five years left to run. He transfers the entire balance of the term to Ann. The assignment document provides that, if Ann fails to perform any of the obligations under the lease, Tom may enter and terminate her estate. In some states, this is treated as a sublease, and Tom is said to have a contingent reversion. Other states, however, more strictly follow the common law system of estates and hold that this is an assignment because there is no common law estate such as a contingent reversion. Thus, the entire estate has been transferred to Ann. (Tom's power of termination is not a reversion. See Chapter 2, p. 60–64.)

B. TENANT'S RIGHT TO TRANSFER— RESTRICTIONS

A tenancy for a term or a periodic tenancy in land is a freely alienable estate. Thus, the tenant may assign or sublease it without the landlord's consent. However, landlords can restrict a tenant's right to assign or sublet by a lease provision. The landlord has a sufficient interest in the property to justify such a restraint on alienation, although courts generally construe such lease provisions as narrowly as possible. Most such clauses are written as forfeiture restraints, which purport to terminate the tenancy at the landlord's election if the tenant improperly has attempted to transfer his interest. On restraints on alienation see Chapter 2, p. 99–101.

1. Landlord's Right to be Unreasonable

Most lease provisions that restrict assignments and subleases state that the tenant shall not assign or sublet without the landlord's consent. If the provision does not expressly provide that the landlord cannot unreasonably withhold consent, most courts will not add such a requirement. However, some courts impose an obligation not to withhold consent unreasonably even if it is not expressed in the lease. Courts disagree whether the landlord may condition her assent on receiving whatever rent increase the transferee has agreed to pay the transferor. A court may regard such a demand as unreasonable unless the lease specifically permits her to do so. In jurisdictions that require a landlord to mitigate damages after a tenant abandons, a court effectively may impose a duty to consent to a reasonable transfer if an unreasonable refusal to approve a legitimate transferee caused the tenant's departure and then offer of the same transferee in mitigation of his damages.

Illustration: Tom proposes to assign to Ann, but Lil unreasonably refuses to consent. Lil's arbitrary refusal may be valid unless the no-assignment clause requires her to be reasonable. However, if Tom now abandons and offers Ann as a tenant again, Lil's second refusal to accept Ann may constitute a failure to mitigate damages. In a state where Lil has a duty to mitigate damages, her second refusal may terminate Tom's continuing liability for rent.

2. Effect of Consenting to the First Assignment

The Rule in Dumpor's Case (1603) is that, once a landlord consents to one assignment, she waives any right to prohibit subsequent assignments. Thus, the assignee subsequently could assign without consent. Many courts today have rejected the Rule. In those jurisdictions that still follow it, a lease provision can negate it. For example, the original lease may provide that consent to one assignment does not constitute consent to further assignments.

C. EFFECT OF AN ASSIGNMENT

1. Effect on the Tenant

A tenant does not end his lease liabilities by assigning the lease. Rights may be assigned but not duties. The tenant remains in privity of contract with the landlord despite the assignment. Therefore, the tenant remains bound on all promises made to the landlord in the lease.

Illustration: Tom assigned his lease to Ann, but Ann fails to pay rent. Even though Lil accepted Ann as an assignee, Tom is still liable for the rent based on his promise to pay contained in the original lease.

2. Effect on the Assignee

A lease assignment transfers the tenant's rights under the lease to the assignee, but it does not automatically impose the burdens of the lease. The assignee is personally liable for the tenant's covenants only if the assignee "assumes" these burdens or if they are covenants that "run with the land." Covenants that run with the land are covered in more detail in Chapter 6. If the assignee assumes the tenant's lease obligations, the landlord becomes a third party beneficiary of this assumption agreement and can enforce it against the assignee.

Illustration: Tom's lease contained a covenant that he would insure the premises. Under the applicable state's law, this type of covenant does not run with the land. Tom assigned to Ann who did not assume. If Ann does not insure the premises, Lil has no recourse against her. But since Tom remains liable on his original promise to insure, Lil may seek relief against him.

Illustration: Tom's lease contained a covenant that he would insure the premises. Tom assigned to Ann who assumed. If Ann fails to insure, Lil may proceed directly against her based on the assumption agreement. Lil also may sue Tom on the covenant in the original lease. If Lil sues Tom, Tom can sue Ann for breach of the assumption agreement.

Illustration: In Tom's lease, he gave a covenant to repair, which runs with the land under the applicable state's law. Tom assigned the lease to Ann who did not assume. If Ann does not repair, Lil may sue Tom or Ann. Lil may sue Tom because the original lease between them created privity of contract. Lil also may sue Ann because the covenant ran with the land to Ann. If Lil elects to sue Tom, he can recover from Ann.

3. Effect on the Landlord

When the tenant assigns the lease, all rights there-under are transferred to the assignee even if the assignee does not assume. Thus, the assignee, rather than the tenant, now can enforce the landlord's covenants.

Illustration: Tom's lease contained a covenant by Lil to insure. Tom assigned to Ann. Lil does not insure. Ann may enforce the covenant against Lil. If the covenant runs with the land, the benefit automatically runs to Ann. Even if the covenant does not run, Tom assigned its benefit to Ann. Therefore, only Ann can enforce the covenant; Tom no longer has standing.

Illustration: Tom's lease contained a covenant by Lil to supply heat to the premises and a covenant by Tom not to assign the lease without Lil's consent. Tom assigned his lease to Ann without Lil's consent. Ann may compel Lil to supply heat. Although the wrongful assignment permits Lil to terminate the tenancy, the assignment is valid if she does not do so. In that case, Ann receives the benefits of all covenants made by Lil to Tom.

4. Effect of a Second Assignment

An assuming assignee has the same duties to the landlord as the original tenant and, thus, remains liable on the lease covenants after a later assignment. In contrast, a nonassuming assignee is liable only on covenants that run with the land and then only while he has the right to possess the land. Once the nonassuming assignee assigns, no risk of future liability exists because he has no privity of contract or privity of estate with the landlord.

Illustration: Tom's lease contained a covenant that he would insure the premises. Under the applicable state's law, this covenant does not run with the land. Tom assigned to Ann who assumed. Ann then assigned to Bob who assumed. If Bob does not insure the premises, Lil may sue Tom, Ann, or Bob. Ann's liability under the assumption does not end when Ann assigns, just as Tom's liability survived the first assignment.

Illustration: Tom's lease contained the same covenant that he would insure the premises, and this covenant does not run with the land. Tom assigned to Ann who assumed. Ann then assigned to Bob who did not assume. If Bob does not insure, Lil may sue Tom or Ann but not Bob.

Illustration: Tom's lease contained the same covenant that he would insure the premises, and this covenant does not run with the land. Tom assigned to Ann who did not assume. Ann then assigned to Bob who also did not assume. If Bob does not insure, Lil's only remedy is against Tom.

Illustration: Tom's lease contained the same covenant that he would insure the premises, and this covenant does not run with the land. Tom assigned to Ann who did not assume. Ann then assigned to Bob who did assume. If the assumption agreement is valid, Lil can sue Tom or Bob. However, courts in many states hold that Bob assumed no obligation because Ann was not personally responsible. In these jurisdictions, Lil could sue only Tom.

Illustration: Tom's lease contained his covenant to repair, which runs with the land. Tom assigned to Ann who did not assume. Ann then assigned to Bob who also did not assume. If Bob does not repair, Lil may sue Tom or Bob but not Ann. Tom is liable on the original promise (privity of contract). Bob is liable because the covenant runs with the land, and he now owns the leasehold (privity of estate). Ann is not liable because she never assumed (no privity of contract) and because she no longer has an interest in the land (no privity of estate).

D. EFFECT OF A SUBLEASE

A sublease does not transfer the tenant's rights or duties to the subtenant. Instead, the tenant remains a tenant of the landlord, and the subtenant becomes a tenant of the tenant. The subtenant does not become a tenant of the landlord. No legal relationship exists between the subtenant and the landlord because no privity of estate or privity of contract exists between them. Therefore, at law, neither can directly enforce lease obligations against the other.

Illustration: Tom sublet to Sue. The original lease contained Tom's covenant to insure. If Sue does not insure, Lil has no remedy at law against her. But Tom remains liable on his covenant to Lil, and Lil may proceed against him. If Lil is entitled to terminate the tenancy for the failure to insure, termination of Tom's leasehold necessarily also terminates Sue's subleasehold.

Illustration: Tom sublet to Sue. In the sublease, Sue covenanted to insure the premises. If Sue does not insure, Tom can enforce the covenant. Lil cannot enforce the covenant because it was made to Tom, and no privity of contract or privity of estate exists between Lil and Sue. Possibly, Lil can be treated as a third party beneficiary of Sue's promise.

Illustration: Tom sublet to Sue. The original lease contained Tom's covenant to insure, and Sue assumed that obligation. If Sue fails to insure, Lil may sue her, because Lil is a third party beneficiary of Sue's assumption agreement.

Illustration: Tom sublet to Sue. The original lease contained Tom's covenant to repair, which runs with the land. Sue does not repair. Lil cannot sue Sue because, even though the covenant runs, it runs only with the estate (Tom's leasehold), and Tom has not transferred that estate to Sue.

See Chapter 6, p. 230–31. Tom has carved out a smaller and different estate for Sue. Lil's only legal relief is against Tom, who is in both privity of estate and privity of contract with Lil. However, Lil may be able to enforce the covenant against Sue as an equitable servitude if Sue had notice. See Chapter 6, p. 243–47.

CHAPTER FIVE

EASEMENTS

I. NATURE OF EASEMENTS

A. EASEMENTS DISTINGUISHED FROM POSSESSORY INTERESTS

"Owners" and tenants usually are regarded as having a possessory interest in property. In general, possessors may act as they please on their property and can exclude everyone else from it even though their presence would not directly injure the possessor. (The word "owner" has been placed in quotation marks here because a person may "own" an easement. The term "owner" is used here to refer to a person holding a possessory freehold estate in the land. "Tenant," of course, refers to a person holding a possessory non-freehold estate in land).

The holder of an easement is known as the dominant tenant (represented by "Dita" in the illustrations). The dominant tenant does not have the right to possess the property, but only a right to make some use of it. Thus, property subject to an easement is always possessed by someone other than the dominant tenant. In this context, the possessor is known as the servient tenant (usually represented by "Steve" in the illustrations).

1. No Right to Exclude

Possession generally includes the right to exclude others from the property. Because an easement is a nonpossessory interest, normally it does not include the right to exclude others or to stop them from also enjoying the property. However, an "exclusive" easement gives the dominant tenant the right to prevent the servient tenant from permitting others to use the easement.

Illustration: Steve, owning property in fee simple, granted a right of way on a road across it to Dita. She has an easement, not a possessory interest, in Steve's property. She may use the road, but she may not stop others from also using it, except to the extent that their use interferes with her use. In contrast, Steve, as possessor, may exclude everyone except Dita from crossing his property, even though their crossings constitute no real injury to Steve. As possessor, Steve also may continue to use the road himself, so long as he does not interfere with Dita. Had Steve leased or sold the road to Dita, thereby transferring full possession to her, she could have excluded Steve and all others from using the road even without showing that their use interfered with her use of the road.

Illustration: Lil leased her property to Tom for ten years. The lease restricts Tom to residential uses of the property. Tom has a possessory interest in the property and not just an easement. While Tom's possessory interest is limited in its use, Lil did not retain any untransferred use rights. Otherwise, she could run a business on the property so long as it did not interfere with Tom's residential use. Because Tom has possession, he may exclude all others, including Lil, from the premises.

2. "Right" and "Privilege" as used in this Chapter

Technically, the freedom to perform an act without penalty, such as the freedom to walk across land or to fish from it, is a "privilege," rather than a "right." Strictly speaking, a right is the ability to demand that others perform or not perform certain acts, such as the right to be paid and the right to exclude. However, where common usage is to the contrary, the word "right" will be used in the text to refer to what more properly should be called a privilege. For example, the texts refers to the "right to fish" and a "right of way" though, as a matter of law, these are privileges, rather than rights. See Restatement of Property §§ 1–5.

B. EASEMENTS DISTINGUISHED FROM OTHER NONPOSSESSORY INTERESTS

1. Profits

The owner of a profit has the right to remove some part or product of the soil of the servient estate. The common law profits were (a) turbary—the right to remove turf for use as fuel; (b) piscary—the right to fish; (c) estovers—the right to cut timber for fuel; and (d) pasture—the right to graze animals. Contemporary interests in land that sometimes are called profits are the right to mine coal or other minerals, to drill for oil or gas, or to cut timber. Generally, a profit includes incidental easements. For example, a profit to mine coal includes the incidental right to enter into the mine.

Virtually no material legal difference exists between easements and profits. Both generally come under the same rules. Under the new Restatement Third, easements and profits (as well as covenants running with the land) are categorized together as "servitudes" and generally are subject to the same rules.

2. Natural Rights in Land

By virtue of possession alone, a possessor has certain rights in neighboring lands. But these "natural rights" are different from an easement. No person acquires an easement in another's land merely by virtue of owning or possessing some other land. An easement must be created by some special act.

Illustration: Martin owns Lot 1, and Nora owns the adjacent Lot 2. Merely by virtue of owning Lot 1, Martin can prevent Nora from excavating so close to the lot line that the natural support her lot provides to his lot would be removed. See Chapter 15, p. 396–97.

Illustration: The owner of a downstream lot may be able to enjoin the owners of upstream lots from polluting the stream or from taking more than their fair share of water. See Chapter 14, p. 392–93.

3. Licenses

Easements may be categorized according to their duration in the same manner as estates. For instance, easements can be created in fee simple, for life, or for a certain term. However, there is no easement equivalent to the tenancy at will. When a use of land is terminable at the will of the servient tenant, it is a license, rather than an easement. The primary distinction between a license and an easement is that the former is terminable at will and the latter is not. A license is a revocable nonpossessory right to use land for a limited purpose, such as parking a car in a parking lot.

II. TYPES OF EASEMENTS

A. APPURTENANT OR IN GROSS

An appurtenant easement is intended to benefit a particular parcel of land (dominant estate or dominant tenement), rather than a particular individual. In contrast, an in gross easement is intended to benefit a particular individual regardless of whether she owns any land. The land that is subject to an appurtenant or in gross easement is called the servient estate or servient tenement.

Illustration: Steve granted Dita the right to swim in a pond on Steve's property. Dita is not a neighbor. This is probably an easement in gross. Dita may enjoy swimming in the pond regardless of what property she owns or whether she owns any property at all.

Illustration: Dita owned a large parcel of land adjacent to a stream. She sold the part of the property directly contiguous to the stream to Steve but reserved an easement to cross from her remaining property to the stream. Her easement is appurtenant. It was created to benefit the use of her retained parcel. When she sells the retained parcel, she no longer can use the easement.

An appurtenant easement is connected to the dominant estate even if the dominant and servient parcels are not adjacent. An easement may be appurtenant even though the two parcels are quite far from each other.

Illustration: Dita owns a parcel of land far upstream from Steve's land. Steve granted Dita the right to flood his property. The easement is appurtenant even though the parcels are separated if this privilege is connected to ownership of the upstream parcel, rather than given to Dita for use even after she sells her land.

1. No Dominant Tenement when the Easement is in Gross

An appurtenant easement always benefits some land held by the dominant tenant. An in gross easement does not necessarily benefit any particular parcel of land. An in gross easement is intended to benefit only its holder, though it incidentally may enhance her use of a parcel of land. Thus, when an easement is in gross, there is no dominant tenement although there is always a dominant tenant.

2. Profits

A profit may be appurtenant or in gross according to the same criteria as for easements.

Illustration: Steve granted Dita a profit to mine coal on his land. This profit is probably in gross since Dita may enjoy the privilege of mining regardless of what property she owns.

Illustration: Steve granted Dita a profit drain water from a lake on Steve's land to irrigate Dita's land. This profit is probably appurtenant because it is for the benefit of a particular parcel of land.

B. AFFIRMATIVE, NEGATIVE, OR SPURIOUS

An easement is affirmative when it entitles the dominant tenant to use the servient tenement for a particular purpose. It is negative when it entitles the dominant tenant to prevent the servient tenant from using the property in a particular way.

Illustration: Steve granted a right of way to Dita. Without this easement, Dita would be guilty of trespass if she walked across Steve's land. With the easement, however, Dita may cross without being liable for trespass. This easement is affirmative.

Illustration: Steve granted Dita an easement of view over his property. Without this easement, Steve could build on his property in a way that blocked Dita's view. After granting the easement, Steve no longer has this right. Dita has a negative easement.

The term "spurious easement" is sometimes used when the servient tenant agrees to perform an affirmative obligation. However, as its name indicates, it is not really an easement. Instead, its enforcement usually must be based on some theory other than easement law. One reason that these cannot be easements is that courts do not permit private parties to create "novel interests" in land. Easements can be created only for uses authorized by the courts or legislatures.

Illustration: Steve agreed with Dita that he would plant and care for a tree on his property. Dita does not have an easement in Steve's property. A negative easement would permit Dita to restrain, not compel, Steve from some use. Nor is this an affirmative easement, since Dita does not have the right to enter Steve's property to plant or care for the tree herself.

III.   CREATION OF EASEMENTS
AND LICENSES

A.   BY EXPRESS WORDS—GRANT
AND RESERVATION

The most usual way to convey an easement is by a deed or other written conveyance ("I grant to you a right of way across my lot."). Instead, when a landowner transfers his land and wishes to retain certain rights in it, he normally gives a deed that conveys title to the land but reserves an easement in it ("I grant Lot 1 to you but reserve a right of way across it from Lot 2 to the road."). The Restatement of Property provides that words of contract, as well as words of conveyance, may create an easement. Restatement (Third) of Property (Servitudes) § 2.1 (1998) (hereafter "Restatement of Servitudes"). Thus, an agreement providing for one party to have a right of way over the property of another is as effective as a deed.

At common law, the grantor had to "reserve" rather than "except" the easement, since only physical parts of the property could be excepted. At common law, the grantor also could reserve an easement only for herself and not for a third party. If she wanted a third party to have the benefit of the easement, she had to convey it directly to the third party. Alternatively, she could reserve it to herself and then transfer it to the third party if it was transferable. The Restatement of Servitudes, if followed by the jurisdiction, permits a servitude to be reserved for the benefit of a third party. Restatement of Servitudes § 2.6.

1. Formalities and Failure to Comply with Them—Licenses

Creation of an easement generally requires the same formalities as the transfer or creation of other interests in land. Usually, a writing, signature, and delivery of the document are necessary. When an attempt to create an easement fails because of noncompliance with the necessary formalities, the grantee acquires a license. Thus, the interest is revocable, subject only to those defenses prohibiting immediate revocation. See Section VII of this Chapter.

Illustration: Steve orally granted Dita a right of way across his property for ten years. The Statute of Frauds requires a signed writing to convey an interest in land exceeding one year. As a result, Steve's grant did not give Dita an easement, but it did give her a license to cross his land. Therefore, Dita will not be trespassing when she crosses his land, but Steve may revoke her privilege to do so at any time. This license is akin to the tenancy at will that is created when a grantee enters property under a void deed. See Chapter 4, p. 133.

2. Formal Creation of Licenses

Not all licenses arise because of inadequate attempts to create an easement. A revocable privilege of use may be precisely what the parties intend.

Illustration: Steve delivered to Dita a written and signed instrument that provided: "You may walk across my property until I change my mind." Even if the document complies with all the formalities for a conveyance, it creates only a license because it expressly makes the interest revocable.

3. Other Revocable Rights to Use

A license can arise not only from a failed attempt to create an easement or from an express declaration of revocability, but also because the parties have created an interest too limited to be characterized as an easement.

Illustration: Steve invited Dita to a party at his house. This was a license, even if the invitation was written and says that it is irrevocable. The right to enter land that is created by a party invitation is too slight to be an easement.

Illustration: Steve sold Dita a ticket to watch a sporting event on his property. Despite the enforceable contract underlying the ticket, it created only a license. If Steve breaches the contract by refusing Dita admission, she has only an action for damages.

B. BY IMPLICATION—QUASI–EASEMENT

In limited circumstances, a court will imply an easement as a matter of law. Generally, a court will imply an easement only if the circumstances indicate that the dominant and servient tenants must have intended to create an easement, though they failed to do so expressly. An implied easement will be created only if an express easement could have been created.

Illustration: Dita owned a large parcel of land. A house on the rear half of the parcel had access to a public road only over a driveway running from the house across the front half of the parcel. Dita sold the front half of the parcel to Steve without expressly reserving a right of way over it. Since Dita could have reserved such an easement and since it appears that such an easement would have been reserved had the parties thought about it, a court probably will hold that an easement was created by implied reservation.

1. Severance of Parcels

An implied easement can be created only when the grantor conveys only a part of the property she owns or when she divides the entire property among separate grantees. In either case, an earlier ownership has been severed into multiple ownership.

In the following illustrations, assume that Owen began by owning a large parcel of land with a house on the rear half and a driveway running from it over the front half of the land to a public street.

Illustration: Owen conveyed the rear half to Dita and retained the front half. Under these circumstances, an easement can be implied in favor of Dita's half over the driveway on Owen's half.

Illustration: Owen conveyed the rear half to Dita and the front half to Steve. Under these circumstances, an easement can be implied in favor of Dita's half over the driveway on Steve's half.

Illustration: Owen conveyed the entire parcel to Dita. An easement will not be implied over the neighboring parcel even if a driveway from Owen's house crosses it. If Owen did not have an easement across the neighboring parcel, he could not have conveyed an express easement across it to Dita. Therefore, an implied easement cannot be created. Conversely, if Owen had an appurtenant easement over the neighboring land, the transfer of Owen's lot to Dita automatically would transfer the existing easement to Dita. It would not be created by implication.

Illustration: Owen conveyed the front half to Steve. Because of the circumstances existing when Owen gave the conveyance, an implied easement in favor of the rear half was not implied at that time. Owen later conveyed the rear half to Dita. An implied easement cannot be created as a result of this second conveyance regardless of the circumstances, because the severance of ownership already had occurred. When Owen conveyed the rear half to Dita, he could not create an express easement over the front half for her because he no longer owned that portion of the property.

Illustration: Owen conveyed the front half to Steve. Because of the circumstances existing when Owen gave the conveyance, an implied easement in favor of Owen's retained half was not implied at that time. Owen later conveyed the rear half to Dita. Dita then conveyed it to Edna. Because an easement was not implied over the front half when its ownership was severed from the rear half, an easement over it will not be created by implication or by express language merely because the rear half has been sold. Once the front half is separately owned, its owner (Steve) must consent to the creation of an easement over it.

a. Implied Grant and Implied Reservation

An implied easement can be created by grant or by reservation.

Illustration: Dita owned a parcel of land with a house on the rear half and a driveway running from the house over the front half of the lot to the street. Dita sold the front half of the lot to Steve. If an easement is implied from the circumstances of this conveyance, the easement was *reserved* by Dita for her retained parcel.

Illustration: Steve owned a parcel of land with a house on the rear half and a driveway running from the house over the front half of the lot to the street. Steve sold the rear half of the lot to Dita. If an easement is implied from the circumstances of this conveyance, the easement was *granted* by Steve to Dita together with the rear half of the lot.

Illustration: Dita and Steve owned adjacent lots. For several months, Dita drove across Steve's lot without his permission to get to a road, leaving a well-worn path visible on Steve's land. Dita then sold her lot to Ann. Ann has no easement over Steve's lot. Dita could not have conveyed an easement to Ann because she did not own one over Steve's lot. An implied easement can be created only if an express easement could have been.

2. Prior Use

An easement is implied at the time of severance only if the use existed before the severance. Such prior use was not an easement because the user also owned the property subject to the use, so that the right to use did not exist as a separate interest in another's property. The term "quasi-easement" refers to a use that would have been an easement if the dominant and servient properties had been owned separately. Thus, for an easement to be created by implication, a quasi-easement must have existed before the severance.

Illustration: Dita owned a parcel of land with a house on the rear half and a driveway running from the house over the front half of the lot to the street. Dita sold the front half to Steve. Since the driveway and Dita's use of it existed as a quasi-easement before Dita conveyed to Steve, a court may imply an easement in her favor.

Illustration: Dita owned a parcel of land with a house on the rear half. After Dita sold the front half of the parcel to Steve, she first began to drive across it. A quasi-easement did not exist before the conveyance. Consequently, a court will not imply an easement in Dita's favor.

3. Characteristics of the Prior Use

A preexisting use will not necessarily be converted into an easement after severance. Courts generally use adjectives such as "apparent," "continuous," "permanent," "necessary," or "beneficial" to indicate the characteristics that the quasi-easement must have to be converted into an easement.

a. Apparent

Since the basis for implying an easement is an assumption that the parties would have created one by express language had they considered the matter, the quasi-easement generally must be apparent to justify such an inference. However, apparent does not necessarily mean visible. Uses that are discoverable by an inspection also can be apparent.

Illustration: When Dita sold the front half of her property to Steve, a paved driveway ran across it to Dita's house on the rear half. Even though Dita was not actually driving over the driveway when Steve purchased, the driveway is apparent, and an easement over it may be implied in favor of Dita.

Illustration: Owen owns two houses. Both houses are connected to a public sewer by a sewer pipe that runs under the front house. Although the sewer pipe is underground, an inspection by a plumber would reveal that fact. Consequently, a court may hold that the pipe is apparent. Thus, when Owen sells either house, an easement under the front house in favor of the rear house may be implied. The Restatement of Servitudes goes further than the traditional common law rule and provides that underground utilities serving either parcel need not be apparent or known to create an easement by implication. Restatement § 2.12, comment g.

b. Permanent—Continuous

Unless there are indications that the preexisting use was permanent and would continue after the severance, no basis exists for assuming that the parties necessarily would have intended to create an easement had they thought about it. Thus, courts require that the quasi-easement be permanent or continuous. The Restatement of Servitudes incorporates this requirement by stating that the prior use must not be "merely temporary or casual." Restatement § 2.12.

Illustration: When Dita sold the front half of her property to Steve, she drove across it to reach her house on the rear half. However, there is no driveway or other indication of use. Since no evidence exists that Dita regularly used the front half for passage to the rear half, an easement of passage will not be implied.

Illustration: Dita paved a road from her house on the rear half of her property across the front half. When she sold the front half to Steve, an easement of passage might be implied since a paved driveway indicates a permanent burden on the front half in favor of the rear half.

c. *Necessary—Beneficial*

When a court creates an implied easement, it not only confers a property interest on one party, it also deprives the other party of an interest without her consent. Therefore, courts are reluctant to do so unless it serves some significant purpose. They require that the easement be necessary or beneficial to the owner of the prospective dominant parcel.

Many courts require strict necessity to create a reserved easement, but only mere convenience to the dominant parcel to create an easement by implied grant. An easement by implied reservation gives the grantor an easement in the property he granted even though, as the drafter of the deed, he had the full opportunity to expressly reserve an easement. Moreover, the deed often contains covenants of title that warrant the title to be free of any easement not expressly disclosed in the deed. Thus, courts are more reluctant to imply a reserved easement in favor of the grantor than a granted easement to the grantee.

Illustration: Steve's house on the rear half of his lot is connected to a driveway that runs across the front half to the street. Steve sold the rear half to Dita. Even though Dita could build a new driveway on her property that runs to a different street, a court may imply an easement by grant in her favor because of the cost to build a new driveway.

Illustration: Dita's house on the rear half of her lot is connected to a driveway that runs across the front half to the street. Dita sold the front half to Steve. Although Dita could build a driveway on her retained property that runs to a different street, it would be expensive. Courts that require absolute necessity to create an implied reserved easement will not create the easement because Dita can gain access by other means, albeit at a heavy cost.

C.   BY NECESSITY

When land is subdivided in a way that leaves a part of it without access to a road, an easement of passage (way by necessity) is implied across the other part or parts. This implication rests on a public policy against useless (landlocked) land. Consequently, the implication does not depend on the parties' actions, the circumstances of the conveyance, or any prior quasi-easement. However, it may be defeated by contrary language in the deed that subdivided the land. A way by necessity lasts only for so long as the necessity exists.

Illustration: Dita granted Steve the front half of her land. As a result, the rear half became landlocked. Even though a quasi-easement did not exist before the severance, an easement of access now exists over Steve's land.

1. Implied from a Plat

If a subdivider shows a home buyer in a newly created subdivision a map (plat) of the area that shows her house as fronting on a public street, she has a legitimate expectation that the subdivider will construct the streets and open them for public use. Courts enforce this expectation by creating an implied easement of access over the streets shown on the map. Some courts imply the easement over all the streets in the subdivision (beneficial or full enjoyment rule), whereas others limit the easement to those streets necessary for access from the property to the nearest public way (narrow or necessary rule). An intermediate rule makes the scope of the easement as extensive as necessary to protect the market value of the buyer's property. The Restatement of Servitudes provides that mapped streets imply an easement to use the street and that mapping of amenities, such as parks and beaches, implies the creation of servitudes in those lands for that purpose. Restatement § 2.13. For the implication of other servitudes from a general plan, see Chapter 6.

D. BY PRESCRIPTION

The doctrine of prescriptive easements is analogous to the doctrine of adverse possession. Most of the rules and concepts applicable to adverse possession are applicable to prescription as well. See Chapter 1. Those principles will be mentioned only briefly here.

Adverse possession depends on the statutes of limitations governing possessory actions. Since ejectment does not lie for adverse use, that statute of limitations is inapplicable to prescription. The doctrine of prescriptive easements arises only by judicial analogy to adverse possession, rather than as a direct result of legislation.

The original judicial rationale for the creation of prescriptive easements was the fiction that a use that had continued long enough probably had commenced with the grant of an easement that since had gotten lost. The possessor's failure to stop the adverse use was taken as proof that the possessor long ago had given permission to the user. Courts generally have abandoned this theory, although in some cases a few of the standards of prescription derive from that old view. For example, some courts require that the use be "peaceable." Today, most states strictly analogize prescriptive easements to adverse possession and only modify the rules to conform them to the special characteristics of easements.

The Restatement of Servitudes § 2.17 states that prescriptive use should include actions taken pursuant to the terms of "an intended but imperfectly created servitude," such as when the absence of a writing defeats the creation of a legal easement, but the intended beneficiary thereafter used the property as if she were entitled to do so.

1. Prescriptive Use v. Prescriptive Possession

Many activities can be viewed either as a use of the property or as possession of the property. Thus, a long continued activity may lead to a finding of either adverse possession or a prescriptive easement. The property owner's behavior during the prescriptive period may be the controlling factor.

Illustration: Dita regularly grazes her cattle on Steve's land. Her use could ripen into either adverse possession of the property or a prescriptive easement to graze. The outcome probably depends on whether Steve also uses the property during the same time period. If Steve is also using the property, Dita cannot claim title by adverse possession since her possession is neither exclusive nor uninterrupted. But, under these same circumstances, Dita can claim a prescriptive right to graze. On the other hand, if Steve does not use the land and it is primarily grazing land, Dita's same acts could give her title by adverse possession.

2. Elements of Prescription

a. *Adverse, Hostile*

These requirements, borrowed from adverse possession, have the same meaning in this context. They generally ignore the user's state of mind but require that her activities are taken without the owner's permission. In some jurisdictions, an owner may establish that all uses are permissive by posting a sign on the property to that effect, which may be easier than constantly monitoring the property. In some jurisdictions, an owner is presumed to have given permission to others to use unenclosed and unimproved land.

b. *Payment of Taxes*

Many states limit adverse possession to situations in which the possessor has paid property taxes during the limitations period. However, since easements are rarely assessed or taxed separately, this is usually not a requirement for prescription.

c. *Exclusive*

It is a general requirement of adverse possession that the claimant's possession be exclusive. Although courts frequently state that a prescriptive easement also requires the use to be exclusive, this does not mean that no one else can make any use of the property during the prescriptive period. At most, it means that the user claims a special right to carry on the use. Thus, a person walking over the property under the claim that it is a public right of way may fail to qualify as a prescriptive user.

d. *Uninterrupted*

An adverse possession is interrupted by the actual or judicial taking of possession by the owner or someone else. But possession in another does not necessarily conflict with an adverse use and will not automatically interrupt a ripening prescriptive easement. Only the actual interruption of the use is sufficient to prevent prescription.

Illustration: Dita consistently walked across Steve's property for twenty-five years. During that time, Steve also used the property for various purposes, such as walking and grazing cattle. Steve's use and possession of the property did not interrupt Dita's use, so she may claim a prescriptive easement.

Illustration: Dita walked across Steve's property until Steve erected a fence barring her. The fence interrupted Dita's use and prevented her from acquiring a prescriptive easement if it occurred before the statute of limitations expired.

(1) Ineffective Interruptions

An interruption stops prescription only if it effectively interrupts the use. However, under the lost grant theory, even an ineffectual interruption could bar prescription by refuting the inference of a lost grant having been given by the servient tenant.

Illustration: Dita consistently walked across Steve's property. Steve built a fence to stop her, but she knocked it down and continued crossing. Steve did not interrupt Dita's use.

Illustration: Dita consistently walked across Steve's property. Steve informed Dita that she could continue to do so. Steve's grant of permission did not stop the statute of limitations. Steve cannot eliminate the adverseness of Dita's use by unilaterally consenting to it.

3. Prescriptive Easements as Appurtenant or in Gross

Depending on the circumstances, a prescriptive easement can be either appurtenant or in gross.

Illustration: Dita consistently walked from her property across Steve's property to get to the road. Dita acquired an appurtenant easement.

Illustration: Dita consistently fished in a lake owned by Steve. Dita does not live near Steve and changed residences several times during the prescriptive period. Dita probably acquired an in gross easement.

a. Negative Prescriptive Easements

Generally, acquiring a negative easement by prescription is impossible since the alleged dominant tenant has not conducted an activity that was wrongful as to the servient tenant.

Illustration: Dita has looked out from her windows over Steve's land for thirty years. She now seeks to enjoin him from building in a manner that would interfere with her claimed easement of view. Dita will fail since her enjoyment of the view was not wrongful as to Steve. As a property owner, Dita was privileged to look over Steve's property, and he could not have enjoined her from doing so. Her privileged act cannot ripen into a right to stop Steve from engaging in his privileged act of building. Steve has no duty not to build as a result of having failed to build in the past. However, the English doctrine of "ancient lights" dictates a contrary result. And under the new Restatement's use of prescription to cure imperfectly created servitudes, an oral grant of an easement of view by Steve, coupled with thirty years of looking by Dita, would ripen into a prescriptive easement.

Illustration: Dita erected a building on her land twenty-five years ago. The building is so heavy that it would have subsided if Steve had excavated on his adjoining land. Dita has not thereby acquired an easement of support. Steve has not had a cause of action against Dita for the past twenty-five years. She was privileged to build her building, and he was privileged to excavate. His failure to exercise his privilege for the past twenty-five years has not caused him to lose it, and Dita's continued exercise of her privilege for that time did not convert it into a right to demand that Steve not exercise his privilege to excavate. Steve is under no duty to support her building by not excavating. See Chapter 15 on support.

IV. TRANSFER OF EASEMENTS

A. TRANSFER OF AN EASEMENT'S BURDEN

When the servient tenement is transferred, the burden of the easement transfers with it because an owner cannot convey more than she has. Thus, the easement's burden always "runs with the land." However, this doctrine is subject to the operation of the recording acts. See Chapter 10.

B. TRANSFER OF AN EASEMENT'S BENEFIT

An appurtenant easement always benefits a dominant tenement, but an in gross easement has no dominant tenement. It has only a dominant tenant. Thus, the rules for transfer of an easement's benefit differ according to the nature of the easement.

1. Transfer of an In Gross Easement's Benefit

Originally, the benefit of an in gross easement was nontransferable. It was regarded as conferring too slight a benefit compared to the burden on the servient tenement to warrant the extensive clouding of title that transferability would entail. Because in gross easements of a commercial nature do have a significant benefit, however, the modern view is to permit them to be transferred.

2. Transfer of an Appurtenant Easement's Benefit

An appurtenant easement's benefit is automatically transferred with the dominant tenement, unless the grant expressly provides otherwise. Thus, an appurtenant easement "runs with the land." Excluding the easement from the transfer of the dominant estate may leave the easement with the transferor or it may destroy the easement.

Illustration: Dita had an appurtenant right of way easement across Steve's property. When Dita sold her land, the buyer obtained both the land and the easement appurtenant to it, even if the deed did not expressly grant the easement.

Illustration: Dita had an appurtenant right of way easement across Steve's property. When Dita sold her property, she expressly excepted the right of way from the grant. The easement was either extinguished or converted it into an in gross easement held by Dita. The result depends on whether the easement's creator intended that it could exist independent of the former dominant tenement.

Illustration: Dita had an appurtenant right of way easement across Steve's property. She purported to grant the right of way to Ann without conveying her land to Ann. Ann did not acquire the right of way over Steve's property, because the easement would be changed impermissibly from appurtenant to in gross.

3. Transferability Affected by the Creating Language

The parties can modify the foregoing rules by providing otherwise in the instrument by which the easement was created. A transferable easement can be made nontransferable, and a nontransferable easement can be made transferable.

Illustration: Steve's deed to Dita said: "I give you the right to walk from your property across my property. However, if you ever convey your property, this right will expire." Although this easement is appurtenant, it is not transferable with the dominant tenement.

Illustration: Steve's deed to Dita said: "I give you the right to swim in my lake, wherever you reside. You may transfer this right to other members of your family." Although this is a noncommercial easement in gross, it is transferable under the circumstances specified in the deed.

V. SUBDIVISION OF EASEMENTS

A. SUBDIVISION OF THE BURDEN

When the servient tenement is subdivided, each part of the property remains subject to the easement, unless the easement is located on only some parts of the servient tenement. A servient owner has no greater power to extinguish an easement by subdividing the property than she does by transferring it. See p. 213.

Illustration: Steve's property was subject to an easement of passage that crossed the property from east to west. Steve subdivided his land into western and eastern parcels. Both parcels remain subject to the easement.

Illustration: Steve's property was subject to an easement of passage that crossed the property from east to west along its northerly boundary. Steve subdivided his land into northern and southern parcels. The northern parcel is subject to the easement, but the southern parcel is not since that part of the property was never subject it.

B. SUBDIVISION OF THE BENEFIT

The distinction between appurtenant and in gross easements is relevant to this issue, as it was to the transfer of an easement's benefits. See p. 213.

1.   Subdivision of an In Gross Easement's Benefit

In jurisdictions where in gross easements are not transferable or are transferable only if commercial, the easement's benefits may not be subdivided or apportioned if they could not be transferred. In jurisdictions where transfers are allowed, no clear standard governs the easement's subdivisibility. However, an exclusive easement is generally more readily subdivisible than a nonexclusive easement, and other terms in the grant may furnish additional guidance as to the parties' intent. For prescriptive easements, a court must determine whether the servient tenant's original acquiescence reasonably can be enlarged to encompass a use by more than one dominant tenant.

2.   Subdivision of an In Gross Profit's Benefit

Some courts apply different standards to the subdivisibility of an in gross profit. In some jurisdictions, a profit in gross is subdivisible if it is admeasurable, i.e. quantifiable. In others, the Rule of Mountjoy's Case is applied to permit subdivision of a profit only when it will continue to be worked as a common stock.

Illustration: Dita has the right to mine fifty tons of coal a month from Steve's land. Since this is an admeasurable profit, some states will permit her to subdivide, so long as no more than fifty tons of coal are removed per month. In other jurisdictions, Dita may subdivide the profit only if all the takers mine the coal jointly and not through separate operations.

3. Subdivision of an Appurtenant Easement's Benefit

An appurtenant easement's benefit automatically is subdivided when the dominant tenement is subdivided unless the original grant prohibits subdivision or the subdividing grants expressly negate a transfer of the benefit.

Illustration: Steve granted Dita a right of way across his property. Dita subdivided her lot into three parcels and conveyed one each to Ann, Bob, and Cathy. Ann, Bob, and Cathy all have rights of way across Steve's property.

Illustration: Steve granted Dita a right of way across his property from her existing house. Dita subdivided her land into three parcels and conveyed one each to Ann, Bob, and Cathy. Ann received the parcel with the house. Only Ann has a right of way across Steve's property.

Illustration: Steve granted Dita a right of way across his property. Dita subdivided her lot into three parcels and conveyed one each to Ann, Bob, and Cathy. In the deeds to Bob and Cathy, Dita expressly excepted the right of way across Steve's property from the grant. Only Ann has a right of way.

VI. SCOPE OF EASEMENTS

This section concerns the variety of activities that are permitted to the dominant and servient tenants with regard to the easement.

A. VARIATIONS BY THE DOMINANT TENANT

No grant or reservation of an easement sets forth with total precision the exact nature of the activity that the dominant tenant may undertake or restrain. Consequently, courts frequently must determine whether some new activity is within the easement's scope. The following series illustrations indicate some of the ways in which a dominant tenant may seek to vary an easement's benefit.

Location of the Benefit–Illustration: Dita has a right of way from her house across Steve's land. She wants to relocate the house elsewhere on her property and continue to use the right of way.

Enlargement of the Benefit–Illustration: Dita has the right to run water in a ditch across Steve's property to irrigate her land. She now seeks to run water in the ditch to irrigate the parcel adjacent to her land as well.

Location of the Burden–Illustration: Dita has a right of way located along the northern boundary of Steve's property. She now wants to cross along the southern boundary of Steve's property instead.

Activity on the Dominant Tenement–Illustration: Dita has a right to run water in a ditch across Steve's property to water her cattle. She now seeks to run water in the ditch for irrigation instead.

Activity on the Servient Tenement–Illustration: Dita has a right of way over Steve's property. She now seeks to (1) drive, rather than walk, across the property, (2) cross at night instead of during the day, (3) cross twice a day instead of once a day, or (4) bring friends with her instead of crossing alone.

1. Standards for Determining Whether the Variation is Allowable

a. When there is Explicit Language

If the language that created the easement is explicit as to any matter, the dominant tenant cannot deviate from what has been specified.

Illustration: Steve granted Dita a right of way ten feet wide across the north end of his property. Dita cannot widen the path or relocate it even though the change would not harm Steve.

Illustration: Steve granted Dita the right to run water in a ditch across his property for irrigation purposes only. Dita cannot use the water for any non-irrigation purposes, even though Steve would not be injured by the change.

b. When there is no Explicit Language

When the language that created the easement does not specify whether the new activity is allowable, no single rule resolves the question. Some authorities look at a variety of factors, including the circumstances of the original grant, the consideration paid for it, and the prior and subsequent uses of the servient tenement. Others follow a "rule of reason," which permits only reasonable rights and burdens. Both approaches attempt to do what the parties would have done if they considered the matter and acted reasonably about it.

Illustration: Dita has a right of way across Steve's property. The grant of the right of way does not specify a mode of transportation. Dita originally rode a horse across Steve's property but now seeks to drive a car instead. Some authorities would look at the circumstances of the grant (whether the parties had cars at the time, whether the road was paved), how much Dita paid for the easement, and whether a car was ever driven over the road before or after the easement was given. Courts applying the rule of reason would assess whether driving a car is a reasonable activity for Dita and whether it would be unreasonably burdensome to Steve.

An implied easement is the most difficult to interpret with regard to scope. In general, the circumstances that were considered to determine whether the easement was created will determine its nature and extent.

c. When the Easement is Prescriptive

With a prescriptive easement, the only factor to consider is the previous use, because there is no writing. However, courts agree that the use is not limited to the precise original use. Rather, the prescriptive use is used as a guide to determine whether the servient tenant would have acquiesced to the new use, as well as to the original use.

Illustration: Dita walked across Steve's property at 5 p.m. every day for twenty-five years. Now she wants to walk across his property at 6 p.m. Based on Steve's failure to stop Dita at 5 p.m., a court might conclude that Steve would not have stopped her at 6 p.m. Thus, Dita may now cross at 6 p.m.

Illustration: Dita walked across Steve's property every day for twenty-five years. Now she wants to drive a car across his property instead. A court might conclude that Steve would have stopped Dita from crossing if she had driven, rather than walked. Thus, Dita will not be allowed to drive.

2. Changes Caused by Development of the Dominant Tenement

Courts generally hold that use of the easement can change when the dominant tenement is developed if the development is normal or reasonable and if the new activity is reasonably required by the dominant tenant. This holding is based on the assumption that, when the easement was created, the parties must have anticipated that changes would occur and would have agreed in advance to changes in the easement's use if they had thought about it. However, while a reasonable servient tenant probably would agree to normal development of the dominant tenement, he probably would not consent to a change that unreasonably burdened his own property, even if it were the result of normal growth of the dominant tenement.

Illustration: Steve granted a right of way to Dita when she used her land as a farm. The entire area now is becoming residential. Dita has built several houses on her property and seeks to use the right of way for access to all the houses. This use should be allowed, because this development of Dita's property is reasonable, the right of way is reasonably required by the houses for access, and the new use does not increase the burden on the servient estate.

Illustration: Steve granted a right of way to Dita when she used her land as a farm. Valuable minerals now have been found on Dita's land and on other nearby properties, and extensive mining activity has begun. Dita wants to use the right of way for trucks to carry the ores. Although mining may be a reasonable use of Dita's land, the additional noise and disruption caused by the trucks substantially increase the burden on the servient estate. Therefore, a court should enjoin this new use. However, many courts consider only Dita's use and do not consider the burden on the servient estate. In return, the dominant tenant, rather than the servient tenant, is obliged to keep the easement in repair, though injured third parties still may be able to recover against the servient tenant, because he possesses the land.

B. VARIATIONS BY THE SERVIENT TENANT

1. Nature of the Dominant Tenant's Rights

An easement holder has rights of use rather than

rights of possession. Therefore, a dominant tenant
may not sue in trespass or ejectment. Instead, she is
limited to a cause of action for unreasonable interference with the easement. Therefore, harm is a far more
essential element to protect an easement than to protect possession.

Illustration: Dita has a right of way over a road on Steve's
land. Ann has started walking on the same road without
anyone's consent. Dita can obtain judicial relief against Ann
only if she can show that Ann's activity unreasonably interferes with her right of way. But Steve can recover from Ann
in trespass without showing any direct injury from her
activity.

2. Nature of the Servient Tenant's Rights

By granting a particular use to a dominant tenant,
the servient tenant does not lose the right to use the
property in the same way or in any other way, so long
as he does not unreasonably interfere with the dominant tenant's use.

Illustration: Steve granted a right of way to Dita. Steve
may continue to walk on the road and to do any other act he
pleases on the road, so long as it does not unreasonably
hinder Dita's right of passage.

a. Third Parties' Rights

Since the servient tenant retains the right to make
all noninterfering uses of the property, she may permit others to make similar uses.

Illustration: Steve gave Dita a right of way across his
property. Steve may permit Ann to use the same road so

long as her use does not unreasonably hamper Dita's use. Both Dita and Ann are now dominant tenants.

VII. TERMINATION OF EASEMENTS

As described in this section, easements can be terminated in a variety of ways, thereby eliminating the burden on the servient estate.

A. TERMINATION BY LANGUAGE IN THE GRANT

An easement may be created for a limited or conditional duration. When the time passes or the condition occurs, the easement ends.

Illustration: Steve granted Dita the right to cross his property for so long as she lives in the house next door. Once Dita moves, the easement ends.

Illustration: Dita's ten-year lease of a house included the right to walk across the adjacent lot owned by the landlord, Steve. When the lease expires, the easement is terminated.

Illustration: Steve granted Dita the right to park in his garage. A fire destroyed the garage, and Steve elected not to rebuild. Dita's easement ended, because it implicitly was conditioned on the continued existence of the structure that was the servient tenement.

1. Termination of Licenses

A license usually expires when it is revoked. However, if it is a license only because the parties failed to comply with the necessary formalities for an easement (see p. 199), the license is irrevocable if the licensee expended time or money in reasonable reliance on it.

Consequently, it cannot be terminated at the licensor's will. The Restatement of Servitudes treats reasonable reliance as creating an exception to the Statute of Frauds (§ 2.9) or as creating an easement by estoppel (§ 2.10).

Illustration: Steve orally granted Dita the permanent right to maintain a sewer pipe under his land. In reliance on Steve's grant, Dita built and installed the pipe. The grant created a license because it was oral even though the parties intended to create an irrevocable interest. But Dita's expenditure of time and money made the license irrevocable. Steve is estopped to revoke Dita's interest.

Illustration: Steve executed a written grant to Dita that stated: "You may drive across my property until I change my mind." Dita then paved the road on Steve's property. Steve may revoke, because Dita's expenditure of money was not made in reasonable reliance on a permanent grant. The grant was of a license because of the grant's express language of revocability and not because the parties failed to comply with the Statute of Frauds.

a. Duration of Irrevocable Licenses

A license that is irrevocable because of estoppel may be terminated when conditions have changed or when the licensee has recovered the value of her reliance.

B. MERGER

When the dominant tenant acquires the servient tenement, the easement merges into the fee title and is extinguished because an owner cannot have an easement in her own property. Similarly, when the servient tenant of an appurtenant easement acquires the dominant tenement, the easement is extinguished by merger.

Illustration: Dita had a right of way across Steve's land. She then bought Steve's land. As the owner of the servient tenement, she has the right to cross it without needing an easement. Therefore, the easement is extinguished.

1. Temporary Merger or Reseparation

If the dominant tenant acquires only a temporary possessory interest in the servient estate, the easement is merely suspended until the possessory interest ends. On the other hand, if the easement was extinguished by a complete merger of the parcels, it is not revived if they subsequently are separated again. However, a new easement may be implied from the severance.

Illustration: Dita had a right of way across Steve's land. Dita then rented Steve's land for five years. During the lease term, Dita did not have an easement, but the easement resumed when the term expired.

Illustration: Dita acquired a right of way easement across Steve's land. She then purchased Steve's land and later sold her original parcel to Ann. The deed to Ann did not expressly convey a right of way over Dita's retained parcel. Ann did not acquire an easement because it was extinguished when Dita acquired the servient tenement. However, an implied easement might have been created if an apparent, continuous, and necessary quasi-easement existed when Dita conveyed to Ann. See p. 181–85.

C. RELEASE (ABANDONMENT)

An easement is formally extinguished by a release deed from the dominant tenant to the servient tenant.

The deed transfers the easement back to the servient tenant, and the easement merges into the larger possessory estate. All the formalities for the creation of an easement apply to the release of an easement. Therefore, an oral statement by the dominant tenant that purports to terminate the easement or to transfer it to the servient tenant is ineffective for lack of compliance with the Statute of Frauds. However, under principles somewhat similar to the abandonment and surrender of leaseholds (see Chapter 4, p. 145), easements can be terminated by operation of law under certain circumstances.

1.   By Words Alone

A mere oral attempt to terminate an easement is ineffective, because it violates the Statute of Frauds.

2.   By Nonuse Alone

Mere nonuse by the dominant tenant does not terminate an easement. The holder of a property right does not have to exercise it to keep it alive. However, in some jurisdictions, prescriptive easements are terminated by a period of nonuse equal to the limitations period to create such easements.

3.   By Words and Nonuse

An easement may be terminated by the dominant tenant's oral statements signifying an intent to abandon followed by nonuse of the easement. The nonuse makes up for the lack of a writing if the nonuse continues long enough to substantiate the statement of intent. The duration of nonuse must be long enough to verify the intent to abandon. Easements can be terminated in such cases because their destruction creates no void in ownership. The servient tenant merely is restored to unburdened, complete ownership.

4. By Words and Inconsistent Acts

An easement may be terminated by the dominant tenant's oral statements coupled with significant acts by her that are inconsistent with the continuance of the easement.

Illustration: Dita had a right of way on a road across Steve's property. She told Steve that she no longer would use the road and then built a fence blocking her access to the road. The easement is extinguished by the combination of Dita's statements and acts.

5. By Inconsistent Acts Alone

Sometimes, the dominant tenant's actions may be so permanent and inconsistent with continuation of the easement that an intent to abandon may be inferred, and the easement is thereby terminated.

Illustration: Dita had an easement of view across Steve's property. She tore down her house and erected a permanent windowless building on her property. Even though she made no statements, an intent to abandon may be inferred, and her easement is terminated.

6. By Words of the Dominant Tenant and Acts of the Servient Tenant—Estoppel

An easement may be terminated by the dominant tenant's oral statement followed by acts of the servient tenant in reliance on the statement. The servient tenant's acts cannot prove the dominant tenant's intent to abandon. If these acts involve an expenditure of money or other detrimental reliance, the dominant tenant is estopped from reasserting the easement. This result may be viewed as a parol license to the servient tenant to terminate the easement, which becomes irrevocable by virtue of his reliance. See p. 223.

Illustration: Dita told Steve that she was giving up her right of way across his land. In reliance on this statement, Steve erected a building across the road. Dita is estopped to assert that the easement was not terminated.

Illustration: Dita stopped using her right of way across Steve's land, and Steve plowed up the road. Dita is not estopped from claiming her easement, because she made no statements inducing reliance by Steve and because Steve will not be harmed if the road is reopened.

D. ADVERSE USE

The dominant tenant has a cause of action for unreasonable interference with the easement by the servient tenant or any third party. However, if the dominant tenant does not assert this cause of action in a timely fashion, it is lost. The rules concerning adverse possession and prescriptive easements are applicable.

Illustration: Dita had a right of way across Steve's land. Steve erected a fence barring Dita from access for twenty-five years. Dita has lost her easement.

Illustration: Dita had a right of way across Steve's land. Steve walked across the same road for twenty-five years. Dita has not lost her easement unless Steve's actions unreasonably interfered with her passage.

Illustration: Dita had a right of way across Steve's land, but she has not used it for twenty-five years. Nonuse alone does not destroy the easement. Steve must have acted adversely to her interest during the period of nonuse to destroy the easement.

Although some courts hold that an easement in a building is destroyed when the servient tenant intentionally destroys it, the majority view is that termination occurs only if the destruction was accidental or the structure had become so obsolete that the servient owner was forced to destroy it. This result is reached on the ground that the building's continued existence was an implied condition to the easement (i.e. "You may cross through my building so long as there is a building.").

E. INVALIDITY

Like other interests in land, easements and profits are invalid if they violate the Rule Against Perpetuities, especially if they are in gross and, therefore, not tied to the duration of a dominant tenement. However, the Restatement of Servitudes (§ 3.3), the Uniform Common Interest Ownership Act (§ 2–103), and the Uniform Condominium Act (§ 2–103) propose that the Rule be inapplicable to servitudes and to the power to create them. The rule against restraints on alienation also may invalidate easements and profits, although public purposes such as historic preservation may make the restrictions reasonable.

CHAPTER SIX

COVENANTS RUNNING WITH THE LAND

An interest "runs with the land" when a subsequent owner of the land has the burden or benefit of that interest. Thus, an appurtenant easement runs with the land since the servient tenement remains subject to it after being transferred, and the dominant tenement retains the benefit after being transferred. Therefore, a property owner may have the right to walk across another's land because of an easement between their predecessors in title, regardless of whether the current owners ratified the transaction. The burden of this easement (the inability to stop the other from walking) ran with the servient tenement, and the benefit of the easement (the privilege of crossing) ran with the dominant tenement. When an easement is in gross, its benefit cannot run with land because there is no dominant tenement, but its burden can.

Covenants (promises) respecting land may run with the land in a roughly similar manner to easements. When a covenant runs with the land, the land remains burdened or benefited by it even though it is no longer owned by the person who made or received the covenant. The covenant continues despite changes in ownership. Thus, running covenants transfer duties and rights in a way not permitted by traditional contract law.

Illustration: Prudence (the promisor) covenanted with Peter (the promisee) that she would not sell liquor on her property. Prudence sold her property to Ann. If the requirements for a covenant to run with the land are met, Ann may not sell liquor on the property even though she neither made nor assumed the covenant. However, if the covenant does not run with the land, Ann is not bound by it.

I. COVENANTS COMPARED TO OTHER INTERESTS THAT BIND FUTURE OWNERS

A. EASEMENTS

Although easements run with the land, the types of activities for which an easement could be created has always been somewhat limited, and courts have resisted attempts to create new kinds of easements. Restrictions that are too novel to qualify as easements or that are "spurious" (see Chapter 5, p. 197) cannot be characterized as easements. Thus, courts had to create a different type of interest—the covenant running with the land—to make these types of agreements enforceable between remote owners of the affected properties.

Generally, parties creating an easement use conveyancing language, such as "I grant" or "I reserve." In contrast, parties creating a covenant use promissory language, such as "I promise" or "I agree." However, regardless of the language used, a court is free to determine the real character of the interest independent of the creating language. The Restatement of Servitudes permits a servitude to be created "by contract or conveyance." § 2.1.

A duty to refrain from acting can be either a negative easement or a covenant, but an affirmative obligation can only be a covenant and not an easement. A covenant, whether affirmative or negative, can never be acquired prescriptively. To avoid confusion, easements and covenants will be treated in this Chapter as distinct property interests, rather than as nominal categories of servitudes.

Illustration: Prudence promised Peter that (1) she would not construct any structures in her garden that blocked Peter's view, (2) Peter could enter the garden to smell the flowers, and (3) Prudence would water the plants regularly. In the above examples, (1) is a negative easement of view that prohibits Prudence from building certain types of structures on her land; (2) is an affirmative easement that entitles Peter to perform an otherwise unprivileged act on Prudence's land; and (3) is a covenant because it imposes a duty on Prudence to perform an act she otherwise would not be required to do. Without a writing, Peter could acquire only the second right by prescription since neither the failure to build in a certain way nor the continued watering would oblige Prudence to continue if she had not promised to do so. Of course, once granted, all of Peter's rights may be lost by prescription.

B. DEFEASIBLE ESTATES

The owner of a defeasible estate owns her land subject to a condition, and she cannot convey the land free from that condition. In that sense, the condition on her estate runs with the land. However, the benefit of the condition is itself an interest in land and is transferable in its own right. It does not run with any other land.

Illustration: Owen conveyed to Ann in fee simple, subject to the condition that he could re-enter and forfeit her estate if liquor was ever sold on the premises. Ann has a fee simple subject to condition subsequent. If Ann conveys the property to Bob, Bob will have the same estate subject to the same condition and, thus, cannot sell liquor there. Owen has a power of termination, which is itself a property interest. He may transfer this interest without transferring any other property. However, the harshness of the forfeiture remedy sometimes will cause a court to construe the restriction as a covenant if the language is ambiguous. In this way, the promise will still run with the land but with a less drastic remedy.

C. CONTRACT ASSIGNMENT AND ASSUMPTION

Courts accepted the concept of covenants running with the land before contract law permitted rights to be assigned and duties to be delegated. When contract law had evolved to incorporate these concepts, courts continued to recognize covenants running with the land. The most important difference between these two sources of rights and duties is that contract law requires the remote purchaser of the burdened land to agree to the burden. In contrast, a purchaser of land encumbered by a covenant is bound even if he does not agree.

Illustration: Prudence covenanted that she would not use her land to compete with Peter's business. Peter then sold his land and business to Ann. If the benefit of this covenant does not run with the land, the benefit is transferred to Ann only if Peter assigns it to her. If the benefit of the covenant does run with the land, it is transferred to Ann along with the property without the need for any assignment.

Illustration: Prudence agreed to water Peter's lawn every day. Prudence then sold her property to Ann. If the burden of this covenant does not run with the land, Ann must water Peter's lawn only if she "assumed" the covenant ("Ann hereby assumes the obligation of the covenant."). If the burden of the covenant does run with the land, Ann is bound even if she did not assume it.

II. REQUIREMENTS FOR A COVENANT TO RUN WITH THE LAND

A covenant can run with the land only if it satisfies the requirements described in this section.

A. THE COVENANT MUST BE AN ENFORCEABLE PROMISE

Originally, a covenant was a promise made under seal. Today, the requirement of a seal has vanished in most jurisdictions, but contract law has many other important rules concerning the enforceability of promises. For example, consideration must be given, and the promise cannot be for an illegal purpose. If the covenant would be unenforceable between the covenanting parties, the covenant cannot run to bind their successors. In a majority of jurisdictions, covenants that run with the land must be in writing. However, the doctrines of estoppel and part performance may excuse the lack of a writing. When the covenant is in a deed, it is enforceable against the grantee if she accepted the deed even though she did not sign it.

B. THE PARTIES MUST HAVE INTEND-ED THAT THE COVENANT RUN— "*ASSIGNS*"

A covenant will not run unless the original parties intended that it should. The parties need not manifest their intent in any particular manner. However, the court in Spencer's Case (1583) held that a covenant concerning something not yet in esse (not yet in existence) will not run unless the "assigns" of the parties are specifically mentioned. A reference to the covenantor "and his assigns" is a common method today for expressing the intent that the covenant run with the land.

Illustration: Prudence covenanted to build and maintain a fence between Peter's and her lots. Since the fence does not yet exist, this covenant would not run under Spencer's Case unless Prudence expressly stated in the covenant that she covenanted for herself and for her "assigns." However, if the fence already existed and the covenant only concerned maintenance, any language indicating an intent that the covenant burden her successors would be sufficient.

C. THE PROMISE MUST *TOUCH AND CONCERN* THE LAND

Courts will enforce a covenant against future owners only if it "touches and concerns" the land. In

Spencer's Case, the court said that a covenant that was "merely collateral to the land" would not run despite the parties' contrary intent. In another case, the court held that the covenant "must affect the nature, quality, or value of the thing demised or the mode of occupying it." A commonly cited standard is that a covenant touches and concerns land when the promisor's or promisee's legal relations concerning land are decreased or increased, i.e. the promise makes ownership more or less valuable. However, several courts have noted that this standard is more question-begging than helpful.

1. Burden v. Benefit

Any covenant concerning the use of land consists of two parts that may affect land in different ways. A covenant can impose a burden (the promisor's obligation) and confer a benefit (the benefit it creates for the promisee or for some third person). Therefore, the question whether the covenant touches and concerns land may be a two part question: (1) does the covenant's burden touch and concern land and (2) does the covenant's benefit touch and concern land. Just as an easement may be appurtenant (the benefit touches a dominant tenement) or in gross (the benefit does not touch a dominant tenement), a covenant may only burden land, may only benefit land, or may burden and benefit separate parcels. In general, a burden that can be performed only by the person who owns or possesses the burdened land touches and concerns that land. Conversely, only a benefit that will be enjoyed by the current owner or possessor of the benefited land touches and concerns that land.

Illustration: Prudence covenanted with Peter that she would not sell liquor on her land. She made this promise because Peter has moral objections to alcohol. The covenant's burden touches Prudence's land, because it deprives her of a use that otherwise would be available to her. But the covenant's benefit does not necessarily touch land.

Illustration: Prudence covenanted to water Peter's lawn every day. The covenant touches Peter's land because it benefits the land, rather than Peter himself. The only person interested in having the covenant enforced is the owner of the lawn. But the covenant's burden does not touch Prudence's land, since Prudence can perform this covenant regardless of whether she owns any property.

2. Money Covenants

In the early common law, courts held that covenants to pay money did not touch and concern land. Today, however, most courts recognize that payments of money can be a substitute method of performing an act that would touch and concern land. For example, a covenant to pay for property insurance may be a substitute for a covenant to keep the premises in good repair if the proceeds are to be used for restoration of the property, rather than for the covenantee's personal enrichment. Similarly, a covenant to pay assessments in a private subdivision may be a substitute for a covenant to maintain the common areas if the assessments must be used for maintenance. Therefore, courts today look at the reason for the money covenant to determine whether it touches and concerns land.

3. Touching v. Running

Even if a covenant touches and concerns a parcel of land, when should its burden run to bind successors of the promisor? Similarly, when should the benefit run to successors of the promisee? These questions must be considered separately.

a. *Requirement for the Burden to Run*

One view is that a covenant's burden runs if it touches the promisor's land even if it does not benefit the promisee's land. This "liberal" view has the virtues of simplicity and directness. It focuses only on the qualities of the covenant to determine whether the burden runs. A different view is that the burden runs only if both the burden and the benefit touch land. This more restrictive view derives from the old English prohibition against easements in gross and the policy that one parcel of land should not be restricted unless some other parcel is proportionally benefited. On the other hand, it is much easier to identify and locate subsequent owners of benefited land than it is to identify and locate subsequent owners of covenants in gross who may not own any land in the vicinity of the burdened land.

Covenant not to Compete—Illustration: Prudence promised not to sell liquor on her land in competition with Peter's tavern. Courts in many states hold that the covenant's benefit does not touch and concern land since it does not increase Peter's physical enjoyment of his land, but only the amount of money that he can make on it. However, the burden clearly touches and concerns Prudence's land, since it restricts her use of it. Thus, this may be characterized as a burden that touches and concerns the land but as a benefit that does not. Under the more liberal view, the burden may run. Under the second view, it may not.

Covenant to Insure—Illustration: Prudence promised to pay to keep Peter's premises insured. Many courts hold that the burden of Prudence's covenant runs only if Peter is obligated to use the proceeds to repair the premises. Such a requirement converts Prudence's promise to pay money into a promise to pay for or make repairs, which obviously benefits land. Under this analysis, her burden runs only if his benefit touches.

b. Requirement for the Benefit to Run

The requirement that the covenant's burden runs only if both the benefit and burden touch and concern land does not necessarily apply for the benefit to run. Since the benefit's running does not hamper land's alienability or utility to the same degree, it may be permitted to run even if the burden does not touch land.

Illustration: Prudence covenanted to water a tree on Peter's property. This benefit touches and concerns Peter's property. Therefore, it should run to and be enforceable by future owners of Peter's property, even though the covenant's burden does not affect any land owned by Prudence.

Illustration: Prudence covenanted with Peter not to engage in any competing business on her land. In some states, the benefit of such a covenant is considered not to touch land and will not run with Peter's land. A benefit never runs if it does not touch or concern the land.

III. REQUIREMENTS CONCERNING THE PARTIES—*PRIVITY*

A. REQUIREMENTS CONCERNING THE ORIGINAL PARTIES TO THE COVENANT—*HORIZONTAL PRIVITY*

1. Privity Necessary for the Burden to Run

In England and in many American jurisdictions, a covenant's burden runs with the land at law only if the original covenanting parties were in "privity of estate." The meaning of privity of estate in this context varies among the jurisdictions.

a. *Tenurial Relation*

England and perhaps Massachusetts follow the most narrow notion of privity. They require that the covenanting parties have a tenurial relationship, which probably exists today only between a landlord and tenant.

b. *Mutual Simultaneous Interests*

Under a slightly less strict view of privity, the covenanting parties both must have interests in the same land. Thus, they may co-own the property, or they may be dominant and servient tenants of an easement in the property.

c. *Privity Through a Deed*

A more liberal view is that privity exists between the grantor and grantee of an estate in land. A covenant contained in a deed that transfers an estate in the land satisfies this requirement.

d.   *Lack of Privity*

The most liberal view is that privity is not required between the covenanting parties. Under such a standard, agreements between neighbors may run with the land. For example, neighboring property owners may agree to use their land for residential purposes only. This mutual granting of covenants fails all the other privity tests mentioned above.

2.   Privity not Required for the Benefit to Run

Most states require privity of estate only for the covenant's burden to run but not for the covenant's benefit. The Restatement of Servitudes entirely eliminates the privity requirement for the creation of a servitude. § 2.4. It also provides that prescription may cure the absence of privity if state law requires it. § 2.17.

Illustration: Prudence and Peter are neighbors who agree that Prudence will not erect any structure on her land over thirty feet high. Because they are not in privity of estate, the burden of this covenant may not run at law to bind Prudence's successors, but that the benefit may run to Peter's successors. Therefore, Prudence would be bound by the covenant even after Peter transfers his land, but her successors in interest would not be bound even while Peter still owns his land.

B.   REQUIREMENTS CONCERNING THE LITIGANTS—*VERTICAL PRIVITY*

1.   Requirement for the Burden to Run

A covenant's burden generally runs at law only to those who acquire the entire estates of the covenanting parties. Therefore, it is more accurate to say that a covenant runs with the estate, rather than with the land.

Illustration: Peter conveyed fee title to land to Prudence. The deed included a covenant that Prudence would not erect any structure over thirty feet high. Prudence then rented her property to Tom. At law, the covenant's burden does not bind Tom because he has not acquired Prudence's entire estate.

Illustration: Peter conveyed land to Prudence. The deed included a covenant that Prudence would not erect any structures over thirty feet high. Prudence then conveyed the same land to Ann. The covenant's burden binds Ann because she acquired Prudence's entire fee simple estate.

Illustration: Peter conveyed two acres of land to Prudence. The deed included a covenant that Prudence would not erect any structure over thirty feet high. Prudence then sold one acre to Ann. The burden binds Ann, because she acquired Prudence's entire estate (fee simple) in a part of the property. The physical division of land is not a division of the estate.

Illustration: Prudence covenanted in a lease with her landlord that she would keep the premises in repair. Prudence assigned the lease to Ann. Ann is bound, since the assignment transfers Prudence's entire leasehold estate to Ann.

Illustration: Prudence covenanted in a lease with her landlord that she would keep the premises in repair. Prudence sublet the premises to Stan. Stan is not bound at law, since a subtenant does not succeed to the tenant's entire estate.

2. Not a Requirement for the Benefit to Run

Many states require vertical privity only for the burden to run at law. For the benefit to run, states usually do not require such privity.

Illustration: Peter conveyed land to Prudence. The deed included a covenant that Prudence would not to erect any structure over thirty feet high. Peter then rented his neighboring property to Tom. Tom may enforce the covenant even though he has not succeeded to Peter's entire estate.

Illustration: Prudence covenanted in a lease with her tenant, Peter, that she would supply heat to his apartment. Peter then sublet to Sue. Even though Sue is only a subtenant and did not succeed to Peter's entire leasehold estate, she may be able to enforce the covenant against Prudence.

IV.   RUNNING OF COVENANTS IN EQUITY—*EQUITABLE SERVITUDES*

A.   POLICY UNDERLYING EQUITABLE SERVITUDES

The legal requirements for a covenant to run are sufficiently difficult that they often defeat the covenanting parties' attempts to bind successors. In England, where the privity requirement is satisfied only by tenurial relationships, land cannot be transferred with enforceable restrictions in the deed. In the United States, privity requirements often prevent neighbors from making binding agreements. One reason these legal rules have survived despite their undesirable effects is that an alternative enforcement device has long been available—enforcement in a court of equity.

In 1848, the English Court of Chancery decided *Tulk v. Moxhay,* which involved a grantee's covenant in a deed that he would not build on the granted property. The grantee-covenantor then sold the property to the defendant, who refused to comply with the covenant. Since the original covenanting parties did not have a landlord-tenant relationship, horizontal privity did not exist, and the covenant did not run at law to bind the successor of the burdened land. Notwithstanding the absence of the necessary privity, the court held that the covenant bound the subsequent owner. The equitable interest created by the court in *Tulk* is called an equitable servitude.

The court in *Tulk* gave two reasons that the defendant was subject to the burden. First, if it did not bind successors, the original grantee-covenantor could sell the land for appreciably more than he had paid for it. Thus, the grantee-covenantor would be unjustly enriched. Second, if the defendant, knowing of the covenant, could acquire the land free of it, he would destroy a benefit for which the original grantor-covenantee had contracted. Thus, the court also was concerned about a wrongful interference with a contractual relationship. For these two reasons, the court held that the covenantee had an equity in the covenantor's property, which bound any subsequent taker who had notice of it.

B. RULES CONCERNING EQUITABLE SERVITUDES

1. Applicability of Rules for Covenants Running at Law

The legal requirements of privity and of touch and concern have limited or different application to equitable enforcement of a burden.

a.   Horizontal Privity

Under *Tulk v. Moxhay,* the original parties need not have been in privity for a burden to be enforceable in equity against subsequent owners.

Illustration: Prudence covenanted with her neighbor, Peter, that she would not use her property for business purposes. Prudence then sold to Ann who knew of the covenant. Although Peter could not enforce the covenant against Ann at law, it is enforceable against her in equity.

b.   Vertical Privity

Succession to a covenanting party's entire estate is not required for equitable enforcement of a burden.

Illustration: Prudence covenanted with her neighbor, Peter, that she would not use her land for business purposes. Prudence then leased the property to Tom who was aware of the covenant. Peter may enforce the promise in equity against Tom even though he did not acquire Prudence's fee interest.

Illustration: Prudence covenanted with her landlord, Peter, not to use the premises for business purposes. Prudence then sublet her property to Sue, who was aware of the covenant. Peter may enforce the covenant in equity against Sue, even though Sue subleased and, therefore, is not in privity of estate with Peter.

c.   Touch and Concern

The touch and concern requirement is construed as diversely in equity as in law. (See Chapter 6, p. 235). In England, a covenant's burden is unenforceable, even in equity, unless the covenant's benefit also touches and concerns land. However, in the United States, courts often do not require the benefit to touch and concern land for either the benefit or the burden to run. However, if the burden does not touch and concern land, a court probably will hold that it does not run.

Illustration: Prudence covenanted that she would not use her land in competition with Peter's use of his land. Prudence then sold her property to Ann who was aware of the covenant. In many jurisdictions, the covenant's benefit is deemed not to touch and concern the covenantee's property, although its burden touches and concerns the covenantor's land. Therefore, in England, the burden would not bind Ann, even in equity. But, in the United States, Ann probably would be bound by an equitable servitude.

Illustration: Prudence covenanted that she would not use her land in competition with Peter's use of his land. Peter then sold his land to Bob. Unless Peter and Prudence intended that only Peter could enforce this covenant, Bob probably can enforce it against Prudence, even though the benefit does not touch and concern land, either because equity permits the covenant to run or because Peter impliedly assigned it to Bob.

Illustration: Prudence covenanted with Peter that she would maintain his garden. Prudence then sold her property to Ann who was aware of the covenant. Since the burden does not touch and concern land, Ann probably is not bound.

2. Special Equitable Requirements

Although the traditional legal requirements for a covenant to run are eliminated or attenuated in equity, equity adds some special requirements before it will enforce a covenant against a remote taker.

a. Notice

Equity imposes a covenant's burden only if the covenantor's successor took with notice of it. The notice may be actual or constructive.

b. Negative Covenants Only

In a few jurisdictions, equity will not enforce affirmative covenants, i.e. covenants that require the covenantor to perform an act. Only negative covenants—those that prohibit the covenantor from acting in a certain manner—are enforceable. However, most modern courts do not make this distinction and will enforce either kind of covenant.

V. ENFORCEMENT OF NEIGHBORHOOD RESTRICTIONS

This section covers the problems that subdivision owners have in enforcing restrictions against each other when the original subdivision developer inserted similar restrictions in all or most deeds but no longer can enforce the restrictions itself. In all the illustrations in this section, "CG Company" refers to the common grantor, a corporation sometimes referred to as "it," that sold all the lots in the subdivision in numerical order to alphabetically listed buyers.

A. ENFORCEMENT BY LATER GRANTEES AGAINST EARLIER GRANTEES—RUNNING OF THE BENEFIT

When a prior grantee gave a covenant restricting her lot, a later grantee from the same common grantor usually can enforce the covenant. The benefit of the earlier covenant touched the common grantor's retained land and ran with the part that later was conveyed to the subsequent grantee.

Illustration: CG Company conveyed Lot 1 to Ann, who covenanted to restrict it to residential purposes. CG Company then conveyed Lot 2 to Bob. Bob may enforce the covenant against Ann. Ann's covenant benefited CG's retained land, which included Lot 2. The benefit of Ann's covenant ran with Lot 2 when CG conveyed it to Bob.

B. ENFORCEMENT BY EARLIER GRANTEES AGAINST LATER GRANTEES—ALTERNATIVE THEORIES

A prior grantee sometimes can enforce restrictions against a subsequent grantee from the same common owner. The prior grantee's enforcement right rests on one of three theories, depending on whether the covenant was given by the common owner, the subsequent grantee, or the prior grantee.

1. Enforcement of a Covenant Given by the Common Owner to the Prior Grantee—*Running of the Burden*

When the common owner covenants with the prior grantee to restrict all its retained property for the benefit of the prior grantee's lot, the covenant burdens all the common owner's retained land and binds subsequent grantees. This theory does not apply to land that was not in the subdivision when the covenant was made. Because that land was owned by someone else when the covenant was given, the covenantor probably did not intend that the prior grantee should receive the benefit of a covenant that later burdened that property.

Illustration: CG Company conveyed Lot 1 to Ann and covenanted that it would restrict all its remaining land to residential purposes. CG then conveyed Lot 2 to Bob. Ann may enjoin Bob from using his lot for nonresidential uses if he took with notice of CG's covenant. If Lot 2 was not part of the subdivision when CG gave Ann its covenant, Bob may not enforce it against her.

2. Enforcement of a Covenant Given by a Subsequent Grantee to the Common Owner— *Third Party Beneficiary*

A prior grantee may be able to enforce a covenant given by a subsequent grantee to the common owner if the covenant was intended for the prior grantee's benefit. Since the prior grantee is not the promisee or a successor to land owned by the promisee when the covenant was given, the covenant's benefit did not run with the land to the prior grantee. Instead, the prior grantee is a third party beneficiary of the covenant if it was intended to benefit prior grantees.

Illustration: CG Company conveyed Lot 1 to Ann. CG Company then conveyed Lot 2 to Bob, who covenanted that he would restrict his land to residential purposes for the benefit of all lots in the subdivision. Ann may enforce Bob's covenant as a third party beneficiary of his promise. She is an immediate beneficiary of his promise and is not required to show that either the burden or the benefit of Bob's covenant runs.

a. *When Third Party Beneficiary Theory Applies*

Many deed covenants specify the burden but fail to specify what property is to be benefited. When a prior grantee seeks to enforce such a covenant, he must show that he "impliedly" was intended to be a third party beneficiary of the covenant. Courts in some states will not allow a prior grantee to make this showing, perhaps due to the old common law prohibition against reserving conditions in strangers. However, courts in other states grant third party beneficiary status whenever adequate extrinsic evidence supports it.

Illustration: CG Company conveyed Lot 1 to Ann. CG Company then conveyed Lot 2 to Bob. Bob covenanted to restrict his land to residential purposes, but the covenant did not state what land was intended to receive the covenant's benefit. Witnesses testify that CG told Bob that the covenant was intended to benefit all other lots in the subdivision and that Bob agreed. Under these circumstances, some courts will permit Ann to enforce the covenant, though she is not expressly designated as the covenant's beneficiary.

3. Enforcement of a Restriction When the Prior Grantee has Covenanted with the Common Owner—*Implied Reciprocal Servitudes*

Some courts hold that, when a grantee covenants to the common grantor that the land just granted will be restricted in some manner, a reciprocal restriction is created by implication against the grantor's retained land in favor of the lot just conveyed. Thus, an "implied reciprocal servitude" burdens the retained land and binds subsequent takers with notice.

Illustration: CG Company conveyed Lot 1 to Ann. Ann covenanted in the deed to restrict Lot 1 to residential purposes. CG Company then conveyed Lot 2 to Bob without such a restriction specified in the deed. Ann may be able to limit Bob to residential purposes based on an implied recip-rocal servitude. A court might hold that, when Ann cove-nanted with CG, CG impliedly covenanted back to Ann that its retained land also would be restricted. The reciprocal burden that attached to Lot 2 ran with the land to Bob, if he took with notice of the burden.

a.   *Reliance by the Prior Grantee*

Some authorities state that reciprocal servitudes can be implied only if the prior grantee purchased in reliance on similar restrictions being imposed on the remaining lots. To these authorities, reliance furnishes the basis for the implication of a reciprocal servitude.

C.   SIGNIFICANCE OF A COMMON PLAN

A neighborhood scheme (a common plan) may be essential to the recognition of an implied reciprocal servitude.

1.   To Find Notice

A common plan may satisfy the jurisdiction's notice requirement. A recorded map or plat that shows uni-form restrictions in the subdivision may provide rec-ord notice of the restrictions. The mere physical exis-tence of uniform structures or landscaping also may provide inquiry notice as to the cause for such unifor-mity.

2.   To Apply Third Party Beneficiary Theory

Under this view, a prior grantee may not enforce a covenant unless a common plan exists. Without a common plan, only subsequent grantees can enforce the covenant. The Restatement of Servitudes provides that each lot included in the general plan is impliedly benefited from all servitudes it creates. § 2.14(a).

3. To Imply Reciprocal Servitudes

Under this view, a subsequent grantee is not subject to the burden of an implied reciprocal covenant unless a common plan exists. Without a common plan, a subsequent grantee is subject only to express covenants.

4. To Burden Benefited Lots

Under this view, a prior grantee is not subject to a covenant's burden if a reciprocal covenant is not implied in her favor because of the absence of a common plan.

Illustration: CG Company conveyed Lot 1 to Ann, Lot 2 to Bob, and Lot 3 to Cindy. The deeds to Ann and Bob include building restrictions, but the deed to Cindy does not. If no general building plan exists in the neighborhood, Cindy's lot is not subject to an implied reciprocal servitude. If Cindy's lot is not burdened, Bob's lot also may not be burdened since it is not benefited. Thus, Ann cannot enforce the restriction against either Bob or Cindy under this view.

Illustration: CG Company conveyed Lot 1 to Ann with a restriction in her deed, then conveyed Lot 2 to Bob with no restriction, and then conveyed Lot 3 to Cindy with a restriction similar to Ann's. Ann can enforce the restriction against Bob if a court will imply a reciprocal servitude against him, which may depend on the existence of a common plan. Ann also can enforce the restriction against Cindy, either as an implied reciprocal servitude or as a third party beneficiary of Cindy's promise to CG, which may require the existence of a common plan. Bob can enforce the restriction against Ann as the successor to a lot benefited by Ann's covenant, though he may have to show a common plan because his lot is not similarly restricted. Bob also can enforce the restriction against Cindy under a third party beneficiary theory. He cannot use the implied reciprocal argument against Cindy, since he did not make a promise from which a reciprocal servitude may be implied. Similarly, he cannot claim to be the beneficiary of a reciprocal servitude implied from Ann's covenant to CG. Cindy can enforce the restriction against Ann as a successor to Lot 3, which was benefited by Ann's covenant. Cindy cannot enforce the restriction against Bob, since he never gave a covenant. A court probably would not treat Cindy as a third party beneficiary of any reciprocal servitude implied against Bob from Ann's promise. A court also is unlikely to retroactively imply a reciprocal servitude against Bob based on Cindy's promise to CG.

D. ENFORCEMENT BY THE HOMEOWNERS' ASSOCIATION

If the common owner wants to create a homeowners' association and grant it power to enforce the common restrictions, she can convey a parcel of land to the association, such as for a community club house, and then state in each deed to a lot in the development that the restrictions are for that parcel's benefit. If the common owner has not yet created the association, the designated parcel still can be expressly benefited by the deed restrictions. When the common owner creates the association and conveys the designated parcel to it, the benefit of the deed restrictions will run with the parcel. Even without owning a benefited parcel, the association may be able to enforce the restrictions as assignee of the original covenantee. However, it may have difficulty enforcing covenants against successor owners if the jurisdiction requires it to own land that is touched by the covenant's benefit.

Once the common grantor has sold all the land in the subdivision, a court probably would hold that she no longer can enforce, release, or modify the covenants.

E.   EFFECT OF OMISSION IN LATER DEEDS

If the restriction was recorded in the public property records, future purchasers of the property are bound or benefited by it even if the deed by which they acquired title did not mention it. The recorded document provides constructive, if not actual, notice of the restriction.

VI.   TERMINATION OF RESTRICTIONS

A.   TERMINATION BY THE COVENANTING PARTIES' ACTS

1.   Restricted Duration

If the covenant is expressly limited, such as for twenty years or until termination, modification, or renewal by a majority vote of the affected property owners, expiration of that time period terminates the restriction. Statutes also may limit the life of such interests.

2. Release

The beneficiary can terminate a covenant's obligations by release (retransfer of the interest) or by rescission (cancellation of the agreement). The release only binds the releasor. Other beneficiaries are not bound by the release or rescission.

Illustration: CG Company conveyed Lot 1 to Ann with a covenant that it would restrict all retained lots to residential use. CG Company then conveyed Lot 2 to Bob and obtained his covenant to restrict his parcel to residential use. CG Company later released Bob from his covenant. Ann still can stop Bob from using his property for a commercial use. The release ended only Bob's obligations to CG. Bob still has a duty to Ann based on CG's covenant to Ann, which ran with the land to bind Bob. CG's subsequent release could not affect Ann.

3. Merger

Covenants are destroyed when the benefited and burdened parcels are merged in one ownership in the same way that easements terminate by merger of the dominant and servient tenements.

4. Abandonment

A common owner who initially includes restrictions in the deeds but then ceases to do so for the remaining lots may be deemed to have abandoned the common plan, thereby terminating the covenants that were created. Even when covenants were included in all the deeds, widespread and tolerated noncompliance by the lot owners may have the same effect.

5. Prescription

A covenantor or his successor may be sued by the covenantee or her successor if he refuses to honor the covenant. Like other lawsuits, this type of action is subject to the statute of limitations. Therefore, a covenant that has been violated for too long may be lost by prescription.

6. Estoppel

Covenants may be terminated by estoppel in the same fashion as easements. This defense, like laches, unclean hands, acquiescence, and changed conditions, is equitable and may merely prohibit enforcement by injunction without necessarily prohibiting a legal remedy for damages.

7. Laches

A court will deny equitable relief when the plaintiff seeking to enforce a covenant has waited too long to the detriment of the burdened property's owner.

8. Unclean Hands

A court will deny equitable relief to the owner of a benefited parcel if he has violated a similar covenant imposed on his land.

9. Acquiescence

A court will deny equitable relief to the owner of a benefited parcel if she has permitted too many other lot owners to breach their covenants.

B. TERMINATION RESULTING FROM EXTERNAL ACTS

1. Changed Conditions

Most courts will not enforce a covenant (at least in equity) when changed neighborhood conditions greatly have diminished the covenant's benefits. However, the changed conditions normally must have occurred within the neighborhood borders. External changes are an insufficient justification to terminate the restriction for border lots to prevent a domino series of violations from occurring. A change in the restricted parcels' zoning classification does not constitute an adequate changed condition unless the zoning ordinance now prohibits the uses permitted by the covenant.

Illustration: When Prudence agreed with Peter to restrict her adjacent property to residential purposes, the entire neighborhood was residential. Neighborhood conditions now have changed. Her house is the only remaining residential structure, and her lot would be worth substantially more for a commercial use. Under the circumstances, the slight benefit to Peter no longer may justify the heavy burden imposed on Prudence. Therefore, a court might not enforce the covenant against her.

2. Governmental Acquisition

If the government acquires the burdened property by eminent domain, it takes it free of all private restrictions. As a result, compensation may be owed to the covenantee, as well as to the covenantor, as occurs when property subject to a lease or an easement is taken by eminent domain.

When the government sells the property at a tax sale because the owner failed to pay the property taxes, courts are split as to whether the new owner remains subject to pre-existing restrictive covenants.

C. LEGAL INVALIDITY

Like easements and profits, covenants that violate the rule against unreasonable restraints on alienation are invalid. Covenants also are invalid if they violate the Rule Against Perpetuities, although the Rule is less likely to be applied to servitudes than to estates in land. Covenants are invalid if they restrain trade in violation of the antitrust laws, such as covenants not to compete and tying arrangements that force members of a subdivision to pay for common recreational facilities even if they do not want them. Courts increasingly are applying modern rules against unconscionability to agreements affecting land. Restatement of Servitudes § 3.7. Finally, covenants are invalid if they discriminate against classes of people protected by federal, state, or local law.

PART TWO
CONVEYANCING

Introduction

Part Two is concerned with the problems that arise incident to the transfer of interests in land. Landlord-tenant law could be regarded as a branch of conveyancing, since it involves the transfer of a leasehold estate from landlord to tenant. However, it has been treated as a separate topic because the problems involved in that context generally deal with the parties' relations after the conveyance has occurred (i.e. after the lease has been executed). The creation and transfer of easements also could be treated as a conveyancing topic. However, the conveyancing aspects of easements generally are incidental to other issues. Adverse possession is not a question of conveyancing at all, since the title acquired by the adverse possessor is an original title and is not one conveyed by the former owner.

CHAPTER SEVEN

REAL ESTATE BROKERS
I. THE BROKER'S ROLE

A. ECONOMIC FUNCTION OF BROKERS

Property can be conveyed without a broker's assistance, but the buyer and seller generally find it to be more convenient to have a broker assist them. Therefore, most real estate sales involve a broker. Unlike many other retail industries, the broker does not carry her own inventory. Rather than buying and selling land herself, she acts as an agent for the buyer or seller.

In most cases, the seller retains the broker, and that is the assumption in all the Illustrations in this Chapter. For rental properties, the landlord usually retains the broker. Even when the buyer or tenant retains the broker's services, she still may receive her commission from the seller or landlord.

B. WHO MAY ACT AS A BROKER

A broker must be licensed by the state regulatory agency. To obtain a license, a broker must possess certain minimum academic credentials, such as some college education, pass a qualifying exam, and satisfy character and fitness requirements. The broker also may have to satisfy continuing education requirements and have a certain amount of experience in real estate marketing. Real estate salespersons hold inferior licenses that entitle them to perform broker services only under the auspices and supervision of a licensed broker.

Engaging in brokers' activities without a license may trigger criminal or civil liability and prevents the agent from collecting a commission that otherwise would be due. A "finder" exception permits an unlicensed person to recover compensation for introducing a buyer and seller to one another. However, any additional activity, such as participating in the negotiations, makes one a broker, rather than a finder, and requires a license.

C. BROKERS' SERVICES

A property owner hires a broker to locate potential buyers. Thus, the broker is the seller's agent to solicit potential buyers to make purchase offers to the seller, which he then may accept or reject. The broker is not an agent to offer the property for sale to buyers, who then could accept an offer made by the broker on the seller's behalf and thereby form a sales contract.

This Chapter deals with the contract between the broker and the seller or buyer. The contract between the seller and the buyer is covered in the next chapter. The two contracts often are confused. For instance, a property owner may employ a broker and agree to pay her a commission if she finds someone who will offer the seller $100,000 for his house. If the broker finds such a person, the seller can reject the offer, but he may owe the broker a commission since she performed her part of the contract.

D. BROKERS' OTHER LEGAL OBLIGATIONS

1. Discrimination

Federal, state, and local civil rights and licensing laws prohibit brokers from discriminating against protected classes of persons. Brokers are prohibited from (1) discriminating in rendering services or in advertising (e.g. "no children" signs), (2) racial steering (directing prospective buyers to certain areas based on their race), and (3) blockbusting (attempting to trigger panic sales by spreading rumors in a neighborhood that members of a protected class are moving into the area). Sanctions may include damages, fines, and loss of license.

2. Practicing Law

Brokers may not practice law by giving legal advice or by drafting contracts, deeds, mortgages, and other documents. However, in many jurisdictions, brokers are permitted to fill out simple legal forms incidental to the services they have rendered as brokers in a transaction.

3. Antitrust

Brokers may not conspire to fix commission rates or otherwise to eliminate competition. A local multiple listing service's refusal to admit "discount brokers" also may violate federal or state antitrust statutes.

II. LISTING AGREEMENTS AND COMMISSIONS

The employment contract between a broker and her principal is called a listing agreement. In the listing agreement, the seller authorizes the broker to act as his agent in showing (listing) the property to potential purchasers. Absent an express agreement between the seller and broker, the broker may be unable to collect a commission after finding a buyer. Some states require that listing agreements be in writing, although the Statute of Frauds does not apply because a listing agreement is an employment contract and does not convey an interest in land.

A. TYPES OF LISTING AGREEMENTS

Listing agreements are classified according to the circumstances under which the seller must pay a commission to his broker.

1. Open Listing

A broker earns a commission under an open listing agreement only if she is the "procuring cause" of the purchase. Thus, she is not entitled to a commission if the seller or someone else finds the buyer. "Procuring cause" is a question of fact. In some states, the standard is satisfied if the broker was the first person to notify the buyer or someone connected with the buyer about the property's availability. In other states, the broker must play a much more significant role to be considered the procuring cause.

2. Exclusive Listing

If the broker is entitled to a commission even when someone else is the procuring cause of the sale, the agreement is an exclusive listing. If the seller is not liable if he finds the buyer, the agreement is an "exclusive agency" listing. If the seller is liable even if he finds the buyer, the agreement is an "exclusive right to sell" listing.

B. EARNING A COMMISSION

Under most listing agreements, the broker earns the commission when she has presented a "ready, willing, and able purchaser" to the seller. The agreement usually does not define the adjectives "ready, willing, and able," but they are commonly understood to describe a person who wants to purchase the property on the terms specified in the listing agreement and who is capable of performing the contract of sale, such as by paying the purchase price.

1. Lesser and Contingent Offers

When a prospective buyer makes an offer that satisfies the terms in the listing agreement, the broker has earned the commission even if the seller does not accept the offer. But it is rare for a buyer to make a perfect offer. If the offer is for less than the asking price, no commission is yet earned because the purchaser is not "ready, willing, and able" to purchase on the seller's terms. However, if the seller accepts the offer, the broker is then entitled to her commission.

If the buyer's offer is contingent on getting a mortgage loan, selling her current house, or some other condition, she is not yet "ready, willing, and able" to purchase, and no commission is yet due. Even if the seller accepts the offer, whether the buyer will complete the deal is unknown. Thus, until the contingency is removed, the broker has not earned the commission.

2. Completing the Sale as a Condition Precedent

If the broker earns her commission by finding a ready, willing, and able buyer, she is entitled to the commission even if the sale is not completed. She may demand her commission from the seller even though the buyer subsequently defaults. To avoid this result, some states require that the buyer of a residential property must close the sale before the broker's right to a commission vests. These states reason that this result is consistent with sellers' expectations, especially because sellers normally anticipate paying the commission from the sale proceeds. The seller and broker always can include a condition of closing in the listing agreement.

a. *Closing as a Condition or Mere Calendar Event*

Many sales contracts between sellers and buyers contain a provision that revises the broker's commission right by providing for its payment at the closing. This type of provision is valid if the broker also signs it, but a court then has to determine whether the provision abrogated the broker's earlier entitlement to a commission for having produced a ready, willing, and able buyer or whether it merely postponed the time of its payment to the closing.

III. BROKER LIABILITY

Brokers are involved in such complicated legal relations with sellers and buyers that they frequently are involved in litigation with them. The more common legal theories behind such lawsuits are listed below.

A. CONTRACT

The listing agreement usually is written as a bilateral contract between the broker and the seller to prevent the seller from revoking just before completion by the broker. However, to make it bilateral, the broker must make some promise to the seller. She cannot promise success since that is too unpredictable, but she can promise to use diligence or best efforts to find a buyer. Lack of diligence then may make her liable, perhaps in an amount equal to the harm suffered by the seller because a timely sale was not made.

B. LICENSING STANDARDS

Licensing statutes frequently set standards of conduct for brokers to retain their licenses. Courts may treat such statutory standards as grounds for imposing civil liability when the broker's violation causes harm. Thus, a broker's lack of "honesty," a common statutory standard, may cause not only suspension or revocation of a broker's license, but also may subject her to economic liability to the injured party.

Illustration: The broker tells the seller that the buyer has offered $90,000 but tells the buyer that the seller insists on receiving $100,000. The broker keeps the $10,000 difference. She may lose her license and may be liable to one or both parties for this breach of the statutory duty of honesty.

C. NEGLIGENCE AND FRAUD

As professionals, brokers are held to a high standard of care and will be liable for malpractice when their conduct falls below that standard. If the broker is the seller's agent, she clearly owes him a duty of care, but lack of privity between the buyer and broker may limit her liability to the buyer to cases of fraud or deceit.

Illustration: The broker did not advise the seller to insist that the buyer's promissory note be secured by a mortgage and did not advise the buyer to test the soil for contamination before buying, which harmed both parties. The broker is liable to the seller if a jury decides that due care required her to give him such advice. But in many states, she is liable to the buyer only if the buyer can show that the broker knew of the contamination and intentionally concealed it or failed to disclose it.

D. AGENCY

An agent owes fiduciary duties of loyalty, integrity, and good faith to her principal. Thus, as the seller's agent, the broker is prohibited from putting the buyer's interests or her own interests above the seller's. She may not side with the buyer against the seller in the negotiations. Furthermore, she cannot acquire the seller's property for her own account unless her involvement in any such acquisition is fully disclosed to him beforehand.

1. Whose Agent is the Broker

It has been assumed in this Chapter that the broker is the seller's agent because he retained her services and will pay her commission, which are the usual grounds for an agency relationship. After entering into the listing agreement, the broker may put the listing into a "multiple listing file" for distribution to all other brokers who belong to the same service. Under the rules of the multiple listing service, the broker then must split her commission with any other broker who finds a purchaser for the property. A buyer will generally assume that the "showing broker" with whom he has been working is his agent, while the "listing broker" is the seller's agent. But since the showing broker will receive his share of the commission from the seller and since he received his authorization to act from the listing broker, courts normally characterize the showing broker as the seller's subagent, rather than as the buyer's agent. Despite what the buyer thinks, the showing broker's duties are owed to the seller! To avoid this situation, many buyers now are entering into buyer's broker agreements, by which the broker expressly agrees to be the buyer's, rather than the seller's, agent.

CHAPTER EIGHT

CONTRACT OF SALE: VENDOR–PURCHASER

When title to land is transferred pursuant to a contact of sale, a time lag normally occurs between the contract execution (signing) and its consummation. A sales contract is created when the seller and buyer sign an agreement in which the seller promises to convey and the buyer promises to pay. The contract is consummated (is "closed") when the seller delivers a deed to the buyer and the buyer pays the price to the seller. (On escrow closings, see Chapter 9, p. 304). This Chapter is concerned with the parties' relationship during this interim period, during which time they generally are referred to as the vendor and the purchaser ("Van" and "Pearl," respectively, in the Illustrations in this Chapter).

I. FORMATION OF THE RELATIONSHIP—STATUTE OF FRAUDS

The vendor-purchaser relationship arises once the parties have entered into a binding contract for the sale of real property. For the contract to be binding, it must include a manifestation of the parties' intent to be bound, consideration, identification of the parties and of the property, and the purchase price. Since the contract involves the transfer of an interest in land, it is subject to the Statute of Frauds and must be in writing. To satisfy the Statute of Frauds, the writing must include at least the parties' names, a description of the property, words that demonstrate an intent to buy or sell, the terms of the sale, and the signature of the party to be charged.

As with other contracts that are subject to the Statute of Frauds, an oral agreement for the sale of land may be enforceable in equity for specific performance and sometimes at law for damages based on estoppel (inducing detrimental reliance) or part performance. Courts disagree as to what constitutes sufficient part performance to take a case out of the Statute. The most important factors are payment of the purchase price, delivery of possession to the buyer, and improvements made by the buyer to the property. In order of increasing judicial acceptance, courts have found adequate part performance when: (1) the purchaser has paid all or part of the price; (2) the vendor has delivered possession to the purchaser; (3) the vendor has delivered possession, and the purchaser has paid all or part of the price; and (4) the vendor has delivered possession, and the purchaser has made improvements. In all these situations, the acts tend to prove that a contract was made, since they hardly would have been undertaken otherwise.

A. DISCRIMINATION BY THE SELLER

Federal, state, and local laws prohibit sellers from refusing to sell to particular buyers because of their race, color, religion, national origin, handicap, sex, age, marital status, or children. Some laws exempt owners of single family homes from some or all of these requirements, and commercial properties may be regulated differently than residential properties. A seller who violates these laws may be forced to pay damages to the aggrieved buyer and to comply with the law by selling to that buyer.

II. MARKETABLE TITLE (MERCHANTABLE TITLE)

Because of land's special nature, the question of title to any particular parcel always has been a more important and more difficult question than for personal property. The variety of permissible estates in land, the fact that ownership may be subject to leases, easements, restrictive covenants, and other interests, the potential for adverse possession, and the mechanical difficulties surrounding the transfer of land all contribute to make the condition of the vendor's title a matter of great concern to any prospective purchaser. This subsection is concerned with the problems that arise when the vendor's title is subject to some question.

A purchaser of land generally enters into a contract of sale before investigating the title. The purchaser does not want to invest time and money into a title search before knowing whether the vendor and she will agree on the terms of the sale. This is not foolhardy because the doctrine of marketable title permits the purchaser to withdraw from the contract if the title is unmarketable. Unless specifically disclaimed, every contract for the sale of land includes a requirement that the vendor's title be marketable. Otherwise, every offer to purchase would have to be made explicitly contingent on the condition of the vendor's title.

A.   WHAT IS MARKETABLE TITLE

The vendor has a marketable title if he in fact has title free of any encumbrance and free of any doubt. Thus, a title is unmarketable if: (a) the vendor lacks all or part of the claimed title; (b) the title is subject to an encumbrance; or (c) a reasonable possibility exists that (a) or (b) is true.

1.   Title Actually Held by the Vendor

Unless the contract indicates otherwise, the purchaser is entitled to receive an undivided fee simple absolute title to the property being purchased. If the vendor does not have such a title, the purchaser may withdraw from the contract. The vendor is often said to lack a marketable title in such cases, though it could also be said that the vendor merely has a marketable title to less than what he promised to convey.

Illustration: Van and Pearl signed a contract for the sale of Van's land. Pearl then discovered that Van does not own an undivided fee interest. He is only a joint tenant or a tenant in common with some other person. Pearl is not obligated to complete her purchase.

Illustration: Van and Pearl signed a contract for the sale of forty acres. Pearl then discovered that Van has title to only twenty-five acres of the forty-acre parcel. Since Van lacks marketable title to the forty acres he agreed to convey, he may not enforce the contract.

Illustration: Van and Pearl signed a contract for the sale of Van's land. Pearl then discovered that Van has only a life estate in the land, rather than the fee simple. Pearl is not bound to purchase.

Illustration: Van and Pearl signed a contract for the sale of Van's land. Pearl then discovered that Van's fee simple title is subject to the condition subsequent that the estate will be forfeited if liquor is ever sold on the premises. Since Van does not have fee simple absolute title, it is not marketable.

Illustration: Van and Pearl signed a contract for the sale of Van's land. Pearl then discovered that Van previously had given Ann an option to purchase the land that has not yet expired. Van's title is not marketable. If Pearl accepted his deed, she would be compelled to sell the property to Ann if Ann exercised her option.

Illustration: Van and Pearl signed a contract for the sale of a parcel of land. Pearl then discovered that Van has no title to that parcel. Van obviously does not have marketable title.

2. Title Free From Encumbrances

An encumbrance is a property right or interest held by some third person that diminishes the estate's value but does not negate its existence. A marketable title is not subject to any encumbrances. Thus, if the title is subject to an encumbrance, it should be stated as an exception to the marketable title standard in the contract of sale.

a.   Easements

Illustration: If Van's title is subject to an easement, his title is unmarketable. Therefore, Pearl may withdraw from the contract unless it specified that the title was to be conveyed subject to that easement.

(1) Exception for Visible Easements

In many states, easements that are open and notorious, particularly utility easements, are an implied exception to the marketable title requirement. Courts assume that the purchaser observed these easements before she offered to purchase and was willing to take title subject to them.

b.   Covenants and Servitudes

Illustration: If Van's title is subject to a restrictive covenant or equitable servitude, his title is not marketable.

(1) Exception for Superfluous and Obsolete Covenants

A covenant does not render title unmarketable if it merely compels the owner to do what the law itself requires (as where both a covenant and the zoning ordinance impose the same prohibition against commercial activity) or if the covenant is obsolete and no longer enforceable (see Ch. 6, p. 257).

c. Leases

Illustration: If Van's title is subject to an existing lease, his title is unmarketable even if the lease is economically advantageous.

d. Money Obligations

Illustration: If Van's title is subject to a mortgage, judgment lien, assessment lien, mechanic's lien, or any other monetary charge, his title is unmarketable so long as such charge remains an encumbrance.

3. Title Free From Doubt

The purchaser need not prove that the vendor's title actually is bad. A title is unmarketable if any reasonable doubt exists concerning its marketability.

Illustration: A deed from Ann Smith to Paul C. Jones is in Van's chain of title. However, the next deed in the chain is signed Paul Jones, rather than Paul C. Jones. A risk exists that Paul is not the same as Paul C., which—if true—means that Paul had no title to convey. Ann is not required to prove that Paul is not Paul C., only that this question exists.

Illustration: An old mortgage is in Van's chain of title. The mortgage was released of record, but the acknowledgment on the release was defective. Since this defect raises some doubt whether the mortgage still encumbers the property, the title is unmarketable.

4. Circumstances not Affecting Marketability

A title may be marketable even though the property itself is undesirable. Property that is subject to termite infestation, flooding, bad soil conditions, or other physical problem nevertheless may have a marketable title. Zoning and similar governmental restrictions on the use of property do not affect the title's marketability, though in some jurisdictions an existing zoning or code violation may render title unmarketable.

B.   EFFECTS OF TITLE BEING UNMARKETABLE

1. Vendor's Right to Cure Defects

The vendor has no obligation to produce a marketable title until the time set for the closing of escrow (the completion of the contract). Thus, the purchaser is not entitled to withdraw at the instant that some title defect is discovered. In many states, the purchaser must give notice of the defect early enough to give the vendor an opportunity to cure. If the contract does not make time of the essence, the vendor's time to cure may extend for a reasonable time beyond the date set for closing or settlement. If the contract does make time of the essence, the vendor must cure the defect by the date set for the closing of escrow, unless the purchaser did not give adequate advance notice of the defect or otherwise waived the clause.

Illustration: On January 1, Van and Pearl entered into a contract for the sale of Van's property. The sale was to be consummated on March 1. On February 1, Pearl discovered that Van's title was subject to an easement. Pearl may not terminate the contract on February 1. Instead, she should notify Van of the defect.

Illustration: On January 1, Pearl and Van entered into a contract for the sale of Van's land. The sale was to be consummated on March 1. On February 1, Pearl discovered that Van's title was subject to an easement, and gave Van notice to that effect. If Van has removed the easement by

March 1, Pearl cannot withdraw from the contract since Van has marketable title on the closing date.

Illustration: On January 1, Pearl and Van entered into a contract for the sale of Van's land. The sale was to be consummated on March 1. On February 1, Pearl discovered that Van's title was subject to an easement, and she notified Van. Van diligently worked to remove the easement, but he did not succeed by March 1. If time is not of the essence, a court may hold that Pearl is not yet released from the contract and that Van has a reasonable time to clear his title. If time is of the essence, Van's failure to have marketable title on the closing day entitles Pearl to terminate the contract.

Illustration: On January 1, Pearl and Van entered into a contract for the sale of Van's land. The sale was to be consummated on March 1. On February 1, Pearl discovered that Van's title was subject to a mortgage and notified him. Van took no action to remove the mortgage before March 1, but instructed the escrow agent to pay the mortgage from the sale proceeds so that Pearl would acquire title free of it. Unless specifically prohibited by the contract, the vendor normally can use the sale proceeds to remove monetary liens even though, technically, the vendor gets the purchase money before transferring marketable title to the purchaser.

2. Vendor's Right to Specific Performance with Abatement

If the title defect is insignificant and technical only, a vendor may be able to obtain specific performance. However, the purchase price will be abated if the defect reduces the land's value.

3. Purchaser's Right to Terminate

If the vendor does not tender a marketable title at the closing, the purchaser can terminate the contract and recover any consideration paid to the vendor. As already indicated, the purchaser cannot terminate before the closing date if the title is unmarketable, but she can terminate if the title has not been cleared by the closing date if time is of the essence or if a reasonable amount of time has elapsed since the vendor first received notice of the title problems.

4. Purchaser's Right to Damages

A purchaser who withdraws from the contract because of an unmarketable title can recover any down payment made to the vendor and out of pocket expenses incurred in preparing to purchase. Many states also permit the purchaser to recover loss of bargain damages.

5. Purchaser's Right to Specific Performance

A purchaser willing to accept an unmarketable title may do so, and the vendor may not refuse to convey based on flaws in his title. Thus, the purchaser can obtain specific performance of the contract.

a. Specific Performance with Abatement

Generally, if the defect is small and quantifiable, a decree of specific performance against a vendor with a defective title will include an abatement of the price. However, if the defect is substantial, the purchaser may withdraw entirely or may enforce the contract without an abatement, but she cannot force the vendor to sell at a drastically reduced price.

C. WAIVER OF THE RIGHT TO MARKETABLE TITLE

The right to marketable title is implied into a contract for the sale of land unless it expressly provides otherwise. Customarily, the contract expressly states or negates the requirements concerning the title.

1. Complete Waiver of Marketable Title

If the parties are unsure whether the vendor has any title, they explicitly may waive the marketable title requirement. This often occurs when owners are buying a doubtful claim against their own title. The parties sometimes negate the marketable title requirement by providing that the vendor will give only a quitclaim deed. More frequently, however, the contract expressly negates the requirement.

2. Waiver of a Particular Defect

Since some title encumbrances are desirable, a purchaser may be willing to buy subject to them. Such willingness is indicated by a provision in the offer or contract that title is to be "marketable except for * * *." The effect of this provision is to eliminate the purchaser's right to terminate based on the existence of the designated encumbrance.

Illustration: Pearl's offer to buy Van's property stated that "the title is to be free of all liens, except recorded building restrictions that are uniform throughout the neighborhood." After Van accepted the offer, Pearl learns that Van's lot is subject to a set-back requirement that also applies to all other lots in the neighborhood. Although a restrictive covenant normally would make title unmarketable, Pearl cannot terminate the contract because she expressly agreed to take subject to this type of encumbrance.

3. Insurable Title

If the contract of sale requires the vendor to deliver an insurable title, the purchaser must accept his title if a title insurance company is willing to insure it without making any exceptions to the policy's coverage.

4. Waiver by Acceptance of the Deed—Merger

The right to marketable title is a contract right that permits the purchaser to refuse to perform if the proffered title is unsatisfactory. However, if the purchaser completes the contract and accepts the vendor's deed, the right to marketable title is extinguished, and the purchaser has no further action against the vendor based on the contract. Upon consummation, the contract provisions "merge" into the deed, and the purchaser's rights against the vendor thereafter depend on the deed, particularly its title covenants. On title covenants, see Ch. 9, p. 309.

III. EQUITABLE CONVERSION AND THE RISK OF LOSS

Because land is a unique asset, the purchaser under a binding sales contract always can obtain specific performance against an unwilling vendor. This equitable right effectively gives the purchaser an interest in the land itself, as well as personal contract rights against the vendor. Thus, when the agreement becomes binding, the purchaser becomes the equitable owner of the land, and the vendor retains mere legal title. Because the vendor's right under the contract is to receive the purchase price, he holds the property title only as security for payment.

The following sections cover some important consequences of the doctrine of equitable conversion. However, first note that the doctrine is limited in two ways. First, it normally does not relate to possession. Even after a binding sales contract has been executed, the vendor remains entitled to possession. The purchaser may not enter until the vendor has permitted her to do so or until legal title has passed (i.e. the contract has been performed). Second, the requirement of a specifically enforceable purchase agreement means that execution of an option to purchase or a right of first refusal does not trigger equitable conversion. Equitable conversion occurs only after the purchaser exercises an option or pre-emptive right.

A. DEVOLUTION ON DEATH

In earlier times, title to a decedent's real property passed to his heirs, but his personal property passed to his next of kin. Thus, if an owner contracted to sell land but died before the contract was consummated, the doctrine of equitable conversion meant that his next of kin were entitled to receive the purchase price and his heirs would be required to execute the deed to the purchaser. The heirs were not entitled to the money because the land was converted from realty to personalty when the contract was signed. Similarly, the heirs of a dead purchaser are entitled to the land, whereas the purchase price is paid from the personal estate that otherwise would go to the next of kin. Similarly, if the vendor married after contracting to sell land, the spouse could not claim a marital interest because the vendor held the legal title in trust for the purchaser.

B. INJURIES TO THE PROPERTY

If a third party injures the property during the contract period, the doctrine of equitable conversion dictates that the purchaser is the party entitled to bring suit, and the vendor may sue only if the purchaser declines. In contrast, damages for trespass depend on the right to possess, rather than title, so that standing depends on who has possession. Execution of the contract does not by itself entitle the purchaser to possession. A purchaser may sue a vendor in possession for waste, and a vendor may sue a purchaser in possession for impairing the security.

C. CREDITORS

Once a contract of sale is binding, the vendor's creditors can recover from the unpaid balance of the purchase price, but not from the property itself. However, the purchaser's creditors may reach the property to satisfy their claims against her.

D.   RISK OF LOSS FOR INJURIES CAUSED WITHOUT FAULT

In the absence of a contrary contract provision, the risk of innocent losses during the contract period can be allocated between vendor and purchaser in one of three ways.

1.   Majority Rule—Risk on Purchaser

Under a strict application of the doctrine of equitable conversion, the purchaser is the equitable—and, therefore, the real—owner of the property when the contract is executed. Thus, she bears the risk of loss during the contract period and cannot withdraw from the contract merely because the property has been damaged before the closing.

Illustration: On January 1, Pearl and Van contracted for the sale of Van's property. The sale was to close on March 1. On February 1, lightening started a fire that destroyed the premises. Under the majority rule, Pearl is still obligated to complete the contract and pay the entire price, and Van may seek specific performance or damages if she fails to do so.

2.   Minority Rule—Risk on Vendor

The minority (or Massachusetts) rule is that a failure of consideration occurs if the vendor cannot deliver the premises on the closing day in their original condition. This rule treats the continued existence of undamaged property as an implied condition of the contract. Under this rule, the purchaser can withdraw from the contract or obtain specific performance with an abatement of the purchase price if the property is damaged during the escrow period.

Illustration: On January 1, Pearl and Van contracted for the sale of Van's property. The sale was to close on March 1. On February 1, a fire caused $3,000 damage. If Van does not repair by March 1, Pearl can withdraw from the contract or can sue for specific performance with a price abatement of $3,000.

3. Uniform Vendor and Purchaser Risk Act

Some states have enacted the Uniform Vendor and Purchaser Risk Act, which allocates to the vendor the risk of innocent destruction during the contract period unless the purchaser has taken possession. Thus, the Act follows the minority rule unless the purchaser has taken possession.

4. Contrary Agreements

Regardless of which rule the jurisdiction follows, the parties are free to allocate the risk of loss in the contract.

a. Insurance Provisions

Both parties can purchase insurance to protect their interest in the property. If the sales contract provides that the purchaser will insure the property until the close of escrow, a court might interpret the provision as assigning the risk of loss to her. However, since a purchaser can insure her interest even when the vendor bears the risk of loss or vice versa, carrying insurance or agreeing to do so does not automatically determine who bears the risk of loss.

If the purchaser had the risk of loss but the vendor insured the property, most courts hold that the insurance award is in constructive trust for the purchaser and must be used to repair the property or to reduce the purchase price. A court may render a comparable holding when the vendor had the risk of loss, but the purchaser insured the property.

IV. PERFORMANCE

The vendor and purchaser must perform the contract within the time specified in the contract or within a reasonable time if none has been specified and perhaps even if a time has been specified but the contract did not make "time of the essence." The vendor must deliver a deed that conveys title to the purchaser, and the purchaser must pay the entire price.

A. INSTALLMENT LAND CONTRACTS (CONTRACTS FOR DEED)

In the ordinary "marketing" contract considered so far, delivery of the deed and payment of the price are "concurrent conditions," because both must be done at the same time. However, the parties instead may employ an installment land contract, whereby the purchaser pays the price in installments over a period of time, such as five years, before the vendor is required to deliver a deed. However, the purchaser normally has the right to possess even before delivery of the deed. In reality, this arrangement is a form of mortgage financing and should be subject to mortgage law since it is a contract in form only. However, courts often literally enforce installment land contracts, which has significant implications for the vendor's obligation to have marketable title only when the deed must be delivered and for the vendor's remedies when the purchaser breaches. See Section V(B) of this Chapter.

V. NONPERFORMANCE

A. BY THE VENDOR

If the vendor breaches the contract of sale by failing to convey the required title, the purchaser can (1) terminate the contract, recover the money she deposited into escrow or paid to the vendor, and receive a purchaser's lien on the property until she is repaid; (2) bring an action for specific performance with an abatement of the price for minor title defects; or (3) sue for damages in the amount of her expenses and benefit of the bargain damages (the difference between the contract price and the property's market value), where permitted. Courts sometimes limit benefit of the bargain damages to cases in which the vendor acted in bad faith, which generally excludes cases involving an unmarketable title.

B. BY THE PURCHASER

If the purchaser breaches the contract of sale by failing to pay the purchase price, the vendor can (1) terminate the contract and resell the property, though he may be required to refund the purchaser's down payment; (2) bring an action for specific performance, although this remedy is of little use against a purchaser who does not have the funds to perform; (3) sue for actual damages in the amount of his expenses and benefit of the bargain damages (the difference between the contract price and the property's market value), although a court may deny benefit of the bargain damages if the vendor has resold the property for a profit; or (4) retain the purchaser's down payment as liquidated damages if the contract or state law so provides.

CHAPTER NINE

TRANSFER OF TITLE BY DEED: GRANTOR—GRANTEE

To transfer title from a property owner (the grantor) to someone else (the grantee), the grantor normally must execute and deliver an instrument that is effective to pass title. In this Chapter, the feminine pronoun refers to the grantor, and the masculine pronoun refers to the grantee.

I. INSTRUMENTS EFFECTIVE TO PASS TITLE—DEEDS

The Statute of Frauds requires that title to land be transferred by a written instrument. The instrument typically used for this purpose is a deed, a document that states the grantor "grants," "conveys," or "quitclaims" title to the grantee. In many states, statutes provide preferred forms and language for deeds. Generally, three types of deeds are used in the United States.

A. QUITCLAIM DEED

A quitclaim deed usually states that the grantor "quitclaims" or "releases" the property to the grantee. By these words, the grantor makes no representation that she has any property to convey. The deed merely states that the grantor conveys whatever interest, if any, she has in the property. This form of deed is useful for quieting title to property by buying potentially adverse claims, because a grantor is not liable if, in fact, nothing was owned or conveyed. Quitclaim deeds also commonly are used to release mortgages and for intrafamily transfers.

B. GRANT DEED (BARGAIN AND SALE DEED, LIMITED WARRANTY DEED, OR SPECIAL WARRANTY DEED)

A grant deed normally states that the grantor "grants," "conveys," or "bargains and sells" the property to the grantee. In many states, such language is statutorily defined as representations that the grantor owns the property and has not encumbered it or conveyed it to anyone else. In the absence of a statutory definition, these representations are expressly included in the deed.

C. WARRANTY DEED (GENERAL WARRANTY DEED)

A warranty deed states that the grantor "conveys and warrants" the property to the grantee. In many states, this phrase is statutorily defined to provide broad representations concerning the title being conveyed. In the absence of a statutory definition, the deed must expressly state these covenants concerning the title. The covenants are discussed at p. 309.

II. PROPER EXECUTION OF DEEDS

A. SIGNATURE

The Statute of Frauds requires that the grantor sign the deed. The early common law also required the grantor to affix his seal to the deed, but that requirement has been abolished in virtually every jurisdiction. The grantee need not sign or seal the deed, because her acceptance of the deed is deemed to constitute acceptance of its terms.

B. CONSIDERATION

Because a conveyance is not a contract, consideration is unnecessary. A deed may be a gift deed. However, modern deed forms commonly recite that consideration was paid to rebut any inference of a resulting trust (see Chapter 2, p. 79) or to qualify the grantee as a bona fide purchaser under the recording acts (see Chapter 10, p. 352).

C. CONTENTS

A deed must identify the parties, the property, and the estate being conveyed and must contain words of conveyance, such as "conveys" or "bargains and sells," to the grantee.

1. Parties

The grantee should be named or adequately described (e.g. "to my present husband"). The grantee's name can be left blank to be filled in later. However, if the grantor dies before that occurs, the deed may be invalid. Unless the grantor dies, it is usually presumed that the grantee is authorized to fill in any name he wants.

The grantor must sign the deed. If her signature was forged, the deed is entirely void. The deed also is void if the grantor's signature is genuine but was obtained by fraud, such as by representing that she was only signing an autograph book. However, if the fraud was collateral to her signature, such as the grantee falsely promising to pay the grantor, the deed is voidable but not void. A subsequent transfer of the title to a bona fide purchaser may defeat the grantor's later attempt to invalidate the conveyance. If the grantor is not the sole owner, her signature alone will only convey her interest in the property. A conveyance of the fee simple absolute title would require the signatures of any spouse, cotenant, easement holder, or other interest owner.

2. Property Description (Legal Description)

The legal description must be sufficiently detailed to identify the property being conveyed from any other parcel of land. The description can refer to an official survey or to a recorded plat map or can identify each boundary by a metes and bounds description. Any part of the property that the grantor "excepts" (if an existing interest) or "reserves" (if a new interest) also must be described adequately. The most common methods for describing land are the federal survey system, recorded plat maps, and metes and bounds.

a. Federal Survey (Government Survey or Rectangular System)

Meridian lines (north-south) and base lines (east-west) running across most of the country furnish location points for many parcels. In between those lines are subsidiary range lines (north-south) and township lines (east-west) every six miles, creating thirty-six square mile townships. The townships are divided into thirty-six sections that are one square mile and are numbered sequentially from the top right corner of the township across to the top left corner (1 to 6), then down one level and back across to the right (7 to 12), zigzagging back and forth to the bottom, as farmers sometimes plow a field without having to double back. These one square mile (640 acre) sections may be divided into 160 acre quarter sections (e.g. northeast quarter) or into 40 acre quarter-quarter sections (e.g. northwest quarter of the southeast quarter). A description generally reads from the smallest locator to the broadest.

Illustration: "E ½ of NW ¼ of SW ¼, Sec. 8, T 5 N, R 6 W, PB & M" refers to the east half of the northwest quarter of the southwest quarter of Section 8, Township 5 North, Range 6 West of the specified principal base line and meridian. Thus, the property is located in the square mile section bordered by range lines 6 and 7 west and by township lines 5 and 6 north.

b. Plat Maps

Most land development occurs when subdividers acquire agricultural or range land and convert it into
smaller residential or commercial plots. For their own
convenience and to comply with the state subdivision
law, they have surveyors prepare maps of the newly
subdivided parcels. The maps are recorded and provide
the basis for legal descriptions of the new, smaller
parcels, such as "Lot 23 of Block 15 of the New Pines
Subdivision, as recorded in Volume 9, page 150, Official Records of Jones County, Georgia." Recorded
maps of condominium projects ("vertical subdivisions") usually include the height and other dimensions of each unit.

c. Metes and Bounds

Any parcel can be described by identifying a point of
beginning and then giving the direction and length of
each boundary. For example, the description might
state "beginning at the southwesterly intersection of
Oak and Main Streets, then west 25 feet to the fence,
then south 100 feet, then northeast approximately 120
feet back to the beginning." This triangle would be
described with much more detail and precision in a
real deed.

d. Inconsistent Descriptions

In a legal description, a "monument," such as a tree
or fence, is inconsistent with a "course" or "distance"
(25 feet) or an "angle" (west), when they do not lead
to the same place. For example, if one walking 25 feet
west from the tree would go beyond the fence in the

prior paragraph, the monument reference prevails over the course reference. In this hierarchy, map references are between monuments and courses. Name or quantity references, such as "known as Smith Ranch, being 1.03 acres," are lowest in the hierarchy. If uncertainty about property boundaries exists between neighbors, rather than between grantor and grantee, the doctrine of agreed boundaries may furnish a basis of resolution. See Chapter 16.

e.   *Boundaries with Width*

If a boundary is defined by reference to a road or other monument, a presumption exists that the deed refers to the monument's center. However, the presumption does not apply in certain common sense cases, such as when the deed provides otherwise or the grantor's ownership goes only to the near edge.

Illustration: A legal description that states that the property is " * * * bounded on the north by the road" presumably means that the parcel's northern border is the middle of the road, rather than the near (south) or far (north) edge. But if the grantor owns the entire width of the road and no land north of it, the boundary would be the northern edge of the road, rather than the middle. If the grantor owned no part of the road, its southern edge would be the boundary.

f.   *Water Boundaries*

If a river or stream is the boundary, the grantee presumptively takes title up to the middle of it. As the stream changes course over time, the party on one side may gain land (accretion), while the party on the other loses land (reliction) due to the alteration of the boundary line. If the change in the stream is sudden and substantial (avulsion), the boundary does not move but remains where it was before the stream change. Other consequences of owning "riparian" land adjacent to a stream are covered in Chapter 14.

3. Description of the Estate

If the deed does not specify the estate being conveyed, it presumptively transfers a fee simple absolute. The ancient words of limitation "and his heirs" are no longer necessary. Therefore, if a lesser estate is intended, qualifying language must be added, such as "for ten years" or "for life." Similarly, the deed should describe whether multiple grantees are taking as tenants in common, joint tenants, or tenants by the entirety. If the form of cotenancy is not specified, a tenancy in common normally is presumed, unless the parties are married, which may lead to a different presumption. If the estate being conveyed is subject to restrictions, the deed should specify whether they are conditions that can cause forfeiture or mere covenants, permitting only injunctive or monetary relief. These matters are discussed more fully in their appropriate chapters, such as Estates, Concurrent Ownership, and Covenants.

4. Words of Grant

The deed must show the grantor's intent to transfer an interest to the grantee. No technical words are necessary, but "grant," "quitclaim," and "convey" are common terms. The grantor should not use words that indicate an intent to convey only at the grantor's death (e.g. "I leave"), or the deed might have to comply with the more stringent formalities for the creation of a will.

D.   ACKNOWLEDGMENT

Most states do not require that the grantor's signature be acknowledged (notarized) or witnessed. These are common requirements for wills but not for deeds. However, the grantor's signature must be acknowledged for the deed to be recorded in the public property records.

E.   RECORDING

In most states, a deed conveys title when it is delivered. Failure to record the deed does not defeat the passage of title, and many deeds are delivered but intentionally left unrecorded. However, recording provides important advantages to the grantee. See Chapter 10.

III.   DELIVERY OF DEEDS

A deed is ineffective unless and until the grantor delivers it to the grantee. Before delivery, the deed is merely a piece of paper without any legal effect.

A.   WHAT IS DELIVERY

No specific physical acts are required for effective delivery of a deed. Delivery is not necessarily the same as the manual handing over of the document, since a deed may be delivered even though it is not handed over. Alternatively, a deed may be handed to the grantee and yet not have been delivered as a matter of law. For example, the grantor may hand the deed to the grantee solely for his review of the document. The physical acts are significant only as manifestations of the grantor's intent, which is the essential feature of delivery.

Delivery occurs when the grantor properly manifests an intent that a completed or consummated legal act has occurred. The grantor must intend that—as a result of her binding act—the deed has operated to pass title. What distinguishes a will from a deed is that a will operates in the future, whereas a deed operates in the present. In the following Illustrations, "Grace" is the grantor, and "Gene" is the grantee.

Illustration: Grace signs a deed, puts it down, and says to those who are present: "Now I have transferred my property to Gene." Even though Grace has not handed the deed to Gene, it may be considered to be delivered. Grace's statement indicates that she regards the deed as already having transferred the title to Gene, i.e. that she has committed a binding legal act.

Illustration: Grace signs a deed, hands it to Gene, and says: "Hold onto this deed for me because later I may want to deliver it to you to make you the owner of the property." Delivery has not occurred because Grace's statement indicates that she does not regard handing the deed to Gene as sufficient to transfer the title.

A presumption exists that a deed has been delivered when it is in the grantee's possession and a contrary presumption when the grantor retains possession.

However, both presumptions are rebuttable, as the above illustrations indicate. A rebuttable presumption of delivery also exists when the grantor has notarized or recorded the deed. When a deed has been dated and delivered, delivery is presumed to have occurred on the date specified in the deed.

Even after delivery has occurred, the deed is effective to transfer title only if the grantee accepts it. However, acceptance is presumed whenever title would be beneficial to the grantee. Acceptance is presumed to have occurred on the same date the deed was delivered. In fact, the grantee need not even know that delivery has occurred, but he can reject a deed when it would have harmful consequences to him. For example, the property might be contaminated by toxic wastes.

B.   INTENT THAT THE DEED BE PRESENTLY OPERATIVE

Delivery occurs only if the grantor has a present intent that the deed immediately transfer title. If the grantor intends that the deed operate only at some future time, there is no delivery, although delivery may occur in the future.

Illustration: Grace hands Gene her deed and says: "The property is now yours." Delivery has occurred, since she intended that the deed presently operate to transfer title.

Illustration: Grace hands Gene her deed and says: "Record this deed when I die; recording will make the property yours." The deed has not been delivered now, since Grace's intent is that the deed transfer title sometime in the future, rather than immediately. Her statement indicates a belief that recording is essential to transfer title. Although she may be mistaken, it nevertheless demonstrates that she does not intend that the deed operate to transfer title immediately. She has not intended to perform a completed legal act.

Illustration: The granting clause in Grace's deed to Gene states: "To Gene on his 21st birthday." When Gene is 19 years old, Grace hands him the deed and says, "I now give you an interest in my property." Grace has *presently* delivered a *future* interest to Gene. The delivery satisfied the present intent requirement.

1. Effect of Future Events when no Intent Exists to Make the Deed Presently Operative

To satisfy the delivery requirement, the grantor must have a present intent that the deed be operative immediately. If the grantor intends that the deed operate only in the future, there is no delivery now. But when that specified future arrives, the grantor then may have a present intent. At that later moment, the deed can be regarded as delivered. Sometimes it is said that the grantor then has ratified the earlier physical act of delivery.

Illustration: Grace handed her deed to Gene and said: "This deed will make you the owner of the property when you are twenty-one." Grace later attended Gene's twenty-first birthday party and congratulated him on his new ownership of the property. The deed may be regarded as delivered on Gene's birthday. It was not delivered when Grace handed it to Gene, since she then had no present intent. But on his birthday, she intended that the deed then operate, i.e. she had a present intent. Since no particular physical acts are required, the deed was delivered that day even though Grace did not hand the deed to Gene at that time.

2. When the Future Event is the Grantor's Death

A future intent cannot become a present intent when the grantor intends that the deed operate only at her death. When the grantor dies, she cannot have any intent and, thus, cannot deliver a deed.

Illustration: Grace handed Gene her deed and said: "Record this deed when I die, and you will then become the owner of my property." Grace's false belief in the necessity for recording means that the deed was not delivered when she handed it to Gene. Her intent was that the deed not yet operate to pass title. For so long as Grace is alive, she has no present intent that the deed transfer title, because she does not want title to pass until her death. But once she dies, she obviously has no intent, and delivery cannot occur. As a result, Gene will not obtain title from the deed.

Illustration: Grace's safe deposit box is opened at her death and is found to contain a deed to Gene with the following note: "This deed is for Gene, so that he will be taken care of after I am gone." There is no delivery. Grace's note indicates an intent that the deed operate only at her death. Therefore, she had no present intent while she was alive to commit a binding legal act.

C. NO CONDITIONAL DELIVERY TO A GRANTEE

If the grantor validly delivered a deed to a grantee, any conditions that the grantor attempted to place on the delivery are invalid, and delivery is absolute. In most states, there cannot be conditional delivery to a grantee.

Illustration: Grace hands her deed to Gene and says: "I am delivering my deed to you now. The land is now yours, but do not record the deed until after January 1." Since Grace intends to make the instrument presently operative, delivery has occurred. Delivery to a grantee is always absolute, so Gene may record the deed immediately.

Under the rule prohibiting conditional delivery to a grantee, a court may reach one of two results if the grantor hands the deed directly to the grantee and states some conditions. The court may hold that the grantor had a present intent to make the deed operative, so that absolute delivery has occurred free of the condition. Alternatively, the court may hold that the condition negates any present intent, so that delivery has not occurred. Where the condition is the grantor's death, neither result satisfies her intent. Therefore, a sympathetic court may construe the deed as reserving a life estate for the grantor.

Illustration: Grace handed her deed to Gene and said: "Record this deed when I die." There are two possible outcomes. The court may hold that present delivery occurred, so that the nonrecordation condition fails and Gene becomes the owner at once with the right to record. Or the court may hold that Grace did not intend the deed to be operative until after her death, so that the deed was not delivered and Gene receives nothing. Observe that neither resolution effectuates Grace's intent that Gene take the property at her death.

D. DELIVERY TO SOMEONE OTHER THAN THE GRANTEE

1. Grantee's Agent

Delivery to the grantee's agent is the same as delivery directly to the grantee, since the agent is subject to the grantee's control. Therefore, the rule that conditions to a delivery are invalid probably still applies.

Illustration: Grace handed her deed to Gene's wife and said: "Please give this deed to Gene when he gets home, but tell him not to record it until next year." If Gene's wife is regarded as his agent, delivery to her is the same as delivery to Gene, and the condition concerning recording is invalid.

2. Grantor's Agent

The grantor may hand a deed to her own agent for delivery to the grantee at a later time. In that case, delivery occurs when the agent delivers the deed to the grantee if the grantor had a present intent at that time.

Illustration: Grace handed her deed to her husband and said: "Please give this deed to Gene when you see him at the party tonight, unless I change my mind." Grace did not change her mind, and her husband handed the deed to Gene that evening at the party while Grace watched. The deed was delivered at that point. Grace's husband became her agent when she reserved the right to recall the deed. When she handed the deed to him, delivery did not occur, because the reservation indicated that she had no present intent to make the deed operative. But that evening, when her husband handed the deed to Gene, Grace's earlier expressed intent became a present intent, so that delivery then occurred.

Illustration: Grace handed her deed to her husband and said: "Deliver this deed to Gene when I die, unless I have changed my mind." Grace died, and her husband handed the deed to Gene. There is no delivery. Grace's husband was her agent, and an agent's power terminates when the principal dies. Thus, he no longer had authority to hand the deed to Gene. When he handed it to Gene, Grace could not have a present intent to make the deed operative because she was dead.

3. Escrow

A deed may be handed to a third person who is an agent for neither party. Such a person is called an "escrow," "escrow agent," "escrow holder," or "escrowee." A true escrow agent is not subject to the control of either person acting without the other. The grantor places the escrow agent beyond her control by giving up the right to recall the deed from the escrow. This device permits a valid conditional delivery to be made to take effect at some time in the future, even when the condition is the grantor's death. By waiving the right to recall the deed, the grantor manifests an intent to perform a binding legal act. The escrow agent's authority therefore no longer depends on the grantor's continued assent, and the delivery may be completed when the condition occurs.

In the following four Illustrations, assume that the grantor has waived the right to recall the deed and that "Ezra" is the escrow agent.

Illustration: Grace handed her deed to Ezra and said: "Deliver this deed to Gene on his 21st birthday." Ezra delivers the deed to Gene on his 21st birthday. At that moment, valid delivery occurs.

Illustration: Grace handed her deed to Ezra and said: "Deliver this deed to Gene on his 21st birthday." Grace died before Gene turned 21. Ezra delivers the deed to Gene on his 21st birthday. The delivery is valid, even though Grace is dead.

Illustration: Grace handed her deed to Ezra and said: "Deliver this deed to Gene when I die." When Grace dies, Ezra hands the deed to Gene. There is a valid delivery.

Illustration: Grace handed her deed to Ezra and said: "Deliver this deed to Gene when he is 21." However, Grace took the deed back from Ezra when Gene was only 19. Title still passes to Gene on his 21st birthday. Grace's recovery of the deed is irrelevant since a binding legal act occurred when she irrevocably delivered her deed into escrow.

a.   *A Contingency Certain to Occur*

In a few states, a deed cannot be deposited into escrow except upon a contingency that is certain to occur. This rule has been criticized for confusing an unconditional waiver of the right to recall with an allowable conditional event, as shown in the following Illustrations.

Illustration: Grace hands her deed to Ezra and says: "Deliver this deed to Gene when I die. I waive the right to recall it." All jurisdictions agree that Ezra may complete the delivery on Grace's death. She had no right of recall, and the event is certain to occur.

Illustration: Grace hands her deed to Ezra and says: "Deliver this deed to Gene when I die, but I reserve the right to recall it." All jurisdictions agree that Ezra may not complete the delivery on Grace's death. The event is certain, but the right of recall prohibits a transfer after her death.

Illustration: Grace hands her deed to Ezra and says: "Deliver this deed to Gene only if he outlives me. I reserve the right to recall it." All jurisdictions agree that Ezra cannot complete the delivery if Grace dies first. The event is uncertain, and Grace retained a right of recall, so that a true escrow was not created.

Illustration: Grace hands her deed to Ezra and says: "Deliver this deed to Gene only if he outlives me. I waive my right to recall it." Courts in most jurisdictions would hold that Ezra may complete delivery after Grace's death because she put the deed beyond her control. But a minority of courts would hold that the condition's uncertainty prevents the deed from being legally delivered despite the unconditional escrow.

b. An Underlying Contract

In noncommercial cases (i.e. donative situations), a grantor can make a binding delivery into escrow by waiving the right to recall the deed even though no contractual relationship exists between the grantor and grantee. However, in commercial situations, courts in most states hold that the grantor can recall the deed from escrow before delivery to the grantee unless an enforceable contract exists between the grantor and grantee.

Illustration: Grace and Gene orally contracted for Grace to sell her property to Gene for $10,000. Grace deposited her deed into escrow with instructions that it be delivered to Gene if he paid the price within one month. Before the month had passed, Grace revoked her instructions and recalled the deed. Courts in most states would permit Grace to do so, since the oral contract was unenforceable under the Statute of Frauds.

This rule is consistent with the minority view that conditional delivery into escrow cannot occur if the condition is uncertain, because the grantee's payment is not a certain event. The rule also is consistent with the majority view if it is assumed that a commercial grantor never intends to waive the right to recall. Thus, a commercial escrow may not be a "true" escrow because the escrow agent remains subject to the grantor's control until the closing. As the grantor's agent, the escrow agent must honor the grantor's demand to return the deed. The existence of a binding contract between the grantor and grantee does not change the nature of the escrow. The contract merely enables the grantee to obtain a decree of specific performance of the contract and force the grantor to deliver the deed regardless of her state of mind. Once a grantor signs a specifically enforceable contract (see Chapter 8, p. 281), she no longer has the right to change her mind.

Illustration: Grace executed a binding contract with Gene to sell her land to him. Grace then deposited her deed into escrow with proper instructions but later sought to recall the deed before the time for Gene's performance. Whether the escrow agent returns the deed to her is irrelevant, since Gene can specifically enforce the contract and compel Grace to convey regardless of her state of mind. This result is the same even if no escrow had been created. If Grace refuses to deliver a deed to Gene, a court would compel her to do so, and title would pass regardless of her intent.

c.   Relation Back

Generally, a deed deposited into escrow passes title upon delivery from the escrow agent to the grantee. But, when necessary to do justice and effectuate the parties' intent, courts hold that the passage of title relates back to the first delivery.

Illustration: Grace deposited her deed to Gene in escrow and died before escrow closed. Her heirs claim that her title passes to them. However, to protect Gene, a court will hold that the escrow agent's post-death delivery to Gene relates back to Grace's earlier delivery into escrow, so that Gene owns the property, rather than Grace's heirs.

Illustration: Grace deposited her deed into escrow, and Gene died before the escrow closed. A court will hold that the second delivery to Gene's estate relates back to the first delivery, so that legal title passed to Gene when he was alive and then descended to his heirs. This result avoids the rule that a deed is void if it does not convey title to a living grantee.

Illustration: Grace deposited her deed to Gene into escrow but later gave a deed to the same property to Alice. Alice knew of the deed to Gene. The doctrine of relation back gives Gene priority over Alice even though the delivery to her preceded the second delivery to Gene. However, if Alice had been a bona fide purchaser without notice, she might have prevailed under the state recording act. See Chapter 10, p. 352.

Illustration: Grace deposited her deed to Gene into escrow. Her creditors then attempted to attach the property. Courts in some jurisdictions hold that Gene prevails over the creditors by virtue of the relation back doctrine, but others hold that the doctrine will not apply when innocent third parties are involved.

E. EFFECT OF DELIVERY AND NONDELIVERY

1. Delivery

Title transfers when the deed is delivered. What subsequently happens to the document is unimportant, because the deed has performed its function and transferred title. Title is not retransferred by loss, recall, or destruction of the deed.

Illustration: Grace delivered her deed to Gene but later changed her mind and asked Gene to return it to her. Even if Gene returns the deed, title will remain with him. Grace's delivery transferred title to Gene. If the parties now wish to retransfer title to Grace, Gene must execute and deliver his own deed to her; returning her deed is not an adequate substitute. Return of the deed does not undo its earlier delivery.

2. Nondelivery

Until a deed is delivered, it has no effect on title. However, a grantor who negligently has permitted the grantee to possess an undelivered deed may lose the title to an innocent purchaser of the property from the grantee based on estoppel.

Illustration: Grace executed a deed to Gene but did not deliver it. Gene obtained the deed without Grace's knowledge and recorded it. Grace still owns the property. Gene acquired no interest in the land and, therefore, has nothing to transfer to a bona fide purchaser, even though he recorded the deed.

Illustration: Grace handed her deed to Ezra and said: "Deliver this deed to Gene if he graduates from college." Gene did not graduate from college, but Ezra gave him the deed anyway. The deed has not been delivered. Grace remains the owner of the property.

Illustration : Grace handed her deed to Ezra and said: "Deliver this deed to Gene when I die." Ezra instead handed the deed to Alice on Grace's death. Alice is not the owner, because the delivery to her was unauthorized. Gene may compel Ezra and Alice to give the deed to him.

IV. TITLE COVENANTS IN DEEDS

Today, property purchasers commonly protect their title by purchasing title insurance from a title insurance company. A title insurance policy indemnifies the purchaser if the title is not what it was represented to be. However, an older and still useful form of title protection provides recourse against the grantor if the title is defective. This section describes this form of recourse that an aggrieved grantee has against her grantor or a former grantor.

A. DEGREES OF PROTECTION AVAILABLE TO THE GRANTEE

Depending on the kind of deed by which the grantee acquired title, he may have extensive or nonexistent protection against title defects.

1. Warranty Deed

A warranty deed gives the grantee the greatest possible recourse against the grantor for title defects. Such a deed contains up to six title covenants.

2. Statutory Deed

In many states, statutes provide that certain title covenants may be implied from the form of the deed used by the grantor. These covenants often are narrower in scope than the covenants in a full warranty deed and, therefore, afford the grantee less protection.

3. Deed Without Warranties

If the grantor executes a deed that has no express or statutory title covenants, the grantee has no recourse against the grantor for title defects. There are no implied warranties of title in deeds. The most typical form of deed without warranties is the quitclaim deed.

B. SIX COMMON LAW TITLE COVENANTS

A general warranty deed includes all six title covenants that are described in the following subsections. The first three—seisin, right to convey, and against encumbrances—concern the title now held by the grantor and are referred to as "present" covenants. The final three—quiet enjoyment, warranty, and further assurances—protect the grantee at a later time and are called "future" covenants.

1. Covenant of Seisin

This covenant warrants that the grantor "is seised of the premises." As the wording suggests, it warrants that the grantor has seisin, i.e. owns a freehold estate in the property being conveyed. However, it does not represent that the seisin is lawful.

2. Covenant of Right to Convey

Under this covenant, the grantor represents that she has the right to sell and convey the property. This covenant complements the covenant of seisin by protecting the grantee when the grantor has only tortious or wrongful seisin of the property.

3. Covenant Against Encumbrances

This covenant warrants that the property is free and clear from all encumbrances. This covenant is violated if the title is encumbered by a lien (tax lien, assessment lien, mechanic's lien, judgment lien, or mortgage), a lease, or a restriction on use (easement, restrictive covenant, or equitable servitude).

Some courts hold that a visible easement does not violate the covenant on the ground that the grantee must have seen the easement and been willing to take title subject to it. A few other courts extend this exception to include any encumbrance actually known to the grantee, but this is a minority view. Generally, any encumbrance "assumed" by the grantee, such as a mortgage, is excluded from the covenant against encumbrances, as are encumbrances that are beneficial to the grantee, such as a power line easement to serve the property.

4. Covenant of Quiet Enjoyment

Under the covenant of quiet enjoyment, the grantor warrants that the grantee will "quietly enjoy" the property conveyed. The covenant protects the grantee against an eviction by the grantor, the grantor's agents, or any holder of a paramount title.

5. Covenant of Warranty

This covenant operates in conjunction with the covenant of quiet enjoyment. In the covenant of warranty, the grantor covenants to warrant and defend the grantee against any conflicting claims to the property.

6. Covenant of Further Assurances

In this covenant, the grantor promises to execute a document or take other actions necessary to perfect the grantee's title. For example, if the deed from the grantor is defective, the grantee can use this covenant to force the grantor to execute a new one. By virtue of this covenant the grantor also is obligated to transfer to the grantee any adverse interest that he subsequently acquires. Much the same result is obtained under the doctrine of estoppel by deed. See p. 314.

C.   SPECIAL COVENANTS

The six title covenants discussed above are general covenants that cover all exceptions to their absolute warranties. A grantor instead can give a special covenant that warrants against only a limited number of title exceptions. Statutory covenants often are special covenants.

1.   Special Covenants of Right to Convey, Warranty, and Quiet Enjoyment

A typical special covenant warrants only that the grantor personally has not conveyed any interest in the property to any other person. An outstanding interest conveyed by a predecessor of the grantor would not breach this covenant.

2.   Special Covenant Against Encumbrances

A typical special covenant against encumbrances warrants that the grantor has not permitted any encumbrances to burden the title. However, it does not warrant that previous owners kept the title free from them. Thus, the covenant is breached only by an encumbrance that attached to the title during the grantor's period of ownership.

Illustration: Grace conveyed her property to Gene with a special covenant against encumbrances. Gene later discovered that the property is subject to an easement granted by the person who sold the property to Grace. Although the easement is an encumbrance, it attached before Grace owned the property. Therefore, she did not breach her covenant.

3. Estoppel by Deed (After Acquired Title)

Under the doctrine of estoppel by deed, if a grantor purports to convey an interest in land that she does not own but then subsequently acquires, it automatically passes to the grantee without the need for an additional deed. Because this doctrine operates by estoppel, it applies only if the grantor represented in the deed that she had title. Therefore, the doctrine only applies if the grantor gave (1) a full warranty deed, (2) in some states, a deed that contains at least a covenant of warranty, or (3) in other states, a deed that contains no title covenants if it is not a quitclaim deed. The deed estops the grantor from later asserting her after acquired title against the grantee. The after acquired title "feeds" the estoppel. A consequence of the doctrine is that a title searcher may have to check whether the owner of an interest in land ever purported to transfer it before she actually acquired it. See Chapter 10, p. 340.

D.   BREACH OF COVENANT

1.   What Constitutes a Breach

The six title covenants differ in the methods by which they are breached.

a.   *Covenant of Seisin*

This covenant is breached if the grantor did not have seisin when she conveyed. Technically, it is breached even if the grantor owns the property but a potential adverse possessor whose claim has not yet ripened is in possession. Conversely, it is not breached if the grantor does not own but is wrongfully possessing the property as a potential adverse possessor. In this case, the grantor has tortious seisin. The grantee need not be evicted from the land to claim a breach. It is sufficient that the grantor was without seisin.

b.   *Covenant of Right to Convey*

This covenant is breached if the grantor lacks the right to convey the estate that the deed describes. Someone may have a right to convey without necessarily having seisin. Therefore, lack of seisin alone does not breach this covenant. Like the covenant of seisin, the grantee need not be dispossessed from the premises for a breach to occur.

c.   *Covenant Against Encumbrances*

This covenant is breached if there are any encumbrances on the property when it is conveyed. The encumbrance need not actually disturb the grantee's possession or title.

d.   *Covenants of Warranty and Quiet Enjoyment*

These covenants are breached if the grantee is "evicted" by a paramount title or interest. "Eviction" includes not only a physical ouster, but also a constructive eviction, such as paying a paramount lien to avoid a foreclosure.

e.   *Covenant of Further Assurances*

This covenant is breached if the grantor refuses to obtain a release of an encumbrance, when possible, or refuses to convey to the grantee some paramount interest later acquired.

2.   When a Covenant is Breached

The covenants are divided into "present" and "future" covenants. Present covenants are breached, if ever, at the moment of the conveyance to the grantee. Future covenants are breached only when an eviction occurs.

a.   *Present Covenants*

The covenant of seisin is breached at the moment the grantor delivers the deed if he lacked seisin at that time. The covenant of right to convey is breached at the moment of delivery if the grantor lacked the right to convey the property at that time. The covenant against encumbrances is breached at the moment of delivery if the title is encumbered at that time.

b.   *Future Covenants*

The covenants of quiet enjoyment and warranty are breached when a paramount title or encumbrance is asserted against the grantee so that he is actually or constructively evicted. The covenant of further assurances is breached when the grantor refuses to obtain or to supply documents the grantee needs to perfect the title.

E. ENFORCEMENT OF COVENANTS BY A REMOTE GRANTEE (RUNNING WITH THE LAND)

The distinction between present and future covenants controls which covenants "run with the land" so as to protect remote grantees. Since a present covenant is breached immediately or never, it does not run. Future covenants do run because they are not breached until sometime in the future.

1. Covenants of Seisin and Right to Convey

These two covenants warrant present facts about the grantor's title. If the facts are true, the covenants have not been breached and never will be breached. If they are untrue, the covenants were breached at the moment of the conveyance. The cause of action for their breach constitutes personal property, which does not run with the land, except in a minority of states.

Illustration: Grace delivered a deed to Gene that contained covenants of seisin and right to convey. However, Grace previously had conveyed the same property to Ann. Gene executed a deed of this property to Rita, but this deed contained no covenants. Rita has no remedy against Grace or Gene, even though she did not acquire title. She cannot sue Gene since he gave no covenants. Although Grace did give covenants, they are both present covenants and do not run with the land so as to protect Rita. However, courts in a minority of states hold that Gene impliedly assigned his cause of action against Grace to Rita when he purported to transfer the property title to her.

2. Covenant Against Encumbrances

This, too, is a present covenant and does not run with the land. If the property is encumbered when it is conveyed, the grantee has an immediate cause of action against her grantor. But subsequent remote grantees may not sue that grantor for the encumbrance if it still exists when they acquire the property, unless the cause of action was assigned to them. However, a subsequent grantee may sue her own grantor if the title is encumbered and if her deed included a covenant against encumbrances.

Illustration: Grace conveyed her property to Gene with a covenant against encumbrances in the deed. At the time of the conveyance, the title was subject to an easement. Gene then conveyed the property to Rita by a deed that did not contain any covenants. Rita has no remedy. Her deed from Gene contained no covenant against the easement, and Grace's covenant did not run with the land.

3. Covenants of Warranty, Quiet Enjoyment, and Further Assurances

These future covenants run with the land and protect the remote grantee who suffers the injury when the eviction occurs. Once these covenants are breached, they technically no longer run with the land. However, courts often hold that the cause of action arising from the breach is impliedly assigned with each conveyance of the property, thus reaching the same result as if the covenant did run. However, the statute of limitations begins to run from the time of the breach.

Illustration: Grace purported to convey property that she did not own to Gene by a deed containing all six covenants. Gene later gave Rita a deed without covenants for the same property. The true owner appeared and dispossessed Rita. Rita does not have a cause of action against Grace for breach of the covenants of seisin or right to convey because they are present covenants and do not run to her. But Rita may sue Grace for breach of the covenants of quiet enjoyment and warranty after she is evicted. If Rita sells the property to Sam after she is evicted, he will have no cause of action against Grace, since even the future covenants do not run once they are breached.

Illustration: Grace's property was subject to a mortgage when she conveyed it to Gene by full warranty deed. Gene then conveyed the property to Rita by a deed without covenants. The mortgage was not paid, and the mortgagee foreclosed and evicted Rita from the property. Rita may sue Grace for breach of the covenants of quiet enjoyment and warranty, since those ran with the land and were breached when Rita was ousted. But Rita has no cause of action against Grace for breach of the covenant against encumbrances, since that was breached when Grace conveyed to Gene and did not run with the land. Rita cannot sue Gene since he gave no covenants.

F. MEASURE OF DAMAGES

The covenants differ in their measure of damages. In general, however, the covenantor is never liable for more than the amount originally paid by the covenantee for the property. Restitution is the maximum amount owed. In some states, however, damages are based on the property's value on the date of breach, rather than on the purchase price. Damages generally do not include the cost of improvements made by the grantee. However, he may be able to make such a claim on an unjust enrichment theory or under an "innocent improvement" statute.

1. Covenants of Seisin and Right to Convey

When these covenants are breached, the grantee can recover the price he paid for the property or for so much of the property as the deed failed to convey. Courts differ as to whether the grantee can retain the property or must tender it to the grantor as a precondition to recovery. If the grantee buys the outstanding title, he can recover the amount paid for it, not exceeding the amount the grantor received when she sold the property. In a minority of jurisdictions, the grantee can recover up to the property's value on the date of the breach.

2. Covenant Against Encumbrances

Encumbrances are either monetary or nonmonetary. If it is monetary, such as a tax lien or mortgage, the measure of damages is the cost to remove it, but not to exceed the land's value. If the encumbrance is nonmonetary, such as an easement or restrictive covenant, the measure of damages is the reduction in the land's market value caused by the encumbrance. If the grantee buys the encumbrance or pays it off, he can recover the amount he paid, not exceeding the amount the grantor received when she sold the property. In a minority of jurisdictions, the grantee can recover up to the property's value on the date of the breach.

3. Covenants of Warranty, Quiet Enjoyment, and Further Assurances

For a total eviction, the plaintiff can recover the amount he paid for the property. For a partial eviction, he can recover a proportionate amount of the price.

4. Damages for Remote Grantees

Some courts limit recovery against a remote grantor to the amount the plaintiff paid for the property even if it is less than the remote grantor received. If a remote grantee has a cause of action under title covenants made by more than one grantor in the chain of title, the grantee can sue them all but is limited to only one full satisfaction. If a grantor who is sued is the beneficiary of earlier covenants, he has an action against the covenantor for any damages he must pay.

Illustration: For $10,000, Grace conveyed property to Gene by full warranty deed. Gene conveyed it by full warranty deed to Rita for $9,000. Rita conveyed it by full warranty deed to Sam for $11,000. Grace never owned the property, and the real owner evicted Sam. Sam may sue Rita based on her covenants and recover $11,000. He may sue Gene based on the future covenants in the deed to Rita and recover $9,000 (the amount Gene received). He also may sue

Grace on the future covenants in the deed to Gene and recover $10,000. However, Sam's total recovery cannot exceed $11,000 even if he obtains judgments against all three defendants. If Sam recovers from Rita, she may have an action against Gene or Grace. If Sam or Rita recovers from Gene, he may have an action against Grace.

V. DUTIES OF DISCLOSURE

The common law title covenants warrant only the title and not the property's physical condition. The common law implied no warranties of fitness or merchantability. This basic rule still applies to real estate today. However, vendors now often have greater disclosure duties, and commercial vendors may be subject to an implied warranty of fitness.

A. NONDISCLOSURE

A vendor must disclose any material defect known to him and not reasonably discoverable by the purchaser. If the vendor fails to disclose, the purchaser can rescind the contract of sale, sue for damages, and possibly recover for personal injuries suffered as a result of the defect. Brokers, lenders, attorneys, escrow officers, and inspectors also may have a duty to disclose defects known to them and perhaps even defects they may have suspected or should have known about.

B. IMPLIED WARRANTIES IN THE
SALE OF NEW HOMES

A growing number of jurisdictions impose an implied warranty of quality on builder-vendors. The warranty originally applied only to builders of mass-produced homes, but it is expanding to include anyone who builds houses for sale. However, many issues remain to be resolved, including:

1. Statute of Limitations

Does the time to sue commence when the defect was created, when construction was completed, when title was transferred to the buyer, when some indication of the defect first surfaced, or when the buyer finally discovered what the problem was?

2. Plaintiffs

Can only the original purchaser sue, or can a remote purchaser also sue? Does the answer depend on whether and how long the original buyer occupied the property? If a remote buyer is not automatically entitled to sue, can the original buyer assign his cause of action as part of the sale to the remote buyer?

3. Defendants

In addition to the seller, can the buyer recover from the prime contractor in charge of the overall project, the subcontractor that caused the problem, the material supplier who supplied the components, the architect, or the construction lender?

4. Damages

The probable measure of damages to the property is the cost of repairs or diminution of value. Are property damages the buyer's only remedy or can he also recover for personal injuries?

5. Disclaimers

To what degree can a seller protect herself by appropriate language in the contract? Is this a matter for freedom of contract or should it be treated like the warranty of habitability in residential rental housing?

CHAPTER TEN

PRIORITIES: THE RECORDING SYSTEM

This Chapter is concerned with the relative rights of successive transferees of interests in land from the same transferor. Priority problems arise when the transferor (1) grants partial interests in the property to successive transferees, such as when the owner gives a mortgage on the property to one person and then gives a mortgage on the same property to another person, (2) purports to transfer the entire estate to different persons, such as when the owner conveys the property to one person and then conveys the same property to another person, or (3) transfers partial and total interests in the same land, such as when the owner gives a mortgage to one person and then conveys the fee title to another person. The relationship between the transferees is analyzed as a question of priorities–who has the prior and, therefore, superior interest.

In most Illustrations in this section, the transfers are of the entire estate, but the same priority principles generally apply to transfers of partial interests. In these Illustrations, the original transferor is usually the owner and is designated as "Owen." The successive transferees are given names in alphabetical order.

I. COMMON LAW PRIORITIES

At common law, most questions of priority were determined according to the principle "first in time, first in right." The party who took first had the superior interest. This principle was supported by the logical notion that, after the owner gave his interest to the first transferee, he had nothing left to give to the second. The same principles applied to the resolution of priorities between equitable claimants, so long as the equities were otherwise equal. The one exception was that a prior equitable claim would be defeated by a subsequent legal claim held by a bona fide purchaser. In this one case, the earlier claim would lose priority.

Illustration–Competing Legal Claims: Owen delivered a deed to his property to Ann and later delivered a deed to the same property to Bob. Ann prevails over Bob in their competing claims to legal title, since her claim was first in time. Ann owns the property.

Illustration–Competing Equitable Claims: Owen executed a contract to sell his property to Ann and later executed a similar contract to sell it to Bob. Both claims are equitable, since Owen retains legal title. See equitable conversion, Chapter 8, p. 281. As between the competing equitable claims, Ann again prevails because her claim was first in time. Ann has the superior right to buy the property.

Illustration–Prior Legal and Subsequent Equitable Claim: Owen delivered a deed to Ann and later contracted to sell the same property to Bob. Ann's prior legal claim based on her deed prevails over Bob's subsequent equitable claim. Ann owns the property and is not obligated to sell it to Bob.

Illustration–Prior Equitable Claim and Subsequent Legal Claim by a Bona Fide Purchaser: Owen contracted to sell his property to Ann and later delivered a deed of the same property to Bob. If Bob paid value to Owen and had no notice of Ann's claim, he is a bona fide purchaser and will prevail over her even though her claim was prior in time. Bob owns the property and is not obliged to honor the contract and sell it to Ann. This was the only type of case at common law for which priority in time was not the controlling factor in determining priority.

Although the common law principle of priority based on time is logical, it is entirely unworkable. If A prevails over B simply because she took first, there is no sensible way for B to purchase O's property. How can B be sure when he pays his money to O that O has not previously conveyed the property to someone else? A diligent search of the property records regarding O's title would be useless because the common law gives A the title even though she never records her deed.

For this reason, every state has replaced the common law rule with a statutory recording system. The system creates incentives for transferees to record the document by which they acquired an interest in land. The system also generally protects a subsequent transferee against prior unrecorded transfers. The recording statutes do not mandate that every document must be recorded to be effective. Rather, they provide that a recorded document is effective against the entire world because recording provides "constructive notice" of its contents to everyone. Conversely, if a document is not recorded, it will be ineffective against certain protected parties.

II. THE RECORDING SYSTEM–
RECORDING STATUTES

Every state now has a land records system for recording documents affecting land titles and for making the documents available for inspection. Therefore, potential purchasers of an interest in land can check the records to ascertain whether their sellers actually own the land and whether the title is subject to encumbrances. However, a search of the public records is useful only if all title documents have been recorded or if the searcher is protected from previously executed documents that are unrecorded. Therefore, the recording acts take the common law exception that a prior equity is defeated by a subsequent bona fide purchaser of the legal title and apply it to all conflicts, whether involving legal or equitable claimants or both.

A. TYPES OF RECORDING ACTS

Each state has enacted one of the three types of recording acts–notice, notice-race, or race.

1. Notice Acts

Notice statutes provide that an unrecorded instrument is invalid against a subsequent purchaser without notice. These acts protect a purchaser who buys property or an interest in it, such as an easement or mortgage, without notice of prior unrecorded instruments affecting it.

Illustration: Arizona's statute provides in part: "No instrument affecting real property gives notice of its contents to subsequent purchasers or encumbrance holders for valuable consideration without notice, unless recorded as provided by law * * *." Ariz. Rev. Stat. § 33–411(A) (1990).

2.   Notice–Race Acts (Race–Notice Acts)

These statutes provide that an unrecorded conveyance is invalid against a subsequent purchaser who buys without notice of it and records before the prior conveyance is recorded. This type of act protects purchasers who buy without notice of an unrecorded claim, but only if they enhance the reliability of the recording system by recording their conveyance.

Illustration: California's statute provides in part: "Every conveyance of real property * * * is void as against any subsequent purchaser or mortgagee of the same property * * * in good faith and for a valuable consideration, whose conveyance is first duly recorded * * *." Cal. Civ. Code § 1214 (West 1999).

3.   Race Acts

A few statutes base priority on the order in which the documents were recorded. The subsequent grantee can prevail even if she knew about the prior conveyance. The sole question is which instrument was recorded first. Sometimes, these statutes are worded in terms of priority. In other cases, they achieve the same effect by making recordation part of the process of delivery, so that a deed will not pass title until it is recorded.

Illustration: Maryland's statute provides: "No estate of inheritance or freehold, declaration or limitation of use, estate above seven years, or deed may pass or take effect unless the deed granting it is executed and recorded." Md. Code Ann., Real Prop. § 3–101(a) (1986).

Illustration: Ohio's mortgage statute provides in part: "All mortgages * * * shall be recorded * * * and shall take effect at the time they are delivered to the recorder for record. If two or more mortgages pertaining to the same premises are presented for record on the same day, they shall take effect in the order of their presentation. The first mortgage presented shall be the first recorded, and the first mortgage recorded shall have preference." Ohio Rev. Code Ann. § 5301.23(A) (Baldwin 1992).

4. Grace Period Acts

These statutes operate like notice statutes, except that they give a grantee certain length of time to record before any sanction is imposed for nonrecordation. These acts were popular when travel to the recorder's office was difficult and time consuming, but modern communication and transportation methods have rendered them obsolete. Therefore, they will not be considered further.

B. COMPARISON OF THE DIFFERENT TYPES OF STATUTE

This section consists of a series of illustrations indicating those situations in which different types of statutes reach a different result.

1. Race v. Notice

Illustration: Owen deeded his property to Ann, who did not record. Owen then deeded the same property to Bob, who knew about Ann's deed but recorded his deed anyway. In a notice jurisdiction, Ann prevails because Bob took with notice. But in a race jurisdiction, Bob prevails because he recorded first.

Illustration: Owen deeded his property to Ann, who did not record. Owen then deeded the same property to Bob, who did not know about Ann's deed and did not record. Then Ann recorded. In a notice jurisdiction, Bob prevails because he purchased without notice of the prior conveyance to Ann. But in a race jurisdiction, Ann wins because she recorded first.

2.   Race v. Notice–Race

Illustration: Owen deeded his property to Ann, who did not record. Owen then deeded the same property to Bob, who knew about the conveyance to Ann but recorded his deed anyway. In a race jurisdiction, Bob prevails because he recorded first. In a notice-race jurisdiction, Ann prevails because Bob purchased with notice of her interest even though he recorded first.

3.   Notice v. Notice–Race

Illustration: Owen deeded his property to Ann, who did not record. Owen then deeded the same property to Bob, who is without notice of the conveyance to Ann. Ann recorded before Bob. Bob prevails over Ann in a notice jurisdiction, because he was the last to purchase without notice. But he loses in a notice-race jurisdiction, since he not only must purchase without notice but also must record first.

Illustration: Owen deeded his property to Ann, who did not record. Owen then deeded the same property to Bob, who was without notice of the conveyance to Ann and did not record. Bob wins in a notice state, because he purchased without notice. But he loses in a notice-race jurisdiction, because he did not record first. In a notice-race jurisdiction, the prior grantee prevails unless the subsequent purchaser records first. Bob has not recorded, so the prior grantee, Ann, prevails. However, if Bob later records before Ann does, Bob will prevail.

III. MECHANICS OF RECORDING AND SEARCHING TITLE

A.   RECORDING A DOCUMENT

To record a document, it is filed, recorded, and indexed. The recording acts differ as to which steps must be completed before a conveyance is protected from conflicting conveyances.

1. Filing

Recording begins when a duly executed, acknowledged, and delivered document is filed at the recorder's office or other designated depository in the county where the land is located. To be accepted for recording, the document must affect title to land, such as a deed, lease, or mortgage. Depending on whether the jurisdiction follows the doctrine of equitable conversion, a contract for the sale of land may be recordable. An option to purchase land is generally not recordable, because it does not convey a property interest. The document usually must be notarized to be accepted by the recorder. Official documents resulting from legal proceedings affecting land, such as probate or quiet title decrees, judgment or tax liens, and lis pendens, are recordable.

The recorder's office examines only the type of document to determine whether to accept it for recording. No government official determines its validity or effectiveness to pass title or even whether the grantor owns the property involved. All such conflicts are resolved between the claimants. The recorder's office merely serves as a repository for documents. Its gatekeeping function is limited to determining what types of documents can be stored there.

2. Recording

The recorder's office makes a copy of the entire document. This copy is then inserted into the current book of official records. These record books, consisting solely of copies of documents, are kept and labeled in strict numerical order. When one book is filled, a new book is started and is given the next number. For example, a one-page document might appear in Volume 387, page 453 of the Official Records; the next document will appear in Volume 387, page 454.

3. Indexing

If the recorder's office merely maintained chronological books of copied documents, searching title to a particular parcel of land would be extremely difficult, particularly in large cities. Therefore, the recorder's office also maintains a set of indexes, where information concerning each document is entered. Rather than leafing through each record book to find documents, a title searcher can use the indexes to obtain the volume and page numbers where relevant documents are recorded. Most states have name indexes that include a grantor-grantee index and a grantee-grantor index. The grantor-grantee index alphabetically lists all recorded documents by the grantor's name. The index shows the grantor's name, then the grantee's name, then possibly a description of the document and of the property, and the volume and page in the official record where the copy of the document is recorded. A grantee-grantor index contains the same information but is organized alphabetically by the grantee's name. In contrast, a tract index (parcel index) organizes the entries by property description, rather than by the parties' names. Indexes (or "indices") often are limited as to time. Thus, one set of indexes may include documents recorded between 1920 and 1950, another for 1950–70, another for 1970–90, another for each year in 1990, and finally a monthly, weekly, or daily index for the current year.

Illustration: A deed of Blackacre from Owen to Ann that was recorded in 1965 will be indexed in the grantor-grantee index for the decade 1960 under Owen's name. It will be indexed in the grantee-grantor index for the same decade under the Ann's name. It will be indexed in a tract index under Blackacre.

If the recorder's office improperly records or indexes a document, it may not give constructive notice of its contents.

4. Returning the Document

After the document has been recorded and indexed, it is returned to the depositor. The recorder's office keeps only the copy.

B. SEARCHING A TITLE

1. Locating the Present Owner in the Grantee Index

A person searching a title starts with the current seller of the property. If that person truly owns the property, he probably will have taken title by a deed, which would be indexed under his name in the grantee index. Thus, a search for Owen would start in the "O" volume of grantees in the year that Owen claims to have purchased the property. If the year is not known, the title searcher must begin in this year's grantee volume and go back year by year until an entry is found.

2. Locating Prior Owners in the Grantee Index

From the first entry, the name of the previous owner can be ascertained, since it will appear in the grantor column. That name then will be searched in the grantee index, usually starting with the date that she conveyed to the current owner and going back in time until her name appears as grantee from the owner before her. That owner's name is then searched in the grantee index, and the process continues with each owner until the searcher arrives at an indisputable source of title, generally the government. At this point, the searcher may conclude that she has a complete chain of title.

a. *Stopping Short of the Original Source*

Many states have marketable title statutes or title standards that require searchers to go back only a set number of years, such as sixty years. Any title existing at that time is presumed to be valid and need not be further justified, although this can create problems when there are rival "roots of title" for searchers to find.

b. Dealing with Gaps

Supplementary indexes may be necessary to fill in missing links. For instance, if a search shows that Norma received a deed from Michael, but no deed to Michael can be found, the next link may be found in the probate records if they are kept separately. These records might show that Michael inherited the property from Lana by will. A return to the grantee index would then show Lana as a grantee twenty years earlier from Kurt, thereby permitting resumption of the search. A comprehensive recording system should include all records affecting titles in one place, but that is not always the case. Bankruptcy, tax liens, condemnation records, and a variety of other records often are stored separately.

3. Searching for Encumbrances and Other Interests in the Grantor Index

Once the searcher knows the names of all owners in the chain of title, she then must determine whether any owners encumbered or otherwise affected the title during their ownership of the property. This is accomplished by searching each name in the appropriate grantor index, usually during that person's years of ownership, since any such conveyance would appear in the grantor index under that owner's name. Thus, a mortgage or easement given by the owner or a judgment lien or lis pendens filed against the owner would be entered in the index showing the owner as grantor and the other party (mortgagee, dominant tenant, judgment creditor, or plaintiff) as grantee.

4. Following the Subsequent History of Encumbrances

To determine whether those property interests still exist, the searcher then must go through either the grantor or grantee indexes for the years after their creation. If they were canceled, a release document should be indexed under the owner's name as grantee and the interest holder's name as grantor. If no such document exists, the interest still survives of record.

IV.   RECORD NOTICE–CONSTRUCTIVE NOTICE

The recording acts penalize only "unrecorded" documents. If an instrument is properly recorded, it takes priority over subsequent claims, whether those claimants actually look for or see it. When an instrument is properly recorded, it gives "constructive" notice, so that subsequent claimants are charged with notice of its existence regardless of whether they have searched the records. The doctrine of constructive notice means that a subsequent claimant cannot benefit from failing to search the records, because he will be charged with notice of all prior recorded instruments even if he does not have actual knowledge of them.

Not every document that has been filed in the recorder's office and copied into the official records is held to be recorded and to give notice within the meaning of the recording acts. The remainder of this section covers cases in which documents have been copied into the records but are held to be unrecorded or to provide no notice. These situations generally are more readily understood by beginning with illustrations and then by following each illustration with an analysis.

A.   DOCUMENTS THAT CANNOT BE LOCATED

1.   Misindexed Documents

Illustration: Owen conveyed his property to Ann. Ann recorded the deed, but the recorder erroneously indexed it under the name of "Smith" rather than "Owen." Owen then conveyed the property to Bob. Because of the misindexing, Bob will not find the deed to Ann since he will search for the name "Owen" in the grantor-grantee index. For this reason, many courts hold that the deed to Ann is unrecorded, since the index would not alert a person checking Owen's title. However, in some states, the recording statute provides that an instrument is deemed recorded when it is filed in the recorder's office. In that type of jurisdiction, Ann will prevail since her deed is technically recorded even though it cannot be found. In jurisdictions holding for Bob, grantees should return to the recorder's office at a later date to check that their document has been properly indexed. In jurisdictions holding for Ann, however, subsequent purchasers do not have a practical method to avoid this hazard.

2.   Wild Documents (Missing Links)

Illustration: Owen conveyed his property to Ann, who did not record. Ann then conveyed the property to Bob, who did record. Owen then deeds the property to Carol, who did record. Carol should prevail over Bob. Even though Bob's deed was recorded, the nonrecordation of the deed from Owen to Ann means that Bob's deed is not connected in the indexes to any name in the chain of title. It will be indexed with Ann as grantor and Bob as grantee, but the index will not alert Carol to look up their names. When Carol checks Owen's name in the grantor-grantee index, she will find nothing. A wild deed (the deed from Ann to Bob) does not give notice within the meaning of a notice act and is not recorded first within the meaning of a notice-race act.

B. DOCUMENTS THAT ARE DIFFICULT TO LOCATE

1. Late Recorded Document

Illustration: Owen purchased the property in 1965. In 1975, he conveyed the property to Ann, who did not record. In 1985, Owen conveyed the property to Bob, who recorded even though he knew about the conveyance to Ann. In 1986, Ann recorded. In 1995, Bob deeded the property to Carol. The jurisdictions are divided as to whether Ann or Carol will prevail, but a majority hold for Ann.

Argument for Ann. Ann's deed is not in the direct chain of title, but it can be found by an extensive search of the records. A normal search would investigate Owen only for the period 1965–1985, the years when he was the owner of record. But if the search under Owen's name was extended from 1985 to the present, the deed to Ann would be found. In jurisdictions that would hold for Ann, a title searcher must check each owner from the date he acquired title to the present, rather than only to the date he appeared to have transferred title.

Argument for Carol. The rule followed in a minority of jurisdictions is that a purchaser should check each owner only during the time of record ownership and no further. The deed to Ann would not be found by such a search, and Carol would not be charged with notice of Ann's claim. Ann's deed would be treated as unrecorded within the meaning of the recording act.

2. Early Recorded Document–Estoppel by Deed

Illustration: In 1994, Ann conveyed property that she did not then own to Bob. Bob recorded. In 1995, Owen, who did own the property, conveyed it to Ann. Ann recorded. In 1997, Ann conveyed the property to Carol. Carol recorded. In most states, the legal effect of the conveyance from Owen to Ann in 1995 was to transfer title to Ann and then from Ann to Bob under the doctrine of estoppel by deed (see p. 314). By virtue of her deed to Bob, Ann is estopped to assert that she had no title to convey to him. Thus, Bob has title unless Carol prevails under the recording acts. The courts are divided.

Argument for Carol. Although Bob's deed was recorded, it is not in the chain of title. For Carol to discover it, she would have to check each owner in the index for the period before the owner acquired title. In this example, Carol would have to check the index under Ann's name for the time before 1995, which is when the records indicate Ann acquired title. Some jurisdictions hold that Carol should not have this burden, especially because Bob should not have accepted a deed from someone who did not have record title. Bob's deed is out of the chain of title.

Argument for Bob. Other courts hold for Bob because Carol could have discovered his deed by a more diligent search. Therefore, Carol is charged with notice of it. In this type of jurisdiction, a purchaser must check each name in the index back to the commencement of the records, rather than merely back to the date the owner acquired title.

3. Deed Affecting more than One Lot

Illustration: Owen conveyed Lot 1 to Ann and, in the same deed, also gave her an easement over his retained Lot 2. Ann recorded the deed. Owen then conveyed Lot 2 to Bob without mention of Ann's easement. Bob recorded. Bob's property is subject to Ann's easement if he is charged with notice of the contents of Owen's deed to Ann. The courts are divided.

Argument for Ann. The deed from Owen to Ann was recorded and could have been discovered by a diligent search of the index. Bob should examine every deed executed by his grantor to see whether it conveys his property or any interest in his property. Bob has notice of the deed from Owen to Ann and of the easement it creates over his property. In this type of jurisdiction, a purchaser must check all deeds executed by her grantor, even though in the index they appear to relate to different property.

Argument for Bob. Courts in other jurisdictions hold that Bob has notice only of deeds in his own chain of title and that a deed to other property is not in that chain. If the index indicates that a deed concerns other property, the searcher is not required to examine the deed to see if it also affects his property. Under this rule, Ann must ensure that her deed is indexed to refer to both Lots 1 and 2.

C. DOCUMENTS THAT CAN BE LOCATED BUT DO NOT GIVE NOTICE

Through inadvertence, the recorder may record a document that should not have been recorded, either because it is an unrecordable document, such as an option agreement, or because the document was defectively executed. The courts do not agree whether such a document gives notice under the recording act. Some courts hold that it does not give notice, even to a searcher who actually sees it. Other courts hold that a searcher who actually sees it has a duty to investigate its validity. As to the duty to inquire further, see p. 342.

1. Defective Documents

Illustration: Owen conveyed his property to Ann, but his signature on the deed was not acknowledged. Nevertheless, the recorder records the deed. The recorded document clearly shows that the acknowledgment is missing. Owen then conveyed the same property to Bob. In some jurisdictions, Bob will prevail over Ann even though he actually saw Ann's deed when searching the title. The defect defeats the contention that the deed was recorded or gives notice. But in other jurisdictions, if Bob saw the deed, he has a duty to investigate the circumstances to ascertain the nature of Ann's interest. If a reasonable inquiry would disclose her interest, Bob is charged with notice, and Ann will prevail.

2. Nonrecordable Documents

Illustration: Owen contracted to sell his property to Ann. Although the local recording act does not authorize the recordation of executory contracts for the sale of land, Ann delivered the contract to the recorder who recorded and indexed it. Owen then conveyed the same property to Bob. The result here is the same as in the previous illustration. In both cases, the recording of an improper document does not give constructive notice, although persons who actually see it may be charged with notice or with a duty to investigate further.

V. INQUIRY NOTICE

Because recording acts charge subsequent claimants with notice of all documents recorded in the chain of title, every person intending to acquire an interest in property first must search the records to determine its priority. The notice doctrine also imposes on subsequent claimants the obligation to make a reasonable investigation outside the records. The claimant is charged with notice of anything a reasonable inquiry would disclose. Thus, a person may have "inquiry" notice, as well as actual or constructive notice, of prior claims. The duty to investigate the validity of recorded but defective documents is an example of the application of the doctrine of inquiry notice. (See p. 341)

Inquiry notice is not applied in the same absolute fashion as constructive notice. First, some suspicious fact must exist to trigger the initial obligation to make an inquiry. Second, it must be shown that a reasonable inquiry would have revealed the fact in question. If either component is lacking, notice is not imputed. However, if an inquiry was made and did not lead to discovery of the relevant facts, the inquirer is not necessarily protected since the trier of fact can conclude that the inquiry should have been more diligent.

A.   NOTICE BASED ON INFORMATION IN THE RECORDS

1.   References in Recorded Documents to Unrecorded Documents

Some courts require a purchaser to investigate references to other documents that appear in recorded instruments even though the documents to which they refer are unrecorded. If a reasonable search would locate the unrecorded document, the purchaser is charged with notice of it and may not claim to be a bona fide purchaser.

Illustration: Owen mortgaged his property to Mel, but the mortgage was not recorded. Owen then conveyed his property to Ann. His deed stated that title was being conveyed "subject to the mortgage given to Mel." Ann later conveyed the property to Bob by a deed that also said it was "subject to the mortgage given to Mel." The reference to Mel's mortgage obligates Bob to inquire as to Mel's interest. If a reasonable inquiry would reveal Mel's interest, Bob will be charged with notice of it and will take title subject to the mortgage.

2. References in Recorded but Unread Documents to Other Unrecorded Documents

The subsequent claimant need not actually know about the suspicious fact. A properly recorded document that refers to it provides constructive notice. The suspicious fact generates a duty to inquire whether it is actually known or merely constructively known.

Illustration: Owen mortgaged his property to Mel, but the mortgage was not recorded. Owen then conveyed the same property to Ann by a deed that stated that title was being conveyed "subject to the mortgage given to Mel." Ann recorded her deed. Ann then conveyed the property to Bob by a deed that did *not* refer to Mel's mortgage. Bob did not search the records. Bob's title may be subject to the mortgage. Owen's deed to Ann was properly recorded and, therefore, may be held to give notice of its contents. Bob could thus be charged with constructive notice of the reference to Mel. This suspicious fact imposes a duty on Bob to investigate. Otherwise, Bob would have a disincentive for searching the records, which result is not to be encouraged.

3. Indefinite References to Other Documents

In some states, a reference in a document to another document does not create a duty to investigate if the reference is too indefinite as to the parties, date, type of interest, or description of the property involved. In such a case, the purchaser who sees such a reference has no duty to investigate.

Illustration: Owen mortgaged his property to Mel. The mortgage was not recorded. Owen then conveyed the property to Ann, who knew about the mortgage. The deed stated that title was being conveyed "subject to all mortgages, easements, and other interests outstanding against the property." Ann recorded and later conveyed the property to Bob without mentioning the mortgage. The indefinite reference in Owen's deed to Ann (sometimes called a "Mother Hubbard clause") creates no duty to investigate. Therefore, Bob is not charged with notice of Mel's mortgage and takes title free of it.

B. NOTICE BASED ON POSSESSION OF THE PROPERTY

In most states, a property purchaser is charged with notice of any possessor's rights to the property. Thus, a prior unrecorded grantee who is in possession of the property prevails over subsequent purchasers even though nothing appears in the records. The effect of this doctrine is to compel a purchaser to inspect the land, as well as to search the records.

Illustration: Owen conveyed his property to Ann, who did not record. Ann took actual possession of the property. Owen then conveyed the same property to Bob, who searched the records and found no mention of Ann. In most states, Bob will be charged with notice of Ann based on her possession, even though she did not record her deed.

1. Information Charged to the Purchaser–Constructive Notice v. Inquiry Notice

If someone is in possession of the property, a purchaser usually is charged with notice (constructive notice) of that person's interest even if the purchaser did not inspect the property. When someone other than the owner is in possession, courts usually hold that this suspicious fact creates a duty of inquiry concerning the possessor's rights (inquiry notice).

Illustration: Owen conveyed his property to Ann. She did not record or take possession. Owen then conveyed the property to Bob who inspected the property. Since Bob had no notice of any suspicious fact, he had no duty to inquire. Thus, Bob prevails over Ann.

Illustration: Owen conveyed his property to Ann. She did not record but did take possession. Owen then conveyed the property to Bob. Bob inspected the land and saw Ann. Since Bob knew that someone other than Owen possessed the property, Bob had a duty to inquire as to Ann's rights. If a reasonable inquiry would have revealed her unrecorded deed, Bob will be charged with inquiry notice of that fact. Ann then will prevail.

Illustration: Owen conveyed his property to Ann. Ann did not record but did take possession. Owen then conveyed the property to Bob, who did not inspect the property. Since Ann is in possession, Bob is charged with constructive notice of that fact. Bob's constructive notice generates the same duty to inquire as did his actual notice in the previous illustration. If a reasonable inquiry would disclose her claim, she will prevail.

Illustration: Owen conveyed his property to Ann, who did not record. Ann then leased the property to Tom but told him that she was acting as Owen's rental agent. Tom took possession of the property. Owen then conveyed the same property to Bob. In this case, Bob may not be charged with notice of Ann's interest. He is charged with notice of Tom's possession and has a duty to inquire of Tom as to his rights. However, a reasonable inquiry might not disclose Ann's interest. Therefore, Bob might not be charged with notice of it. It is a question of fact whether Bob must ask Ann whether she claims any interest in the property after Tom informs him that she said she was Owen's agent. If the finder of fact concludes that Bob should have inquired of Ann and that Ann would have responded honestly, Bob will be charged with notice of Ann's interest. But if the finder of fact concludes otherwise, no notice of Ann's interest will be imputed to Bob.

2. Inquiry Notice when the Statute Requires Actual Notice

When the recording act provides that unrecorded documents are void only as to persons without "actual" notice of them, strict statutory construction may limit the scope of notice and rule out constructive and inquiry notice. Courts in some states hold that a statutory requirement for actual notice means that the purchaser is not charged with notice of a possessor's rights unless they are actually known to the purchaser. Therefore, the purchaser has no duty to inquire of the possessor even if the purchaser has actual notice of the possession. In other states with similar statutes, courts hold that a purchaser has a duty to inquire of a possessor, but only if the purchaser actually knows about the possession. The purchaser has no initial duty to look for a possessor.

Illustration: Owen conveyed his property to Ann. She did not record but did take possession. Owen then conveyed the same property to Bob. He inspected the land and saw Ann but made no inquiry of her. The recording act provides that an unrecorded deed is void against purchasers without actual notice. Under a restrictive view of actual notice, Bob prevails since he had no obligation to ask Ann about her rights. Under a less restrictive view, since Bob had actual knowledge of Ann's possession, he may be charged with notice of her rights if a reasonable inquiry would have revealed them. But even under this second view, Bob would prevail if he had not visited the property at all and thereby avoided acquiring actual knowledge of Ann's possession. For Bob to be charged with notice of Ann's rights when he never looked at the land, the statute must be interpreted to provide no protection to a person with notice, whether actual or otherwise.

Illustration: Owen conveyed his property to Ann, who did not record. Ann then rented the property to Tom. Tom did not record his lease but did take possession. Owen then conveyed the same property to Bob. Bob searched the records but did not view the land. If the local recording act provides that an unrecorded instrument is void against a purchaser without notice, Ann and Tom should prevail over Bob. Bob is charged with notice of the rights of a person in possession when that possession is inconsistent with the record title. Tom's possession based on a lease from someone other than Owen creates an obligation to investigate and probably would cause Bob to discover Ann's interest in the property. If the recording act referred only to actual notice, Bob might prevail because he did not have actual notice, and the statute created no duty to look.

3. When Possession is not Suspicious

Possession creates a duty to inquire only when it is suspicious. If the possession is consistent with the record title, no duty to inquire exists.

Illustration: Owen conveyed a life estate to Ann and the remainder to Bob. Ann took possession and recorded her deed. Bob conveyed his remainder interest to Ann, but this deed was not recorded. Later Bob conveyed his interest to Carol. Carol should prevail over Ann as to Bob's remainder. Although Ann was in possession, the records indicated that she held a life estate. Therefore, her possession was consistent with the records and created no duty for Carol to ask Ann about her rights. Carol has a remainder after Ann's life estate.

a.   Landlord–Tenant Exception

Because tenants commonly have rights beyond those mentioned in their original leases, many courts require purchasers to inquire of the tenants even though their possession is consistent with the record title.

Illustration: Owen leased property to Tom for five years. The lease was recorded. Owen later gave Tom an option to purchase the property. The option agreement was not recorded. Owen then conveyed the property to Bob. Bob searched the records and saw Tom's lease but did not talk to him. Bob may be charged with notice of Tom's option and would be required to sell if Tom exercises the option to purchase.

C.   NOTICE BASED ON NEIGHBORHOOD CONDITIONS

In the section on constructive notice, it was said that a purchaser may be subject to an interest created in a deed to other property owned by the same grantor even though that interest does not appear in the purchaser's direct chain of title. Similarly, the chapter on covenants running with the land stated that a court may imply a restriction against the grantor's retained land if he restricted other lots in the development. A court may hold that a purchaser has constructive notice or inquiry notice of the restrictions. The court could find constructive notice based on the purchaser's duty to read all deeds given by the grantor.

Alternatively, the court could find inquiry notice based on the uniform development of the neighborhood.

D. HARMLESS NOTICE

A nonrecording interest holder does not automatically prevail over a purchaser if the purchaser or her predecessor in interest had notice of the unrecorded interest.

Illustration: Owen conveyed his property to Ann, who did not record. Owen conveyed the same property to Bob. Bob recorded, but he knew of the conveyance to Ann. Bob then conveyed to Carol, who was without notice, paid value, and recorded. Carol prevails over Ann. Bob was not protected by the recording act because he had notice of Ann's claim, but he acquired an apparent title that gave him the power to divest Ann by conveying to a bona fide purchaser, such as Carol. Carol prevails despite Bob's knowledge.

Illustration: Owen conveyed his property to Ann, who did not record. Owen then conveyed the property to Bob, who did not have notice of the conveyance to Ann, paid value, and recorded. Bob then conveyed the property to Carol. Carol knew of Ann's claim, did not pay value, and did not record. Nevertheless, Carol prevails over Ann. Because Bob qualified as a purchaser for value without notice and recorded first, he divested Ann of her title under any recording act. He had legal title, which he transferred to Carol. Carol need not qualify for protection under any recording act because she took from a real, not an apparent, owner.

VI. PERSONS PROTECTED AGAINST PREVIOUS FAILURES TO RECORD

The recording acts rarely make unrecorded instruments absolutely void. Instead, the statutes normally provide that unrecorded instruments are void as against certain classes of people. Unless a subsequent taker is in the category of protected persons, failure to record the prior instrument is harmless.

A. PERSONS PROTECTED UNDER THE RECORDING STATUTES

1. Persons Protected in a Race State

In a race state, the only persons protected from prior unrecorded instruments are those who record first. If a subsequent grantee buys without notice but does not record, the statute gives no protection against an unrecorded prior grant.

2. Persons Protected in a Notice State

In a notice state, the only persons protected from prior unrecorded instruments are those who purchased without notice of them.

3. Persons Protected in a Notice–Race State

In a notice-race state, the only persons protected from prior unrecorded instruments are those who purchase without notice and who record before the prior instruments are recorded.

B. PURCHASERS WITHOUT NOTICE

Except for race states, the only persons protected from prior unrecorded instruments are those who take without notice of them. The question of notice was covered in the previous two sections.

C. PURCHASERS FOR VALUE

Most states, either by statute or by judicial decision, protect subsequent takers only if they paid value for their interest. Only a person who pays value has "relied" on the records in a meaningful way. Since the recording system is designed to encourage and protect reliance on the records, no reason exists to protect those who would not suffer a loss if their property interest is voided or diminished.

Illustration: Owen conveyed his property to Ann, who did not record. Owen then conveyed the same property to Bob, who searched the records and found no reference to Ann. Bob paid Owen $10,000 for the property. Bob prevails over Ann because he is a bona fide purchaser. Bob paid Owen only because the records did not show Ann's claim. If Bob were to lose to Ann, he would suffer a $10,000 loss because of Ann's failure to record her deed. Bob must prevail to protect the investment he made in reliance on the records.

1. Donees

A donee or beneficiary of a gift deed is not a subsequent purchaser protected by the recording act, since she paid no value and, therefore, did not detrimentally rely on the records.

Illustration: Owen conveyed his property to Ann, who did not record. Owen then executed a gift deed of the same property to Bob. Bob did not have notice of the conveyance to Ann and recorded his deed. Ann prevails over Bob since Bob is not a purchaser for value. He did not give any value in reliance on the records and, therefore, will not be injured if he does not get the property.

Illustration: Owen executed a gift deed of his property to Ann, who did not record. Owen then executed another gift deed of the same property to Bob. Bob did not have notice of the conveyance to Ann and recorded his deed. Ann still prevails over Bob because he did not pay value. Ann's unrecorded deed is void only against subsequent takers for value, and Bob does not qualify. Ann need not have paid value, since Owen had title to convey to her. The issue is not who has the better equities as between Ann and Bob, but whether Ann's legal title is divested under the recording act.

Illustration: Owen conveyed his property to Ann, who did not record. Owen died, and Bob was his heir. Bob conveyed the property to Carl who paid value, did not have notice of the conveyance to Ann, and recorded. Carl prevails over Ann. Ann's failure to record left Owen as the apparent owner with the power to divest her by conveying to a bona fide purchaser. When Owen died, no title descended to Bob, and Bob did not qualify as a bona fide purchaser because he did not pay value. However, Bob did acquire the power to divest Ann since the records showed him as the apparent owner. Therefore, his conveyance to a bona fide purchaser, Carl, is protected by the recording acts.

2. Cancellation of a Prior Debt

Cancellation of a prior debt in return for a conveyance is often regarded as the payment of value. A creditor who accepts a deed in satisfaction of an obligation is regarded as a purchaser for value in some jurisdictions but not in others.

3. Payment of Less than Full Consideration

Courts do not require the subsequent purchaser to pay full consideration, so long as more than a nominal consideration is paid. The necessary amount varies from state to state.

4. Promise to Pay

If the promise to pay can be canceled, courts generally do not treat the promisor as having paid value. But if the promise cannot be canceled, the promisor is treated as having paid the entire amount.

Illustration: Owen conveyed his property to Ann, who did not record. Owen then conveyed the same property to Bob in return for Bob's promissory note for $10,000, which was the full price for the land. Before Bob made any payments on the note, Ann asserted her claim to the property. If the note was made payable to Owen and Owen still has it, Ann should prevail, since Bob can defend against Owen's enforcement of the note based on failure of consideration, especially if Owen's deed contains covenants of title. See Chapter 9, p. 309. However, if the note is negotiable and has been negotiated to a holder in due course who takes free of the defense of failure of consideration, the note cannot be canceled, and Bob will have to pay it. So he prevails over Ann.

5. Payment of Part of the Price–Alternative Solutions

When part of the price has been paid before discovery of an unrecorded prior deed, the payor should be protected according to the amount paid and other circumstances by (a) dividing the land, if possible, (b) giving the subsequent purchaser the entire property with the balance of the price going to the prior unrecorded grantee, or (c) giving the prior grantee the property and giving the subsequent purchaser a lien on it for the amount actually paid. The best result generally depends on the circumstances, as illustrated below.

Illustration–Partition: Owen conveyed two acres of vacant land to Ann, who did not record. Owen then conveyed the same two acres to Bob for a price of $10,000. After Bob paid $5,000 of the price, Ann asserted her interest. A possible remedy would be to give Bob one acre and Ann the other if both acres have the same value. By giving Bob one acre and excusing him from further payment, he receives all the protection he needs.

Illustration–Title to the Subsequent Purchaser: Owen conveyed his one-family house to Ann, who did not record. Owen then conveyed the house to Bob for a price of $100,-000. Bob paid $70,000, took possession, and made improvements before Ann asserted her interest. Under these circumstances, Bob should get title to the entire house but should be required to pay the balance of the price to Ann, rather than to Owen.

Illustration–Title to Prior Purchaser: Owen conveyed his property to Ann, who did not record. Owen then conveyed the same property to Bob for a price of $10,000. When Ann asserted her interest, Bob had not taken possession or made any improvements and had paid only $1,000 of the price. An appropriate remedy under these circumstances would be to give Ann title to the entire property and a lien to Bob for $1,000.

The appropriate remedy also may depend on whether a deed had been delivered to the purchaser. In a few jurisdictions, payments made by a purchaser under a contract for the sale of the property are not protected because title has not yet passed. This rule poses serious problems for purchasers under long term installment contracts who are obliged to pay the price over ten or twenty years before receiving a deed.

D.   ENCUMBRANCERS

The recording acts generally protect persons who take encumbrances on property for value. For example, a mortgagee who loans money and takes a mortgage to secure the debt in reliance on the property records is entitled to have that reliance protected.

Illustration: Owen conveyed his property to Ann, who did not record. Owen then borrowed $10,000 from Bob and gave Bob a note and mortgage on the same property to secure the debt. Bob's mortgage should be protected against Ann's unrecorded deed. Ann owns the property subject to Bob's mortgage. Bob's loan was made in reliance on the records, which showed Owen as the owner. Therefore, Bob should be protected to the extent of his reliance.

1.   If the Encumbrance is not Taken in Reliance on the Records

If a creditor loans money and takes back an unsecured promissory note, she has not relied on the land records at that time since she made the loan without taking an interest in the property as security. If the creditor later requests that the debtor secure the existing note with a mortgage, no reliance on the records occurs either since the money already has been advanced. Therefore, the subsequently secured creditor is not protected against prior unrecorded instruments.

Illustration: Owen conveyed his property to Ann, who did not record. Owen then borrowed $10,000 from Bob and gave him an unsecured promissory note. Later, Bob requested that Owen secure the note with a mortgage on the property, and Owen did so. Then Ann asserted her rights. Ann's title should not be subject to Bob's mortgage because Bob did not give value in reliance on the records. He did not rely on the records when he loaned the money, because he did not take an interest in the land then. When he did seek the land as security, he did not give any new value, since he already had loaned the money.

Illustration: Owen conveyed his property to Ann, who did not record. Owen then borrowed $10,000 from Bob and gave him an unsecured promissory note. When the note became due, Bob agreed to extend the due date only if Owen secured the note with a mortgage on the property, which Owen did. Courts in many states will hold for Bob, because the extension of time constituted new value for the mortgage. Bob gave up his right to collect immediately. Ann owns the property, but it is subject to Bob's mortgage.

E. CREDITORS

1. Unsecured Creditors

Unsecured general creditors are not protected against prior unrecorded conveyances, because they did not give value in reliance on the records.

Illustration: Owen conveyed his property to Ann, who did not record. Owen then borrowed money from Bob and gave him an unsecured promissory note. Bob cannot claim an interest in the property against Ann, since he did not make the loan in reliance on the records. Even without the conveyance to Ann, Bob's unsecured note gives him no interest in the property. That is what is meant by "unsecured."

2. Judgment and Attachment Creditors

Most states authorize a creditor who obtains a judgment to record it, whereupon it becomes a lien on all real property owned by the judgment debtor in the county. If the creditor has attached any property before the judgment, the judgment lien relates back to the date of the attachment. Before the judgment, the attachment creates an attachment lien on the property. In most states, such lien creditors are not protected by the recording acts, because they have not obtained their liens in reliance on the records.

Illustration: Owen conveyed his property to Ann, who did not record. Bob then obtained a judgment against Owen based on nonpayment of an unsecured promissory note. Bob recorded the judgment to make it a lien on Owen's property. Ann's title is not subject to Bob's judgment lien. Bob did not give value in reliance on the property records when he made the loan, since he took an unsecured note. He also did not rely on the records when he sued Owen and obtained a judgment. When Bob recorded the judgment, he gave no new value in reliance on the records. Thus, Bob does not qualify for the recording act's protection.

3. Execution Purchasers

Although most states do not protect judgment creditors, if a creditor executes on the judgment and has the property sold to satisfy it, the purchaser may be a purchaser for value within the meaning of the recording act.

Illustration: Owen conveyed his property to Ann, who did not record. Bob then obtained a judgment against Owen, levied execution on the property, and conducted an execution sale. Carol purchased at the sale for $10,000. Carol will prevail over Ann since she paid value in reliance on the records. Although Bob obtained no lien on property and should not have been able to execute, he had the apparent right to do so because the property records indicated that Owen was the owner. Therefore, Bob could transfer good title to a bona fide purchaser just as Owen could transfer good title to a bona fide purchaser despite his earlier conveyance to Ann.

Courts are divided whether a judgment creditor can become a bona fide purchaser when he buys at his execution sale for the amount of the judgment. Some courts hold that the creditor has given no new value because the bid amount is offset against the judgment. But other courts hold that the creditor thereby pays value because he gives up the judgment in return for the property. An additional reason for protecting the creditor is that, otherwise, the most likely candidate to bid at the execution sale will be virtually excluded.

VII.   RECORDING SYSTEM LIMITATIONS

Not all interests in land derive from written instruments, and not all written instruments affecting interests in land are recordable. The recording acts protect against only interests arising from written instruments and instruments that statutorily are recordable.

A.   INTERESTS NOT ARISING OUT OF WRITTEN INSTRUMENTS

1.   Adverse Possession and Prescriptive Easements

Adverse possession and prescriptive easements give an original, rather than a derivative, title and are not referable to any writing. Consequently, the holder usually does not have a written document and is not subject to the recording act.

Illustration: Paul possessed Owen's land for twenty-five years and satisfied all the elements of adverse possession. Owen then conveyed the property to Ann, who searched the title and found no record of Paul. She also did not see Paul when she inspected the land. In a contest between Paul and Ann, Paul prevails because he does not claim a derivative title under any recordable document and, therefore, is not penalized for failure to record.

Illustration: Dita adversely walked across Owen's land for twenty-five years and acquired a prescriptive right of way easement. Owen then conveyed the property to Bess, who searched the title and found no record of Dita's easement. Bess' title is subject to Dita's easement, since it was not created by a recordable instrument.

2. Easements by Necessity

An easement by necessity is created to serve the public policy that parcels of land should not be land-locked. Typically, the easement is created when a parcel is subdivided in a way that portions of it do not have access to a public road. See Chapter 5, p. 206. The courts are divided whether a subsequent purchaser without notice takes free of or subject to the easement.

Illustration: Dita conveyed all her property to Steve except for one landlocked parcel. Under the circumstances of the conveyance, she acquired an easement of necessity across

Steve's land. Steve conveyed his property to Ann. She searched the title and found no evidence of an easement in favor of Dita. In some jurisdictions, Dita will be held to have an easement over Ann's property on the ground that her easement was not created by a recordable document. But other courts will rule in favor of Ann to avoid penalizing her for Dita's negligent manner of conveying her property.

3.   Easements by Implication

Easements are created by implication when a parcel of land is subdivided under circumstances that permit a court to infer that one parcel was intended to be burdened for the benefit of the other even though an easement was not created expressly. See Chapter 5, p. 200. The courts are divided whether a subsequent purchaser of the servient parcel who is without notice takes free of or subject to the easement.

Illustration: Dita owned two houses that shared a common sewer line that runs from the house on the rear of the lot across the yard of the house on the front of the lot. She conveyed the front house to Steve under circumstances that would cause a court to reserve an implied easement in her favor. Steve later conveyed his house to Ann. She found no evidence of the easement in the records and saw no physical evidence of the pipe on the land. In some jurisdictions, Ann owns her property free of the easement because she took without notice of it. But in others, Dita still has an easement since it was not a recordable interest in land.

B.   INTERESTS ARISING FROM NON-RECORDABLE OR EXCEPTED IN-STRUMENTS

Recording statutes often provide that certain documents, such as short-term leases, need not be recorded to be protected. Additionally, judicial decisions in many states have made certain documents affecting title to property unrecordable, such as executory sales contracts. The failure to record such a document does not penalize the person who acquired an interest from it.

Illustration: In a state with a notice act that applies to transfers of a fee simple, fee tail, life estate, and tenancy of more than seven years, Owen leases his property to Tom for five years. The lease is written but is not recorded. Owen then conveyed the property to Ann. Her title search revealed no evidence of Tom's interest, and she did not see Tom in possession of the property. Ann still takes subject to Tom's lease, since it was not required to be recorded and, therefore, is not penalized for being unrecorded.

Illustration: Owen agreed to sell his property to Ann in a written contract of sale. Under the state's laws, the contract is not recordable. Owen then conveyed the same property to Bob. Even though Bob searched the title and conducted all other reasonable investigations, he should take subject to Ann's contract, since Ann cannot be penalized for not recording what was nonrecordable. However, it is possible to argue that nonrecordable documents do not come under the recording acts at all and, therefore, are governed by the common law. In that case, Ann would lose since her prior equity is defeated by a subsequent bona fide purchaser of the legal title.

CHAPTER ELEVEN

TITLE INSURANCE
I. SEARCHING TITLE

A prudent land purchaser (Pearl in the Illustrations in this Chapter) will have her vendor's (Van) title searched before the settlement or closing of escrow to ascertain whether it is marketable. An attorney or professional abstractor commonly conducts the search and guarantees its accuracy. Thereafter, if a title defect is discovered, the purchaser can recover on this guarantee. Hereafter, the guarantor will be referred to as a title company.

A title insurance policy cannot eliminate existing title defects. If a title company discovers a defect when it searches the title, the defect will be an exception to coverage under the title insurance policy it issues. The title company lists the defect both for its protection and because some courts impose an affirmative obligation of disclosure to the insured. The company insures the accuracy of the search and not the perfection of the title. A title policy guarantees that the title company has found no title defects other than those it has disclosed.

Illustration: In searching Van's property title, the title company discovers that it is subject to a recorded easement. Unless the easement is removed from the title, Pearl's title insurance policy will show that her title is subject to the easement. The company will not have any liability because of the easement. However, if the title also was subject to a previously recorded mortgage that was not shown in the title policy, the title company will be liable for that encumbrance.

Illustration: In searching Van's title on behalf of the bank that intends to make a purchase money mortgage loan to Pearl, the title company discovers an existing recorded mortgage. Thereafter, it can offer to insure the bank's mortgage only as a "second" mortgage, which is inferior to the existing mortgage. But it can insure that the bank's mortgage will not be subject to any other mortgage, if it found no other mortgage of record. See Chapter 12, p. 378.

II. PRELIMINARY TITLE REPORTS AND TITLE INSURANCE

Before the closing, a purchaser often obtains a preliminary title report ("title binder") from the title company that shows the current condition of the vendor's title. If the title is satisfactory, the sale is closed, and the purchaser will receive a title insurance policy that guarantees that she acquired the title described in the preliminary report. If the vendor's title is defective, the purchaser can either take title subject to the defect or require that it be eliminated before closing. She also may agree to new encumbrances on the title.

Illustration: Pearl's preliminary title report shows that Van has marketable title to his property. Therefore, she will close the sale and will receive a title insurance policy that guarantees her ownership of the same marketable title. Usually, Pearl will instruct the closing agent to close the escrow when it can issue such a policy to her. The title company will make a last-minute search of the records before issuing the policy to make sure the title has not changed. The same company often closes the sale and issues the title policy.

Illustration: Pearl's preliminary title report shows that Van's title is subject to a recorded height limitation, which applies throughout the neighborhood and is acceptable to Pearl. She will instruct the closing agent that she will accept a title policy showing title vested in her subject to that restriction.

Illustration: Pearl's preliminary title report shows that Van's title is subject to a mortgage, which is unacceptable to Pearl. She will instruct the closing agent to close escrow only when a title policy can be issued that does not list the mortgage as an exception. The agent can use part of Pearl's purchase price to pay the mortgage if Van agrees. The mortgage then will be eliminated from the title and from the title policy.

Illustration: The preliminary title report shows Van's title to be clear. Pearl is borrowing part of the purchase price from a bank and has promised to give it a mortgage as security. Pearl will instruct the closing agent to obtain a title policy showing title vested in her subject to the bank's mortgage. The bank will direct that its loan funds be disbursed only when a title policy is issued to it showing that it has a valid first mortgage on the property.

III. TITLE RISKS

A. COVERED RISKS

Many title insurance policies guarantee not only the accuracy of the record search, but also the absence of certain "off record" risks, such as nondelivery, forgery, and incompetence.

Illustration: The chain of title for a parcel of property was A to B, B to Van, Van to Pearl. All these deeds were recorded. However, A never delivered the deed to B (or A's signature was forged or A was incompetent to execute a deed at the time). Therefore, B never acquired title to the property, and Van and Pearl did not either. If Pearl's policy insures that she has title, the title company must indemnify her for any loss even though the records did not reveal this problem. In such a case, her title policy performs a true insurance function. However, not all policies provide such broad protection.

B.   EXCLUDED RISKS

Many risks inherent in the recording system are excluded from coverage by title policies. These exclusions or exceptions generally track the cases in which the recording system does not protect a purchaser despite her diligent search of the records.

1.   Grantee's Knowledge of Defects or Failure to Pay Value

Most policies exclude title defects that (1) are unrecorded but are known to the purchaser or (2) will succeed against a purchaser who has not paid value. Since the recording system generally protects only a purchaser for value and without knowledge, the purchaser's failure to qualify for such protection will cause the title company to decline to insure against the defect.

Illustration: Before conveying the property to Pearl, Van gave a mortgage to Walt that was unrecorded. Even though it is unrecorded, Pearl will take subject to it if she either actually knew of it or did not pay value for the deed from Van. Since the title company has no practical method for discovering this mortgage, it cannot afford to insure Pearl against it. Therefore, it is excluded from coverage.

2. Defects Discoverable by Investigation Outside the Records

Title policies also generally exclude risks that can be ascertained only by physically inspecting the premises, such as questions involving boundaries, adverse possession, or rights claimed by persons in possession. The title company usually limits its coverage to those risks that can be ascertained from the property records, because its expertise is in conducting title searches. However, these risks are not completely unascertainable. Therefore, the company may be willing to insure against them for a higher premium. In this case, the company will physically inspect the premises and will issue an endorsement to the title policy. However, since the purchaser usually has inspected the property personally, the endorsement may be an unnecessary expense.

Title policies also normally exclude governmental restrictions on the property, such as zoning, subdivision regulations, environmental laws, and eminent domain. These types of laws are not entered into the official records and, therefore, will not be found by a conventional record search. While most of these restrictions do not make the title legally unmarketable, title insurance companies prefer to avoid disputes with their insureds by specifically excluding them. A person interested in such matters generally must check with all the relevant agencies to discover such restrictions.

3. Subsequent Defects

A title policy excludes defects that arise after it is issued, because the company cannot know or control what will happen to the title in the future. In that sense, title insurance is quite different from most other forms of insurance. Because of this limited coverage, only a one-time premium is paid, rather than an ongoing obligation to pay for continued coverage.

IV. RELIEF UNDER THE POLICY

A. TITLE COMPANY OPTIONS

A title insurance policy usually gives the title company the option to pay the insured for the loss resulting from the defect (up to the policy limit), to pay off or purchase the adverse claim, or to challenge it. The policy usually also provides that the company will be subrogated to any rights the purchaser has against third persons because of the title defect.

Illustration: Pearl's neighbor claims an easement across Pearl's property that was not listed as an exception in her title insurance policy. Pearl's title company may (1) compensate Pearl for the loss of property value caused by the easement, (2) purchase the easement from the neighbor to make Pearl's title conform to her policy, or (3) contest the validity of the neighbor's claim. If Pearl received a warranty deed from Van, the title company may seek to recover from Van as subrogee to Pearl's rights under the title covenants in the deed.

B. DURATION OF COVERAGE

The protection of a title policy may last only for so long as the insured purchaser owns the property. Many policies also protect the insured after she sells the property if she gave title covenants in her deed or accepted a purchase money mortgage from the purchaser. But the policy will not insure the next purchaser. That person must purchase his or her own title policy.

Illustration: Pearl acquired a parcel of land and purchased a title insurance policy for her fee title. Pearl sold the land to Quentin and took a mortgage from him on the land to secure part of the price. In fact, Pearl never owned the land. Therefore, her mortgage is worthless, and she may recover from her title company even though she no longer owns the property. If Quentin sues Pearl based on the title covenants in the deed she gave him, her title policy may protect her in that regard as well.

CHAPTER TWELVE

MORTGAGES

I. SIGNIFICANCE OF A MORTGAGE

A. SECURED AND UNSECURED DEBTS

A promissory note, without more, creates only an unsecured debt. The note is merely written evidence of the debtor's promise to repay the debt. If the debtor breaches that promise, the creditor's only recourse is against him. However, if the debt is secured, the creditor also can satisfy the debt by selling the assets (the "security") that the debtor gave as collateral for the loan. A mortgage is the document used to create a security interest in land in most states. In a mortgage, the debtor is the mortgagor (Mort in the Illustrations), and the creditor is the mortgagee (Marie).

In some jurisdictions, a deed of trust is used instead. Deeds of trust are very similar to mortgages. The main difference is that deeds of trust have three parties to them. The debtor (trustor) conveys the property to a third person (trustee) "in trust" for the creditor (beneficiary). The trustee is instructed to reconvey the property to the trustor when the debt is paid or to sell it on default. Because the mortgage and deed of trust are so similar, this Chapter does not treat the deed of trust separately.

370

Illustration: Mort borrowed $50,000 from Marie and signed two documents, a note and a mortgage. The note says in essence: "I promise to pay you $50,000 by (date)." The mortgage says in essence: "If I do not pay the $50,000, you may sell the property that is the subject of this mortgage and keep enough of the sale proceeds to satisfy the debt."

B. ADVANTAGE OF HOLDING A MORTGAGE

Unsecured creditors always must bring a judicial action to recover when they are not paid. If successful, they obtain a money judgment. The judgment is merely a judicial declaration that the debtor owes the creditor. If the debtor does not pay the judgment, the creditor must have the sheriff seize and sell the judgment debtor's property (execution) or any debts owed to the debtor (garnishment) and use the proceeds to satisfy the judgment. In contrast, a mortgagee avoids the risk of the debtor not having assets to satisfy the judgment. Even if the debtor sells the mortgaged land, it is still subject to the mortgage. And, in over half the states, the mortgagee does not need to bring a judicial action to sell the property.

C. HISTORY OF MORTGAGE LAW

When real property was security for a loan during the early common law, the parties had to comply with the rules of conveyancing and estates in land. Because the law of future interests was more rigid then, extreme care was required. A debtor's promise to convey his property to his creditor if he failed to pay the debt probably would be treated as an attempt to create an illegal springing interest and, therefore, would be void.

1. Fee Simple Subject to Condition Subsequent

In response to that problem, lenders began using a recognized property interest, the fee simple subject to condition subsequent. The mortgagor executed an immediate conveyance of his property to the mortgagee. The conveyance was subject to the condition that, if the mortgagor repaid the debt by the due date, the mortgagee's estate would terminate. Alternatively, lenders sometimes took a conveyance of the fee simple absolute and gave a covenant to reconvey upon timely payment of the debt. These arrangements gave the creditor title to the land for the life of the loan, so that the debtor could not dispose of or otherwise impair the creditor's security. Furthermore, if the debtor failed to pay, the creditor had the fee simple absolute title without the need for any judicial action. See Chapter 2, p. 57.

2. Equity of Redemption

The early mortgages gave the debtor no right to pay late. Once the due date ("law day") passed, the creditor had the fee simple absolute title, and the debtor had no legal remedy to compel the creditor to accept a late payment even if the land's value greatly exceeded the debt. To provide some relief against this potentially harsh result, the court of equity gave a delinquent debtor the right to obtain a decree that permitted him to pay late and thereby "redeem" himself from his default. Over time, this right was characterized as an interest in the property that was called the "equity of redemption." The equity of redemption was regarded as fair to the creditor, because she received interest for the period of delay, and as necessary to avoid a forfeiture by the debtor when the value of the security exceeded the debt.

3. Foreclosure

Once creditors knew that debtors would be entitled to pay their debts late, they needed to know how long that privilege would last. Initially, a creditor's only option was to bring a suit in equity to impose a time limit on this right. Upon petition by a creditor after the debtor was in default, the chancellor would issue a decree providing that, if the debtor did not redeem within a certain period of time, he would be "foreclosed" from doing so.

These early foreclosure decrees merely made the mortgagee's title absolute if the debtor did not redeem in time. These decrees came to be known as strict foreclosure. Although the extra time helped debtors somewhat, they still would be penalized if the property's value exceeded the debt. In an attempt to avoid this unjust enrichment of the creditor, the court of equity began to permit redemption by the debtor even after the strict foreclosure, sometimes even years after it occurred. Therefore, creditors began including a clause in the mortgage that authorized them to sell the land and to keep sufficient proceeds to repay the debt, rather than rely on strict foreclosure.

Today, many states permit creditors to conduct foreclosure sales without first filing judicial foreclosure actions. These sales, known as nonjudicial foreclosure sales, power of sale foreclosures, private sales, or foreclosures by advertisement, generally require language in the loan documents permitting use of this remedy (a "power of sale" clause). The sales usually are subject to significant state regulation, such as required notices and publication of information concerning the sale.

D. MORTGAGOR PROTECTION RULES

1. Deficiency Rules

If a foreclosure sale fails to produce sufficient funds to satisfy the debt, the mortgagee may seek a judgment in the foreclosure action for the balance due under the promissory note (the "deficiency") or may bring an independent action on the note for the deficiency. However, the availability of an action to recover the deficiency may create an inducement for the mortgagee to underbid at the foreclosure sale in order to obtain the property cheaply and then get a judgment against the mortgagor for a large deficiency. To avoid this result, some jurisdictions require a hearing on the value of the mortgaged land and may limit any deficiency judgment to the difference between the debt and this value, regardless of the price paid at the foreclosure sale. Other states entirely prohibit deficiency judgments in certain circumstances, such as when the foreclosure was against a single family residence, farm, or property acquired with the loan proceeds (a purchase money mortgage).

Other jurisdictions require the mortgagee to make an election of remedies. In these jurisdictions, the mortgagee can either foreclose on the property or obtain a judgment for the debt but cannot do both.

Some states give the mortgagor and possibly junior lienors the right to redeem the property even after the foreclosure sale. Because the right was created by statute and was not recognized at common law, it is called the statutory right of redemption. This right usually is exercised by paying the amount bid at the sale, rather than the debt amount. It is designed to deter underbidding. Whereas statutory redemption gives the right to pay the foreclosure purchaser the amount paid at the sale, the equity of redemption gives the right to pay the creditor the amount of the debt before the sale.

2. Waiver Prohibitions

Courts prohibit mortgagees from compelling mortgagors to waive the protections that courts or legislatures have created. It is assumed that any necessitous borrower otherwise automatically would be compelled to waive every form of protection. Therefore, courts hold most such protections to be nonwaivable.

3. Nondiscrimination in Lending

Federal and state statutes prohibit lenders from discriminating against borrowers based on race, color, national origin, religion, sex, age, handicap, or marital status. Lenders also are prohibited from "redlining," which is refusing to make loans secured by property in certain neighborhoods. Lenders also may be required to make loans in poorer neighborhoods if they receive deposits from the residents of those neighborhoods.

E. TITLE OR LIEN

The common law mortgage gave the mortgagee title to the mortgaged land even before default. Although some states still treat mortgages as having this effect, most characterize a mortgage as giving only a lien on the mortgaged property. A lien gives a lender only the right to sell the property after default. The mortgagor retains the title until it is divested by the foreclosure sale.

II. MORTGAGE INSTRUMENTS

Mortgages today rarely are written as conveying a fee simple subject to condition subsequent. Generally, the instrument merely recites that the mortgagor "mortgages" the property to the mortgagee. In many cases, it may not be clear whether a document is a mortgage. For example, the mortgagee may have attempted to disguise the true nature of the document in an attempt to avoid the legal protections afforded mortgagors, such as the statutory right of redemption. Courts generally hold that an instrument is a mortgage if it was intended to serve the mortgage function of securing a debt, but this is not always plain.

Illustration—Absolute Deed: In return for $50,000, Mort gave Marie a deed to his property and received from her an option to repurchase the property one year later for $55,000. A court could decide that this transaction was a loan of $50,000 at 10% interest, even though Mort did not execute a promissory note. If the property was worth $100,000, this result is especially likely. If a court determines that the "option" was really a mortgage, Mort may be able to recover the property even after the option expired according to its terms.

Illustration—Sale and Leaseback: In return for $50,000, Mort gave Marie a deed to his property and received from her a twenty year lease to the property at a rent of $5,000 per year. A court could characterize this transaction as a mortgage with rent substituting for interest. If the arrangement included an option to repurchase twenty years later at an unrealistically low price, this result is all the more likely. If the transaction is determined to constitute a mortgage transaction, Marie may be unable to evict Mort by the normal summary dispossession mechanisms available to a landlord.

III. POSSESSION AND RENTS

Under the early common law mortgage, the mortgagee had a present possessory estate, the fee simple subject to condition subsequent. Today, however, most mortgages permit the mortgagor to retain possession. The mortgagor's right to possession normally continues until a foreclosure sale has occurred, at which time the foreclosure purchaser gets possession, unless the mortgagor has a right to possess during the statutory redemption period. The mortgagor can give the mortgagee possession immediately, in which case the mortgagee must use any rents or profits from the land to reduce the mortgage debt. The mortgage also may permit the mortgagee to take possession upon default, but this right may require court appointment of a receiver.

Mortgages often provide that the rents and profits from the mortgaged property are assigned to the mortgagee but that the mortgagor can collect them for his own account for so long as he remains current on his obligation ("assignment of rents clause"). Once a default occurs, the mortgagee can have a receiver appointed to collect the rents and apply them to pay senior liens, property expenses, and any deficiency judgment following the foreclosure.

IV. PRIORITIES

Mortgages are recordable and are subject to the same priority principles that apply to other real property interests. A mortgage that qualifies for protection under the recording act from any other mortgage is referred to as a senior or first mortgage. Subsequent mortgages are called junior mortgages or second, third, fourth, etc. mortgages, depending on their priority. Sometimes, special priority status is given to a purchase money mortgage.

Priority determines the distribution of the foreclosure sale proceeds and the title acquired by the foreclosure purchaser. When a senior mortgage is foreclosed, the property is sold free and clear of the senior mortgage and any interest that is junior to it. The sale proceeds first are paid to the foreclosing mortgagee. If any surplus remains, it is paid to the junior interest holders in the order of their title priority. When a junior mortgage is foreclosed, the property is sold subject to the senior mortgage, and none of the foreclosure sale proceeds go to the senior mortgagee.

Illustration—Senior Foreclosure: Mort's property is subject to a first mortgage of $50,000 and a second mortgage of $10,000. The property has a fair market value of $55,000. If the first mortgagee forecloses, the title will be sold free of both mortgages, and a bid of up to $55,000 may be made. If $55,000 is paid, $50,000 goes to the first mortgagee, and the remaining $5,000 goes to the second mortgagee, who then has a right to collect the deficiency of $5,000 from Mort. If the land's value was greater and the bid was $65,000, the first mortgagee would receive $50,000, the second mortgagee would receive $10,000, and Mort would receive $5,000.

Illustration—Junior Foreclosure: Assume the same facts as above but that the second mortgagee, rather than the first mortgagee, forecloses. Since title will be subject to the first mortgage, the bid may be only $5,000 if the property has a market value of $55,000. The $5,000 from the sale will go to the second mortgagee, and she may have a right to collect the deficiency from Mort. The first mortgagee will not receive any of the proceeds, since its mortgage is unaffected by the foreclosure. If the property were worth $65,000, there could be a bid of $15,000, in which case the foreclosing second mortgagee would receive $10,000 and Mort would receive $5,000.

V. TRANSFERS BY THE PARTIES

A. TRANSFERS OF THE MORTGAGED PROPERTY

Whether a mortgage conveys a title or a lien, the mortgagor can convey the mortgaged property. A complete prohibition on transfer usually would be an invalid restraint on alienation. However, many mortgages make the entire loan amount immediately due and payable when the property is sold unless the mortgagee consents to the sale. Such "due on sale" clauses generally are enforceable pursuant to federal law.

Absent the exercise of a due on sale clause, a property title remains subject to the mortgage after the title is transferred, if the mortgage was properly recorded. If the mortgage debt is not paid after the transfer, the mortgagee can foreclose, and the transferee will lose the land. However, a transferee is liable for a deficiency judgment after the foreclosure only if he assumed personal liability for the debt, i.e. promised that he would pay the note.

Illustration—Nonassuming Transferee: Mort conveyed his house to Theresa, subject to a mortgage held by Marie. Theresa did not assume the mortgage. The loan now has gone into default. Marie may foreclose and sell Theresa's house. If the sale does not generate enough money to pay the debt, Marie may obtain a deficiency judgment against Mort but not against Theresa.

Illustration—Assuming Transferee: Assume the same facts as above, except that Theresa did assume the debt when she purchased the property. Marie now can sell the property and obtain deficiency judgments against both Mort and Theresa. Mort remains liable because he signed the original note, and Marie has not released him from that obligation. Theresa is liable because she promised Mort that she would pay the debt. Marie is a third party beneficiary of Theresa's promise to Mort. Alternatively, the jurisdiction may treat her as being equitably subrogated to Mort's rights against Theresa.

B. TRANSFERS OF THE MORTGAGE

The mortgagee can transfer the note and mortgage. The mortgage automatically transfers with the note even if the mortgage is not expressly assigned. The transferee may acquire the note as a holder in due course under the Uniform Commercial Code if the note was negotiable and the transfer was by proper negotiation. As a holder in due course, the transferee can enforce the note free from many of the mortgagor's contract defenses, such as failure of consideration or payment to the original lender. Problems arise when the original mortgagee sells participation interests in her loans to others and then goes bankrupt without properly completing (perfecting) her transfer of the documents to the investors. However, these issues usually are outside the scope of a Property Law course.

Lenders often sell their mortgages in the "secondary mortgage market." The mortgage purchasers create large pools of mortgages and sell fractional ownership interests in them or bonds secured by them. The secondary market injects more funds into the real estate market.

*

PART THREE

MISCELLANEOUS PROPERTY DOCTRINES

This Part includes a variety of topics that are taught at scattered places in the Property Law course or sometimes not at all. Air, water, and support sometimes are covered collectively as "incidental rights in land" or with easements. Agreed boundaries may be covered as part of adverse possession or with deeds. Fixtures may be part of landlord-tenant or an advanced mortgages or commercial law course. Trespass and nuisance often are studied in Torts or are treated as parts of adverse possession or land use. Land use may be a separate course and not covered at all in the basic Property Law course.

In this Part, the masculine pronoun refers to the property owner, and the feminine pronoun refers to the other party involved in the transaction, unless the text indicates otherwise.

CHAPTER THIRTEEN

AIRSPACE

Ownership of land generally includes ownership of the airspace above its surface. The advent of air travel has led to different treatment of air rights directly connected with surface uses and air rights in the upper atmosphere.

I. LOWER AIRSPACE

A landowner has the same rights and privileges regarding the lower reaches of the airspace directly over the surface of his land as he has with regard to the surface itself. Thus, he may, for example, convey the airspace, lease it, permit limited uses of it, and resist encroachments in it.

Illustration: Len leases a second floor apartment in his building to Tina. Technically, Tina has a leasehold estate in airspace located between ten and twenty feet over the surface of Len's land. If Tina enters any other second floor apartment without permission, she is trespassing into the airspace of the person entitled to possess it.

Illustration: If Len converts his building into condominiums and conveys a second floor unit to Tina, she will have fee simple title to that airspace. If she occupies a different unit for a long enough time, she may acquire title by adverse possession to that different segment of airspace.

384

Illustration: Stan grants Dita the right to string a power line across his property. She has an easement in the airspace over his property. If Dita installs the power line without Stan's consent and he fails to exercise his legal remedies within the statute of limitations, Dita may acquire a prescriptive easement or title by adverse possession in the space occupied by the line. She also could acquire an interest if she regularly drove golf balls over Stan's land or if the overhanging eaves on her roof intruded into Stan's airspace for a long enough period of time.

II. UPPER AIRSPACE

A. TRESPASS

Congress has declared that the upper airspace is navigable and has given the public the freedom of transit there. Consequently, air flights at high altitudes over privately owned land generally are not trespassory, and surface owners' rights are subject to the public right of air travel. A surface owner retains conventional property rights in the airspace over her land only to the extent that she reasonably can use it. The owner may not be restrained from building a tall building even though it may interfere with air travel, unless it is expressly prohibited by law. Conversely, the owner does not have a trespass action for flights above the land if they are in a part of the airspace higher than the owner could reach through ground construction. A trespass occurs only when the flight is low enough to intrude upon actual or potential ground-based activity. Trespass is covered in Chapter 18.

B.   NUISANCE

A flight over land may be actionable as a nuisance if it disturbs use of the land's surface by virtue of its noise, glare, danger, or other adverse impact. A flight may constitute a nuisance even if it flies only over adjacent land or from a neighboring airport, rather than directly over the plaintiff's land. Courts usually award damages, rather than injunctive relief, in such cases unless the overflight is by a private party for cloud seeding or for some other form of weather modification that is likely to affect the owner's land. Nuisance is covered in Chapter 19.

C.   TAKING

Governmental overflights that render the surface valueless because of their frequency or nuisance-like qualities may constitute a taking of the owner's property, which requires the government to pay just compensation to the owner. Similarly, the noise of takeoffs and landings at a governmentally operated airport may take or damage its neighbors' property. In contrast, a private airline company would not be liable on a taking claim, though it could be liable as a nuisance. Taking of property is covered in Chapter 20.

CHAPTER FOURTEEN

WATER

A person who owns land bordering on a stream, lake, or other body of water can use the water for drinking, swimming, fishing, and other appropriate activities. But the landowner does not own the water. His rights and privileges are usufructuary, rather than proprietary. Water is owned only after it has been taken from the stream or lake or if it is part of a lake or pond entirely surrounded by one owner's land. Rights to use water in a stream are called riparian rights.

Use rights on navigable or tidal bodies of water are subject to public and federal rights in those waterways. The public may be entitled to use such waters for swimming, fishing, boating, and related recreational purposes under the public trust doctrine and may prevent riparian activities that interfere with those uses. Under the Commerce Clause of the U.S. Constitution, the federal government has a navigational servitude in all navigable waterways of the United States. When exercising its rights under the servitude, the government may interfere with riparian uses of water without liability.

I. STREAM WATER

A parcel of land is riparian when any part of it is contiguous to a stream if it extends only a reasonable distance from the water and is within the same watershed. A portion of the land may lose its riparian character if title to it is severed from the rest and no part of the severed portion is contiguous to the stream. Conversely, in some jurisdictions, nonriparian land may become riparian when an adjacent riparian owner acquires it. Land adjacent to a lake is called littoral and is subject to the same riparian rules.

A. PREFERRED USE PRIVILEGES

A riparian owner can use water from the stream for any purpose that does not have a significant effect upon the quantity, quality, or velocity of the flow across lower riparian lands. A riparian owner also can use water for domestic purposes even if it affects downstream users.

Illustration: Ursula, an upstream landowner, draws water from the stream and sells it. Her use does not affect the stream's flow over Don's downstream land. Even though her use of the water is nonriparian, Don may not enjoin it.

Illustration: Ursula draws water from the stream for drinking, bathing, irrigating her garden, and watering her domestic livestock. During the dry season, these diversions stop the water flow over Don's land. Nevertheless, Don cannot enjoin these domestic uses of water.

B. CORRELATIVE USE PRIVILEGES

Any nondomestic use of water by an upper riparian owner that affects the quantity, quality, or flow of a stream is limited by the rights of the lower riparian owners. Two rival doctrines define a lower riparian owner's rights.

1. Natural Flow Doctrine

A lower riparian owner is entitled to receive the stream's natural flow without any significant alteration in quantity, quality, or velocity. The owner need not show any special injury resulting from the alteration of the flow.

2. Reasonable Use Doctrine

A lower riparian owner is entitled to receive as much stream water as she can put to beneficial use, with due regard for the upstream owner's correlative rights. The downstream owner must show some injury resulting from the alteration of the flow.

Illustration: Ursula diverts a significant portion of the stream's water for sale. Since Don does not use the stream water, this alteration of the flow does not affect any of his activities. In a natural flow doctrine jurisdiction, he may enjoin Ursula's diversion. In a reasonable use doctrine jurisdiction, however, he would not get an injunction.

Illustration: Ursula diverts the stream water for various commercial uses, such as for use in her mill or other manufacturing activity, and pollutes the stream with waste products from those uses. These activities affect the flow over Don's land and interfere with his use of the water. If his domestic needs for the water are impaired, he may enjoin Ursula. However, if he needs the water only for commercial purposes, a court ruling on an injunction would compare the social utility of the parties' respective uses and the harm each would suffer from a deprivation of some or all of the water.

The older natural flow doctrine offers the advantages of certainty, since a lower riparian owner prevails merely by showing that the flow has been altered. On the other hand, it is nonutilitarian, often prohibits beneficial water uses, and leads to waste of a valuable resource. It also compels a lower riparian owner to bring suit before he has suffered any injury to avoid the creation of prescriptive rights. In contrast, the majority reasonable use doctrine permits litigation to be postponed until actual harm has occurred and leads to better water use. However, it offers little certainty to the parties, and judicial decrees may require frequent modification as needs change.

C. APPROPRIATION SYSTEMS

Many western states have found the riparian system to be unsuited to their arid conditions and have developed a doctrine of appropriation rights as a substitute or complement to the riparian rules. In an appropriation system, the right to use water is acquired by permit from a government agency. The agency grants the permit if it determines that the appropriator will make a beneficial use of the water. Priority of right to the water is controlled by the date of the permit or appropriation.

Illustration: April obtained a permit to appropriate a certain amount of water per day for her mining activities.

Subsequently, Jerry obtained a permit to use water from the same stream for his mines. If the stream level falls too low to allow both parties to take their full quotas, April will be preferred as the prior appropriator. Jerry may take his full allotment only if it does not interfere with April's rights, regardless of where their respective diversion points are located on the stream.

A nonriparian owner may acquire an appropriation permit. Some states eliminate riparian rights entirely (the "Colorado doctrine") so that even a riparian owner must apply for a permit to use the water crossing his land. Other states permit riparian and appropriation rights to coexist (the "California doctrine"). In these states, a more complicated system of priority is necessary to reconcile the competing claims of various appropriators and riparian owners.

Illustration: Ann acquired riparian land in 1850. Bob obtained a permit to appropriate water for his nonriparian land in 1860. Cathy acquired her lower riparian land in 1870 when it came out of the public domain. Don obtained an appropriation permit in 1880. Applying the California doctrine, Ann's privilege to take water probably has the highest priority. Therefore, she may divert water even if it injures all the others, unless her activities are not reasonable or beneficial. Bob may divert water under his appropriation permit only if it does not interfere with Ann's reasonable needs, but Bob may take water even if it injures Cathy or Don. Cathy may divert water even if it injures Don, but she may not interfere with Bob's appropriation. As a lower riparian owner, Cathy's use would not affect Ann, unless Cathy dams the stream and causes water to back up onto Ann's land. Don may appropriate water only if his use does not injure Ann, Bob, or Cathy. Under the Colorado doctrine, Ann and Cathy would have no rights to water, because they did not obtain appropriation permits. Only Bob and Don would be entitled to water. As the prior appropriator, Bob has superior rights to Don.

II. SURFACE WATER

Unlike still ponds, swamps, or marshes, surface waters normally move from higher to lower ground but, unlike streams, do not follow any clearly defined channel. Surface waters generally result from rain or snow, but sometimes flood waters that separate from the main body of the flood also are treated as surface water. Because such waters are generally unwanted, most litigation concerns a landowner's right to discharge them from her land or to prevent them from crossing her land. In those rare situations when a landowner wants to appropriate surface water, there is a general entitlement to do so.

Three rival doctrines deal with the disposal of surface waters.

A. COMMON ENEMY DOCTRINE

A landowner may dam against surface waters, discharge them back onto upper lands, or deflect them elsewhere. Only the artificial discharge of large quantities of water onto others' lands is prohibited.

B. NATURAL SERVITUDE DOCTRINE

Lower land is servient to the natural drainage from upper land. Thus, a lower landowner cannot obstruct or deflect surface waters. Conversely, the upper land-owner cannot cut channels to drain the water elsewhere. This doctrine, which is derived from the civil law, often is subject to an urban exception to permit interference with the natural flow when it results from grading or construction.

C.   REASONABLE USE DOCTRINE

A landowner may drain surface waters in connection with a reasonable use of the land if a reasonable necessity exists for the draining, reasonable care is exercised to avoid unnecessary injury to others, and the benefit outweighs the harm. This more recent doctrine is designed to directly reach the result that the other two doctrines in fact produce as a result of their exceptions.

Illustration: Surface waters naturally tend to flow from Ursula's upper land to Don's lower land. Under the common enemy rule, Don can erect a barrier to prevent the water from leaving Ursula's land or can cut a channel to make them pass onto Lowell's land below him. Under the natural servitude rule, neither activity would be allowed. Under the reasonable use rule, Don may do either depending on the need to drain his property, the care he takes to avoid unnecessary harm to Ursula or Lowell, and the benefits to him in keeping his land free of the waters as compared to the harm Ursula and Lowell would suffer.

III.   UNDERGROUND WATER

A separate body of law regulates rights regarding diffuse underground water that follows no ascertainable underground channel and either remains still or percolates up to the surface. Underground water that flows in a defined channel is subject to the same rules as streams, but the presumption exists that the water is diffuse, rather than channeled. As with the rest of water law, there are rival rules concerning diffuse underground water.

A.   ABSOLUTE OWNERSHIP DOCTRINE

A landowner has an unqualified right to pump all the water, even if it deprives other landowners over the same underground basin of water for their needs.

B.   REASONABLE USE DOCTRINE

An overlying owner may pump only so much water as reasonably can be used for beneficial uses on his overlying land. How much is reasonable may depend in part on whether the water used will seep back down to recharge the aquifer.

C.   CORRELATIVE RIGHTS DOCTRINE

All overlying owners are joint tenants of the underground basin and are limited to a reasonable proportion of the annual supply for beneficial use on the overlying land.

D. APPROPRIATION

The appropriation system may apply to under-ground water, as well as to stream water, and may permit persons who do not own overlying land to appropriate water from an underground basin.

CHAPTER FIFTEEN

SUPPORT

A landowner is entitled to have his land naturally supported by the adjacent and underlying property of others. Consequently, activity by a neighbor or subsurface owner that causes another's land to subside may be actionable. Support by neighboring land is called lateral. Support by underlying land is called subjacent. The rules relating to the two kinds of support are, for the most part, similar.

I. SUPPORT OF UNIMPROVED LAND

A. ABSOLUTE RIGHT TO SUPPORT

Unimproved land has an absolute right to support. Excavation that causes neighboring unimproved land to subside is actionable even though it was not negligently performed and was essential to the land's use. This absolute right applies only to land in its natural condition and not when the land already has been weakened or improved. Liability exists only when an actual subsidence has occurred because of removal of the surrounding land. If the subsidence is due to removal of water, the matter is governed by water law, rather than by support law.

Illustration: Nora excavated on her lot to build a house on it. As a result, Owen's unimproved land subsided. Nora is liable to him even if the excavation was not performed in a negligent manner.

Illustration: A mining company has the right to remove minerals below the surface of Owen's land. Its underground tunnels caused subsistence of Owen's land. The mining company is liable to Owen even though the tunnels were cut carefully.

Illustration: Excavations on Nora's land reduced the lateral support for Owen's land, but the surface of his land has not subsided. Until some subsidence occurs, Owen does not have a cause of action against Nora. Similarly, if Nora protects Owen's land from subsiding by installing an artificial support, such as a retaining wall, to replace the natural support, Owen has no cause of action against her unless she fails to maintain the retaining wall in an effective condition.

Illustration: Because Owen has discharged great amounts of water onto his land, the natural cohesiveness of the soil has been reduced. If Nora now carefully excavates on her land, she will not be liable to Owen for any subsidence that occurs as a result of his land no longer being in its natural condition.

B. LIABLE PERSONS

A landowner is liable only for her acts or her agents' acts that cause another's land to subside. She is not liable for acts of predecessors, successors, or strangers.

Illustration: Some years earlier, Nora's predecessor excavated on her land, but Owen's land did not subside until after Nora had acquired title. The predecessor may be liable for damages because the statute of limitations on Owen's cause of action did not begin to run until the subsidence. However, Nora is not liable.

Illustration: Some years earlier, Nora excavated on her land. As a result of further excavations by Nora's successor or by other neighbors, Owen's land subsides. He has no cause of action against Nora since intervening acts caused the injury.

Illustration: An earthquake or flood eliminated the natural support that Nora's land previously provided to Owen's land, and his land subsided. He has no cause of action against Nora.

II. SUPPORT OF IMPROVED LAND

A. EXTENT OF THE OBLIGATION

Land improved with buildings is subject to somewhat different rules concerning support. Many courts hold that the absolute obligation of subjacent support continues as before and that a subsurface excavator must furnish support to the surface owner's pre-existing building, as well as to his land. However, the removal of lateral support is actionable only if the land would have subsided even without the buildings on it. Experts may be required to determine whether the pressure of the improvements caused the subsidence or whether their additional weight was offset by the soil removed for their foundations when they were built.

B. MEASURE OF DAMAGES

Courts disagree concerning the measure of damages for an actionable removal of lateral support of improved land. In some jurisdictions, the owner may recover for the injuries to his land but not to his building. The theory behind this rule is that compelling the second improver to pay damages for the first improver's building gives preferential treatment to the first, which is contrary to the policy that all owners should have equal rights to improve. In other jurisdictions, removal of support makes the neighbor liable for injury to the buildings, as well as to the land, on the ground that the building damage was foreseeable. The measure of damages in these cases may be the cost of repairs up to the property's market value, depreciation of market value, or the lesser of those two measures.

A neighbor who negligently or maliciously excavates is liable for harm to the land and to the buildings, regardless of the buildings' weight. A court may find that an excavator acted negligently if she failed to (1) warn the neighbor of the impending excavation so that he could shore up his building first, (2) shore up his building for him, or (3) make adequate preliminary soil studies. On the other hand, the neighbor may be guilty of contributory negligence if the building had an inadequate foundation or was so close to the boundary as to subside inevitably when the adjacent land was improved.

C. STATUTORY CHANGES

Some jurisdictions have statutes that require the excavator to give advance notice to the neighbor of the nature of the excavation and, if she intends to excavate below a certain depth (often eight or twelve feet), to shore up the neighbor's building unless he denies permission to do so.

III. AGREEMENTS REGARDING SUPPORT

A.   RELEASE OF SUPPORT RIGHTS

An owner may release others from their duty to support his land. A release may be implied from the circumstances of a grant. A release of natural support rights does not include a release of liability for negligent or malicious removal of support.

B.   ACQUISITION OF SUPPORT RIGHTS

If an intended building will require additional support from adjoining land, the builder can obtain an easement of support from his neighbor. A support easement may be implied when a building is sold and the supporting adjacent land is retained. No easement of support for a building arises by prescription, since the mere existence of a heavy building creates no cause of action for the neighbor. See Chapter 5, p. 211–12.

CHAPTER SIXTEEN

AGREED BOUNDARIES

I. DIFFICULTIES IN ASCERTAINING BOUNDARIES

Although the boundary description in a deed may be easy to understand, it nevertheless may be difficult to convert the words of the description into lines on the earth. Unless an owner employs a surveyor to mark the property lines, the owner may have only an approximate idea of their location. Adjoining landowners frequently have difficulty settling the precise location of their boundary line.

Illustration: Owen's deed states that his property's northern boundary is one mile north of the stream. The deed of his neighbor, Nora, describes her southern boundary as one mile north of the stream. Although on paper the two boundaries coincide, neither Owen nor Nora know the precise location. To mark the boundary accurately, they must employ a surveyor.

II. AGREEING ON A BOUNDARY

The doctrine of agreed or practically located boundaries permits neighbors, under certain circumstances, to fix a boundary that thereafter is the legal line, even though a subsequent survey may reveal that the true line originally was somewhere else. The doctrine generally applies only when the new boundary line results from a disagreement or uncertainty between the neighbors as to the true line. The doctrine does not apply if they were either certain or mistaken as to the old line when they established the new line.

Illustration—Certainty: Owen and Nora both know that the true boundary line is ten feet north of the road between their properties. However, they find it more convenient to use the road as the boundary, and they orally agree that the road will constitute their legal boundary. The agreement violates the Statute of Frauds and is invalid. If they wish to change the boundary, one must convey the ten foot strip to the other by deed.

Illustration—Mistake: Although the true boundary between the properties is ten feet north of the road, both owners mistakenly believe that the road is the true line. Any action they take based on this mistake will be invalid, and the parties will be relieved from the consequences of their mistake.

Illustration—Disagreement: Owen believes that the boundary is ten feet north of the road, but Nora believes that it is ten feet south of the road. To compromise their difference, they agree that the road will be the boundary. This agreement may be binding, even though oral, and will survive any later discovery that the true boundary was north or south of the road.

Illustration—Uncertainty: Neither Owen nor Nora knows the boundary's location. To settle the matter, they agree that the road will be the boundary. This agreement may be binding, even though oral, and will survive any later discovery that the true boundary was somewhere else. In some jurisdictions, the uncertainty must be justified; the parties cannot be merely too lazy to locate the real line.

III. ACQUIESCENCE

The parties generally must acquiesce in the new boundary line. Acquiescence frequently is the critical component of this doctrine and eliminates the need for proof of any actual prior agreement. Some courts require that the acquiescence continue for the statute of limitations period for adverse possession. In these jurisdictions, the doctrine may function as an alternative theory of relief for the party possessing the disputed strip if one of the elements of adverse possession has not been satisfied. Even without acquiescence or an explicit agreement, the owners may be bound by an "incorrect" line when both purchased from a common grantor who had marked it on the ground and had given deeds that used lot numbers on a map, rather than metes and bounds calls, for the legal descriptions.

IV. EFFECT

Once established, an agreed boundary binds not only the original parties, but also their successors, even though nothing in the property records warns successors of the change.

CHAPTER SEVENTEEN

FIXTURES

A fixture is a tangible object that had been personal property but has become so connected with real property as to become part of it. To be a fixture, the object must retain its original identity even after being affixed to the real property.

Illustration: While sitting on the floor of a plumbing supply store, a toilet is personal property. Once bolted down in a bathroom, it becomes a fixture, which is a type of real property.

Illustration: Paint in a can in a paint store is personal property. When opened and applied to a wall, it becomes real property. It is not a fixture, however, since it no longer has a separate identity.

Illustration: A refrigerator is not a fixture, even though it is plugged into the kitchen wall. It remains personal property, although it could change to real property if it were "built-in" to the kitchen.

I. FACTORS IN DETERMINING WHAT IS A FIXTURE

Courts consider a number of factors in determining whether to classify an item as a fixture: (1) the method of annexation (how firmly and securely the item is annexed to the real property), (2) appropriateness (how well the item has been adapted to the real property and how appropriately it fits), (3) removability (how much removal will harm the realty), and (4) intent (what was the annexor's objective intent, as inferred from the above considerations and from his relationship to the real property, especially whether he owns it).

II. WHEN THE ANNEXOR OWNS THE REAL PROPERTY

In many situations, the person affixing personal property to real property owns both. Nevertheless, it still may be important to determine whether the affixed item is real or personal property for the following reasons.

A. PROPERTY TAXATION

Since real and personal property frequently are taxed at different rates, characterization may be necessary to calculate the tax.

B. EMINENT DOMAIN

When land is taken by eminent domain, the condemning authority may be liable for compensation for real property, but not for personal property.

C. MORTGAGES

A real estate mortgage generally covers all of the mortgagor's originally owned or "after acquired" real property, but not personal property. On foreclosure, personal property assets that have become fixtures are subject to the sale.

D. CONVEYANCES

A contract for the sale of real estate obligates the vendor to convey all real property, but not personal property, to the purchaser. Whether the contract includes items such as wall-to-wall carpeting and window blinds depends on whether they are fixtures. Of course, the contract can include an express provision concerning these types of items.

E. DEATH

At common law, real property descended to the intestate's heirs, while personal property went to the personal representative for his next of kin. That distinction rarely exists today, but a similar issue could arise if the decedent left a will that gave his real and personal property to different people.

III. WHEN THE ANNEXOR DOES NOT OWN THE REAL PROPERTY

The person who owns and annexes personal property to real property may not own the real property. If the item becomes a fixture, title to it passes from the annexor to the real property owner despite any subjective intent to the contrary.

A. TENANTS

If a tenant installs a fixture, it may become the landlord's property and removal by the tenant would constitute waste. Nevertheless, many states permit a tenant to remove trade fixtures and possibly ornamental and domestic fixtures as well. However, removal may be permitted only if it will not cause too much injury to the premises.

B. STRANGERS

A person who enters onto another's real property and affixes chattels generally loses the right to remove them. In some states, a betterment or innocent improver statute provides the right to remove them or to recover their reasonable value from the owner.

C. CHATTEL SELLERS

Personal property often is sold on credit with the seller reserving a security interest in the property until the price is fully paid. The security interest is enforceable between the parties. But if the item becomes a fixture, the rights of other parties may make resolution of the issue more difficult. Section 9–313 of the Uniform Commercial Code establishes the priorities for many such situations. Priority can depend on considerations such as whether the personal property security interest was recorded in the public records, a construction loan was involved, or the goods are readily removable. For example, if the annexor is a tenant, the landlord may have an interest. Similarly, if the real property to which the fixture was attached is subject to a mortgage, the mortgagee may have an interest.

CHAPTER EIGHTEEN

TRESPASS

I. PROTECTION OF POSSESSION

As indicated in the materials on adverse possession, a land possessor has certain rights by virtue of that possession even if she does not own the land. Subject to certain principles of reasonableness, she may protect her possession from intruders by erecting barriers to their entry or by physically expelling them. She also has certain judicial remedies against intruders. When the intrusion amounts to a dispossession, she can bring an action in ejectment. Failure to do so creates a risk of adverse possession. When the intrusion does not amount to a dispossession, the appropriate relief is usually damages for trespass. This Chapter does not provide a complete review of the law of trespass, because it generally is covered in Torts. The emphasis here is on those features of trespass law most relevant to a Property Law course.

II. WHAT IS A TRESPASS

Any intentional intrusion on property possessed by another is a trespass. Liability is absolute. Motive, extent, duration, and harm are irrelevant, though they may affect the amount of damages. A negligent intrusion also can be a trespass, but only if some harm results from it. A nonvolitional intrusion is not a trespass, but mistake as to location does not make the entry nonvolitional.

Illustration: Trish is carried across Paul's land by kidnappers. Although they may be guilty of trespass, she is not, since her entry was nonvolitional.

Illustration: Paul's neighbor walks on his property, because she believes that it is part of her land. She is a trespasser since her entry was intentional, even though she was mistaken as to ownership.

Illustration: Trish negligently runs her car off the road and onto Paul's land. If she harms his land, she is liable for it in trespass.

A. INTRUSIONS OTHER THAN BY THE TRESPASSER

A trespass occurs with a physical intrusion of the land. The trespasser need not personally be the intruder. The intrusion can be by the trespasser's agent or by physical objects that the trespasser sets in motion, such as a rolling car or a fired bullet.

Illustration: Trish's animals wander over Paul's land. At common law, she would be liable for their trespasses. However, many states have altered these rules with fencing statutes. Additionally, generally no liability exists for intrusions by dogs, cats, and other animals whose movements are difficult to control.

B. TOUCHING THE BOUNDARY

A trespass occurs when the trespasser touches a vertical boundary line, even if he does not cross it.

Illustration: Trish piles dirt against the wall of Paul's house, which is on his lot line, or fastens a clothes line to his wall. She is trespassing in both cases.

C. ABOVE AND BELOW THE SURFACE

A trespass may occur above or below the surface since the possessory right extends vertically in both directions from the boundary line on the surface. Therefore, an underground intrusion, such as a slant well, is a trespass, although the depletion of migrant minerals, such as water, oil, or gas, from a common basin by a perpendicular well dug on neighboring land is not. Similarly, an intrusion into airspace by a building, wire, or other object also is a trespass and may lead to the acquisition of prescriptive rights of possession or use. An isolated nonpermanent intrusion, such as firing a gun over land, also is a trespass. Special rules deal with airplanes' overflights. On airspace, see Chapter 13.

III. PRIVILEGED ENTRIES

A. CONSENT

Entry with the possessor's consent is not trespass. The invitation creates a license, which may be oral or implied. Once it expires or is revoked, failure to leave within a reasonable time constitutes a trespass.

Illustration: Trish enters a restaurant to dine. Her entry is not trespassory because the circumstances create the implication that the public is invited to enter. However, if she refuses to leave after closing time, she is guilty of trespass.

B.   SOCIAL NEED

In certain situations, public policy requires a possessor to permit others to enter his land. A possessor's right of undisturbed possession is subject to the general public interest.

Illustration: The police enter Paul's property to break up a fight or to stop a crime from being committed there. The entry is privileged.

Illustration: A building inspector or other public official enters property in furtherance of an official duty. The entry is privileged, although a warrant may be required if the entry would constitute a search or seizure under the Fourth Amendment.

Illustration: Paul's house is on fire. Trish enters to extinguish it before it spreads to her property. She is privileged to do so.

C.   PROPERTY RIGHTS

In certain cases, a person may be entitled to enter another's land to protect certain property interests. This is not a general license to wander freely but is limited to such entry as is necessary to protect the property interest.

Illustration: Paul has fee title subject to condition subsequent, and Trish has the power of termination. After the condition has occurred, Trish can exercise the power by entering onto Paul's land. Her peaceable entry to perfect the power is not a trespass. See Chapter 2, p. 60.

Illustration: As Paul's landlord, Trish may have the right to enter to make sure that he is not committing waste. Such a limited entry is not trespassory. See Chapter 4, p. 135–37.

Title to real property does not constitute an absolute privilege for entry. The owner is privileged to peaceably enter property in another's possession but may not use force to do so. In most jurisdictions, forcible entry creates civil and criminal liability.

Illustration: Because Paul was in arrears on his rent, his landlord broke open the door to his apartment while he was away and removed his belongings. Although the landlord is entitled to have him evicted, she may not commit this forcible entry and trespass.

Illustration: In a dispute between Trish and Paul over the location of their common boundary line, Trish demolished the fence that Paul erected and stepped over it. Trish is guilty of trespass and forcible entry, even though a survey ultimately may show that Paul's fence was encroaching onto her property and that she owned the disputed strip.

IV. REMEDIES

A. NOMINAL DAMAGES

A possessor need not show that he has suffered any harm from the trespass and always may recover at least nominal damages for any trespass. An action for nominal damages is sometimes brought to establish a property right, settle a boundary dispute, or stop the running of the statute of limitations.

B.   COMPENSATORY DAMAGES

A possessor may recover compensatory damages for actual harm suffered from a trespass. If permanent injury has occurred, the measure of damages is either the diminution of the property's value or the cost of restoration. Consequential damages, such as for personal injuries, mental anguish, and lost profits, also may be recovered, subject to the usual tort principles of foreseeability and mitigation of damages. In certain cases, the damages may be based on the benefit received by the trespasser. For example, if a trespasser removes assets from the property, she may be liable for their value or she may be required to return them or pay a royalty for them. A trespasser who improves the property sometimes is allowed to offset the value of her improvements against her trespass liability. Where the trespass is continuing but the injury is not permanent, damages will be awarded only for injuries caused before the date of judgment. The possessor may file subsequent actions against the trespasser for harm caused since the prior judgment.

C.   PUNITIVE DAMAGES

If the trespass is malicious or wanton, courts may impose exemplary or punitive damages on the trespasser. In some jurisdictions, the wrongful cutting of timber subjects a trespasser to double or triple damages.

D. EQUITABLE RELIEF

A court may grant an injunction if damages are difficult to calculate or the harm is irreparable. To eliminate multiple lawsuits, a court also may grant an injunction against trespasses that probably will continue in the future. Occasionally, a court will order removal of an encroaching building but usually only after balancing the hardship to the defendant if the injunction is granted against the hardship to the plaintiff if it is not granted. The denial of an injunction in such a case amounts to the defendant's exercise of a form of private eminent domain. A court also may grant injunctive relief to a future interest holder who currently lacks standing to bring an action for damages.

E. RELIEF ACCORDING TO THE PLAINTIFF'S STATUS

The plaintiff in an action for damages for trespass must either possess the property or hold a present possessory interest in it. The possessory right, not ownership, is protected. Thus, a trespass action may be brought by a tenant, a purchaser in possession under a land contract, a cotenant in possession alone or with others, an adverse possessor, or a mere peaceful possessor of another's property. However, a shopping center owner often cannot exclude political and religious pamphleteers from sidewalks and parking lots despite his ownership, because these areas are treated as public, rather than private, places. A non-possessory interest holder may recover only if she can show some injury to her interest; harm is a prerequisite to any such action because, technically, it does not sound in trespass.

Illustration: Trish entered Paul's apartment without his permission. Paul can recover at least nominal damages from Trish, but his landlord can recover only for any permanent harm Trish caused to the apartment. The landlord's mortgagee may recover only if Trish impaired its security.

Illustration: Trish trespassed over a road on Paul's property. Dita, who has a right of way easement over the road, has a cause of action against Trish only if the intrusion unreasonably interfered with her use of the road.

CHAPTER NINETEEN

NUISANCE

I. NUISANCE v. TRESPASS

A property owner who suffers an unreasonable interference with the use and enjoyment of his property is entitled to relief against the person who caused it. Trespass is the appropriate remedy if a physical invasion caused the interference, whereas nuisance is the action if the invasion is nonphysical. Nuisance differs from trespass in that harm is an essential element of this cause of action, whereas trespass lies for any physical intrusion regardless of harm. Furthermore, trespass is available only to those holding possessory interests, while nuisance protects any property interest. Prescription can be a defense for both physical and nonphysical interferences.

Illustration: Nora works on cars on her property. If she drives the cars onto her neighbor's property, she is guilty of trespass and is liable for at least nominal damages regardless of harm. On the other hand, if the cars make a great deal of noise in Nora's garage, her neighbor may recover in nuisance if he can show that the noise unreasonably interferes with activities on his land. If his land is vacant or if his house is situated far from the noise, he cannot sue for nuisance.

Illustration: If Nora parks her cars on her neighbor's driveway, she has committed a trespass as to him. But she is not liable in trespass to Dita, who has an easement to drive across the driveway, since Dita's property interest is nonpossessory. Dita may recover only if she can show that Nora has unreasonably interfered with her use of the driveway.

II. DETERMINING WHETHER A NUISANCE HAS OCCURRED

Nuisances generally involve some interference with the physical senses, such as smoke, dust, odor, noise, light, or heat, that would interfere with a normal person's use of his property. An activity that is merely visually offensive generally is not an actionable nuisance, although activities that cause fright, such as a funeral parlor, or moral indignation, such as brothels or gambling halls, may be. A nuisance usually involves intentional conduct by the defendant. Negligence generally is irrelevant, although malice may convert an otherwise legitimate activity into a nuisance.

To determine whether the challenged activity is a nuisance, courts generally balance the parties' respective interests by comparing the gravity of the plaintiff's harm with the utility of the defendant's conduct. As components of the gravity of harm, the Restatement of Torts § 827 includes the harm's extent and character, the harmed activity's social value and its suitability to the locale, and the plaintiff's ability to avoid the harm. Factors in determining the utility of the defendant's conduct include its social value and suitability to the locale and the impracticality of preventing the plaintiff's harm. Restatement of Torts § 828. Priority of use is not a complete defense but may be treated as a factor. Thus, it might be relevant that the plaintiff has "come to the nuisance."

III. RELIEF

Damages are the appropriate remedy for a nuisance that has ceased. The plaintiff is entitled to recover for harm to property and person. In the case of a nuisance that threatens to continue indefinitely, an award of damages alone constitutes a form of private eminent domain. The defendant essentially is paying for the property interests it has appropriated from the plaintiff.

If an injunction is sought, courts generally balance the harm to the defendant if the injunction is granted against the benefit to the plaintiff. The factors considered in the balancing are basically the same as for determining whether the defendant's activity constituted a nuisance. However, their weight changes because of the context. Some economists argue that an injunction should be granted only if the defendant can avoid the harm at a lower cost than the plaintiff. The equities of the situation should be relevant only to the question of damages, which can be awarded either to a plaintiff who is denied an injunction or to a defendant who is enjoined.

Illustration: Nora's race track emits such bright light during night racing that it impairs Owen's neighboring drive-in movie business. In deciding whether to enjoin Nora from night racing, a court might compare the relative avoidance costs. If the court determines that it is cheaper for Nora to shield her lights or to give up night racing than for

Owen to build a high wall, it may grant an injunction. The court also could condition the injunction on Owen's compensating Nora if the court decides that equitable principles require this. In such a case, the court effectively has held that Nora is entitled to emit light but should compensate Owen for the interference at a price set by the court, rather than by the parties. This award is a "liability entitlement," rather than a "property entitlement," because of its similarity to a personal injury award for which a judge or jury determines the price of a broken limb. Alternately, the court could deny an injunction to Owen if it determines that he can remedy the problem more cheaply than Nora and if she reimburses him for his avoidance costs. The court also could grant or deny the injunction without reallocating costs. If the problem cannot be eliminated through corrective measures, a court might consider the relative costs of either party's relocating away from the other.

A nuisance imposes an external cost on another's land. An injunction may be regarded as compelling the defendant to internalize that cost or to reverse the externality. When neighboring activities are incompatible, a court is almost inevitably drawn into judicial zoning.

Illustration: Nora's foundry is next to Owen's laboratory. Noise or vibrations from the foundry make laboratory work impossible. Therefore, Nora is imposing an external cost on Owen's land. However, if Owen obtains an injunction that prohibits or limits her foundry's activity, he will have imposed an external cost on her land. Either her work makes his work impossible if she is not enjoined, or his work makes hers impossible if she is enjoined. Either activity is compatible with many other kinds of activities but not with each other. A neutral principle may not exist to resolve this conflict.

IV. PUBLIC NUISANCE

A nuisance is public when it affects a significant portion of the community, rather than just a few neighbors. It often can be remedied only by an action brought by a public official. However, an individual may sue for damages or an injunction if he can show special harm to himself or his property over and above what everyone else is suffering.

CHAPTER TWENTY
LAND USE REGULATION

This Chapter deals with the relationship between a landowner and the general public concerning the activities on his land. The public interest can be manifested by (1) legislative action that regulates land use activities, (2) administrative agency action in granting, denying, or modifying a permit for land uses, and (3) judicial action between the government and a landowner or between the government and neighboring landowners over the validity of a land use regulation or its application to a particular parcel of land. All the Illustrations in this Chapter are based on actual cases or statutes.

I. TYPES OF LAND USE REGULATION

A. ZONING

1. Typical Zoning Devices

Zoning is the most common form of local land use control. The city or county (referred to as the "community" in this Chapter) is divided geographically into zones (districts), and different use regulations apply in each zone. The regulations are set forth in a zoning ordinance. The zoning map graphically depicts each geographic district. Although the regulations differ from district to district, they apply uniformly to all parcels of land within a district.

a. Lot, Building, and Use Regulations

Zoning ordinances generally regulate the size and shape of the land, the size and shape of improvements on the land, and the type of activity that can occur on the land or in its improvements.

(1) Lot Regulations

(a) Minimum Lot Size

Many zoning ordinances establish minimum lot sizes to reduce density. Density limitations are designed to eliminate overcrowding, increase the flow of light and air, facilitate police and fire services, and reduce demands on natural resources. Required lot sizes can range from 2,000 square feet in dense urban areas, five acres in suburban and rural areas, and twenty or more acres in farm communities.

(b) Minimum Frontage

A related form of regulation establishes a minimum width for a parcel's frontage on a public street. In urban areas, the minimum frontage may be as little as twenty feet. In the suburbs, it may be one hundred or two hundred feet. The requirement may be tied to some other variable, such as the parcel's depth or the width of surrounding lots.

(2) Building Regulations

(a) Height

Building heights usually are regulated by number of feet or stories independent of the lot area. However, the height limit may vary according to the topography, such as thirty feet along the coast, or according to use. For example, buildings in commercial zones may be allowed greater height than those in residential zones. Height also may be related to bulk, so that a building may be taller if it is narrower or if it is stepped back as it rises so as to increase the light and view at ground level. The limit also may depend on the heights of adjacent buildings or on the average height of buildings on the block. Special adjustments may be made for buildings erected on sharply sloping ground.

(b) Bulk

(1) Yards. Building bulk generally is regulated as a function of lot size. Front, back, and side yard requirements prohibit a building from occupying the entire parcel by mandating open space along all or part of its perimeter. A front yard regulation, which requires a building to be no less than a specified distance from the front lot line, usually is called a setback regulation. A side yard regulation requires buildings on neighboring properties be detached from one another. Rear yard requirements, which are common in residential districts, may be expressed in absolute numbers or may use averaging principles. For example, front or rear setbacks for a building may have to be

consistent with buildings on adjacent parcels or with the average setback on the block.

Many communities do not have setback requirements, especially in commercial areas, thus permitting contiguous buildings to extend all the way to the lot lines. In dense residential neighborhoods, the front or side yard requirement may be as little as five or ten feet. In more spacious suburbs, the requirements may be as much as fifty feet in front and forty feet along the sides. The requirements generally vary from district to district.

(2) Open Space. Building bulk also may be regulated by a direct open space regulation. This type of regulation prohibits a building from occupying more than a specified percentage of the lot. In the suburbs, the percentage may be as low as twenty percent. The setback requirements described above generally supplement the open space requirements to control the placement of buildings on the lot.

(c) Floor–Area Ratio

A floor-area ratio (FAR) requirement may regulate a building's overall bulk according to the size of the lot without specifying the building's precise shape. For example, a 2:1 ratio permits the lot owner to erect a building containing two square feet of floor space for every one square foot of lot area. The owner can erect a two-story building covering the entire lot, a four-story building covering half the lot, an eight-story building covering a quarter of the lot, and so on. However, height limits and open space and yard requirements may limit the owner's options. Residential

FARs often range from 2:1 to 5:1. In downtown areas, they may vary from 15:1 to 20:1. The Empire State Building's FAR is 25:1. Some ordinances permit the FAR to be increased if the owner provides certain amenities, such as plazas, public parking, or rapid transit access.

(d) Minimum Floor Space

Suburban zoning ordinances often prohibit residential structures from being too small, rather than too large, by requiring a minimum size, such as 1,000 square feet of floor space. If the requirement is designed to exclude the poor, rather than to prevent overcrowding, a court may invalidate it, especially if it is combined with an unjustifiably large minimum lot size requirement. Zoning devices that are designed to exclude lower income people or other classes of persons are called "exclusionary zoning," which is covered at page 475.

Illustration: The Berlin, New Jersey zoning ordinance required a minimum floor space of 1,600 square feet, a minimum lot size of one acre, and a minimum frontage of 200 feet in single family residential zones. The New Jersey Supreme Court invalidated these exclusionary zoning devices in *Home Builders League of South Jersey, Inc. v. Township of Berlin* (1979).

(e) Design and Site Plan Review

A community may impose design controls for new structures by requiring that, as a condition to receiving a building permit, the building plans be submitted to a local review board, which usually is composed of architects. Because courts in some jurisdictions hold that aesthetic considerations alone are an insufficient justification for land use regulations, many design review ordinances state preservation of property values as the primary consideration. To withstand challenges based on vagueness and improper delegation of legislative power to an unelected review board, such ordinances often attempt to prescribe aesthetic standards in considerable detail.

Illustration: The Architectural Board of Review of Cleveland Heights, Ohio was charged with "regulating according to proper architectural principles the design, use of materials, finished grade lines and orientation of all new buildings." *Reid v. Architectural Bd. of Review Cleveland Heights* (1963).

Illustration: The Architectural Board of Ladue, Missouri was authorized to review building plans to ensure that they "conform to certain minimum architectural standards of appearance and conformity with surrounding structures, and that unsightly, grotesque and unsuitable structures, detrimental to the stability of value and welfare of surrounding property structures and residents, and to the general welfare and happiness of the community be avoided, and that appropriate standards of beauty and conformity be fostered and encouraged." *State ex rel. Stoyanoff v. Berkeley* (1970).

Illustration: The Board of Architectural Review of Westchester County, New York was authorized to disapprove an application if it found that the proposed structure would cause "harmful effects" by reason of (1) "monotonous similarity," (2) "striking dissimilarity or visual discord or inappropriateness" to nearby buildings, or (3) "visual offensiveness or other poor qualities of exterior design."

Site plan review is less predictable. A community board may have power to review all aspects of a project and to demand changes as a condition for final approval, even if the plan complies with all zoning and other regulations. Such standardless review gives planners powerful discretionary control. It also significantly changes the nature of land use regulation from its original concept of providing preset standards to all property owners in the district. Under the original view, landowners had the power "as of right" to complete projects that conformed with the standards.

(3) Regulations on Activities

The key feature of traditional zoning is the creation of use districts, which are zones where certain activities are prohibited, though they are permitted in other zones in the community. An original premise behind zoning was that some uses of land are incompatible and must be kept separated for the protection of one or both of them. In particular, residential areas were deemed to need protection from commercial and industrial intrusion.

Zoning originally was "cumulative," meaning that more intense uses (commercial and industrial) were excluded from less intense use (residential) zones, whereas less intense uses were permitted in more intense use zones. Today, commercial and industrial zones often exclude residential uses. This is noncumulative zoning, because the enumerated uses are exclusive in each zone.

Zoning ordinances exclude activities either by explicitly excluding certain uses in a zone or by specifying the only uses that are permitted and excluding all others. Serious questions of validity are raised when a zoning ordinance excludes a lawful use from the entire community.

Illustration: In Weston, Connecticut, the zoning ordinance classified the entire town as residential and agricultural, thereby excluding all commercial activities. The court upheld the ordinance on the ground that "the business and industrial needs of its inhabitants are supplied by other accessible areas in the community at large." *Cadoux v. Planning and Zoning Comm'n of Town of Weston* (1972).

Illustration: The West Whiteland, Pennsylvania zoning ordinance entirely excluded rock quarries. The Pennsylvania Supreme Court invalidated the ordinance because "a zoning ordinance which totally excludes a particular business from an entire municipality must bear a more substantial relationship to the public health, safety, morals and general welfare than an ordinance which merely confines that business to a certain area in the community." *Exton Quarries, Inc. v. Zoning Bd. of Adjustment of West Whiteland Township* (1967).

(a) Residential

Residential uses commonly are separated by housing type. Separate districts may exist for single family, two family (flats or duplexes), and multiple family residences (apartments). Other districts may include or exclude different kinds of residential use, such as hotels, motels, apartment complexes, garden apartments, mobile home parks, boarding houses, fraternity and sorority houses, dormitories, and various forms of institutional housing, such as mental health facilities, orphanages, and halfway houses.

Courts generally have upheld the exclusion of apartment buildings from single family residential zones since the United States Supreme Court first validated zoning in *Village of Euclid v. Ambler Realty Co.* (1926). However, the exclusion of housing that best accommodates low-income persons may be invalid as exclusionary. Exclusionary zoning is covered at p. 475. Constitutional issues involved in single family zoning are covered at p. 464.

(b) Commercial

Most communities have some commercial zones, as well as residential zones. There may be only one commercial category that includes all permitted commercial uses or a variety of categories, such as central district commercial (large department stores), neighborhood commercial, retail, and office. The zoning ordinance may have special rules for garages, gas stations, liquor stores, bars, drive-ins, theaters, and restaurants, because these uses, though beneficial, tend to impose unique burdens on a neighborhood.

Illustration: The Fair Lawn, New Jersey zoning ordinance excluded from certain business zones "drive-in restaurants or refreshment stands, commonly called snack bars, dairy bars, hamburger stands or hot dog stands where customers and patrons are served food, soft drinks, ice cream * * * for their immediate consumption * * * outside the confines of the building or structures in which the business is conducted." *Morris v. Postma* (1964).

Some ordinances put all such uses in one zone, whereas others seek to disperse them.

Illustration: The Detroit, Michigan zoning ordinance prohibited any "adult theater" from being located within 1,000 feet of any other "regulated use" or within 500 feet of a residential area. "Regulated uses" included sexually oriented theaters or bookstores, topless cabarets, bars, hotels, motels, pawnshops, pool halls, second hand stores, shoe-shine parlors, and dance halls. *Young v. American Mini Theatres, Inc.* (1976).

Illustration: The Boston, Massachusetts zoning ordinance created an Adult Entertainment District in which adult book stores and other sexually oriented businesses are allowed. The general prohibition of moving or flashing signs did not apply in this district. Since such uses were forbidden in all other districts, the area become known as the "Combat Zone."

(c) Industrial; Performance Standards

Many zoning ordinances create different zones for the various types of industrial use. Today, many communities have set aside areas as exclusive industrial parks, from which residential and commercial activities are excluded to prevent interferences with the industrial activities. Industrial regulations often are directed at the activity's external effects, rather than at the specific activity being conducted. Thus, "performance standard zoning" regulates externalities, such as smell, noise, smoke, and vibrations, rather than the activity itself.

Illustration: The Lake Success, New York zoning ordinance included a district for uses such as "offices, scientific and research laboratories, assembly, fabrication and finishing of articles of small compass and high value (cameras, watches, electronic instruments), (inside) storage facilities. . . . " The ordinance excluded from this district "any use which will cause smoke, gas, dust, odor or other pollutant, noise perceptible beyond the boundaries of the site of the use, discharge of waste into any watercourse, dissemination of glare, vibration, heat or electromagnetic interference beyond the immediate site, or physical hazard by reason of fire, explosion or radiation * * *." *Brechner v. Incorporated Village of Lake Success* (1960).

2. Mapping

In addition to the zoning ordinance, which describes the bulk, area, and use restrictions, a community also will have a zoning map that shows the location of each zone where such restrictions apply. The boundaries of the different types of districts may overlap. For example, one height limit may apply to all residential districts and a different height limit for all commercial districts. Alternatively, different mapped areas may exist for different purposes, such as height limits on all coastal areas though some parts of the coast are zoned residential and other parts commercial. There may be only one map, with all bulk and area standards dependent on the use district (e.g. a forty foot height limit for all residential zones), or there may be separate (overlay) use and bulk maps.

a. Size of the Zone; Spot Zoning

If a very small area is mapped for a use significantly different from that permitted in the surrounding area, a court may invalidate it as impermissible "spot zoning." Invalidation is especially likely if the classification was created in a rezoning, rather than in the original zoning of the parcel. Rezoning is covered at page 439.

Illustration: In 1951, the Board of Public Works of the City of Paterson, New Jersey amended the zoning ordinance to reclassify a single lot from residential to business in order to permit the lot owner to build a bank on it. The area where the lot was located was the finest residential neighborhood in the city, and the lot had been vacant for forty years. The court invalidated the rezoning. *Conlon v. Board of Pub. Works of City of Paterson* (1953).

b. Zoning Boundaries

If the zoning boundaries do not coincide with the lot lines, a single parcel of land may be in two different zoning districts. In such a case, an ordinance may provide that the entire lot is subject to whichever classification is more (or less) severe or to whichever covers the greater geographic part of the lot. In small communities, mapping can coincide precisely with all existing lot lines. The problem of a split lot also can be avoided by running all zoning lines down the center of public streets, but that would put opposite sides of the same street into different districts, which is generally undesirable. If no corrective action is taken as to a split lot, it will remain subject to two different classifications unless a court holds the mapping to be invalid.

Illustration: Under the zoning map of Cambridge, Massachusetts, the plaintiff's parcel was classified as residential for a one hundred foot strip along the street, but the rest of the parcel was unrestricted. Even though the actual use of the other side of the street was residential, the court held that the city had acted arbitrarily in not running the zoning line along the property's street frontage. *Nectow v. City of Cambridge* (1928).

3. Special Zoning Tools

a. Special Exceptions (Conditional Uses)

Under the traditional zoning system, a use is permitted as a matter of right if the ordinance includes it as an allowable activity, or it is absolutely barred. However, not all activities can be so readily categorized. If the community believes that some activities might be appropriate in a certain zone depending on the circumstances, the zoning ordinance may include a category of conditionally permitted uses for them. These types of uses are allowed only after review by the appropriate zoning agency. These uses usually are called special exceptions or conditional uses, because the zoning agency may permit the use only under certain conditions, such as landscaping the premises to shield the neighbors or limiting the hours of operation. The agency has the discretion to grant, deny, or condition a permit only if the zoning ordinance includes the proposed use as one that can be permitted as a special exception or conditional use.

Illustration: The zoning ordinance of Owatonna, Minnesota permitted drive-in businesses, such as gasoline stations or car lots, as special uses in commercial districts. A permit for this type of special use could be granted only after a public hearing and a two-thirds vote of the city council. *Alexander Co. v. Owatonna* (1946).

Illustration: The zoning ordinance of Millburn, New Jersey provided that a school, hospital, club, or cemetery would be permitted only if the Board of Adjustment found that "as it is proposed to be located, it will not be detrimental to the health, safety and general welfare of the community and is reasonably necessary for the convenience of the community." The permit for this type of structure or use was "subject to such requirements as to front, side and rear yards, and other reasonable conditions as to structure or use as the governing body may see fit to impose." *Tullo v. Millburn Township, Essex County* (1959).

b. *Floating Zones*

A city can create a zoning classification by specifying the standards for it without putting it on the zoning map. A property owner then can apply to an administrative body to have her land reclassified for the uses permitted in that zone. Because the zone has not been mapped, it "floats." Floating zones have been created for industrial parks, mixed apartment-commercial zones, and mobile home parks.

Illustration: The Farmington, Connecticut zoning ordinance provided: "Restricted Apartment zones may be designated on the zoning map and may also be established in any other zone by petition in accordance with the following procedure * * *." The regulations then provided that zoning cannot be approved if it is "inconsistent with the public welfare or * * * does not fully safeguard the appropriate use of the land in the immediate neighborhood [or] unless there is clear evidence of safe and satisfactory means of providing water supply and sewage disposal." There were also "limitations and requirements as to use, area, yards and courts, spaces between structures, building coverage, and building and dwelling size, as well as special requirements for parking areas, access ways and sidewalks, and recreation and open space." *Miss Porter's Sch., Inc. v. Town Plan and Zoning Comm'n of Town of Farmington* (1964).

Illustration: The 1947 zoning ordinance of Tarrytown, New York provided that the boundaries of its apartment zone would be "fixed by amendment of the official village building zone map at such times in the future as such district or class of zone is applied to properties in this village." *Rodgers v. Village of Tarrytown* (1951).

c. Cluster Zoning

To avoid monotonous developments in which each house has the same front and side yards and the same general layout, a community may enact cluster zoning. Cluster zoning permits developers to depart from the standards for individual parcels so long as those standards are maintained with regard to the overall project. For instance, if the ordinance requires fifty percent open space for each lot, a developer of two lots might have the option of clustering two houses on one lot and leaving the other lot entirely open.

Illustration: The zoning ordinance of South Brunswick, New Jersey provided that a subdivider could reduce the minimum lot size and frontage requirements by up to thirty percent for individual lots within the subdivision if: (1) the resulting "net lot density" of the area was no greater than otherwise would be allowed; (2) the development complied "with all other provisions of the zoning ordinance, such as front, rear and side setbacks, size of buildings, etc.;" (3) the subdivider donated a "usable" five acre tract to the city for public purposes; and (4) "if the tract to be subdivided is located in a zone which requires a minimum lot size of 20,000 square feet or less, the developer must donate, exclusive of open drainage water courses, twenty percent of the tract to the township; if the tract to be subdivided is located in a zone which requires a minimum lot size in excess of 20,000 square feet, the developer must donate, exclusive of open drainage water courses, thirty percent of the tract to the township." *Chrinko v. South Brunswick Township Planning Bd.* (1963).

d. Planned Unit Development (PUD)

The same clustering principle may be applied to uses, as well as to bulk and area. If the subdivider is permitted to allocate space for both commercial and residential activities within overall limitations, the project may be a Planned Unit Development. Instead of local officials mapping separate single family residential, apartment, and commercial districts when the zoning ordinance is adopted, the subdivider can map all those activities on a single parcel subject to percentages specified in the ordinance. To reduce the costs of delay and the dangers of inconsistent demands from different reviewing boards, the property may be rezoned to PUD at the same time as the site plan review and perhaps under the aegis of one agency.

Illustration: The zoning ordinance of New Hope, Pennsylvania included a PUD district within which there can be "single family attached or detached dwellings, apartments, accessory private garages, public or private parks and recreation areas including golf courses, swimming pools, ski slopes, etc. (so long as these facilities do not produce noise, glare, odor, air pollution, etc., detrimental to existing or prospective adjacent structures); a municipal building; a school; churches; art galleries; professional offices; certain types of signs; a theater (but not a drive-in); motels and hotels; and a restaurant. The ordinance then sets overall density requirements. The PUD district may have a maximum of eighty percent of the land devoted to residential uses, a maximum of twenty percent for the permitted commercial uses and closed recreational facilities, and must have a minimum of twenty percent for open spaces. The residential density shall not exceed ten units per acre, nor shall any such unit contain more than two bedrooms. All structures within the district must not exceed minimum height standards set up in the ordinance. Finally, although there are no traditional 'setback' and 'side yard' requirements, ordinance 160 does require that there be 24 feet between structures, and that no townhouse structure contain more than twelve dwelling units." *Cheney v. Village 2 at New Hope, Inc.* (1968).

e. Holding Zones

A holding zone is a restrictive use classification that is designed to render land practically undevelopable . When a community is not yet ready to classify all the land within its borders, it may zone some areas very restrictively, not because it believes the zoning to be appropriate to the area, but because it prevents development until the comprehensive plan is finished. For example, it may restrict a zone to single family residences with a minimum lot size of ten acres. The same goal can be achieved by interim zoning. Overly restrictive zoning forces owners to apply for a rezoning for any development and, thus, often is called "wait and see" zoning.

4. Zoning Relief

a. *Variances*

A variance permits a landowner to deviate from some aspect of the zoning ordinance's requirements with respect to the lot, building, or use. This relief usually is granted by a special agency, often called a board of adjustment. Usually, there must be circumstances unique to the parcel, the hardship must not be self-inflicted, conditions can be imposed to minimize adverse effects on the neighborhood, and the intent of the comprehensive plan must be preserved. The variance process is designed to prevent regulatory takings lawsuits when enforcement of the zoning ordinance's requirements would inflict an unnecessary hardship on a landowner.

Illustration: The Standard State Zoning Enabling Act authorizes the board of adjustment to grant a "variance from the terms of the ordinance as will not be contrary to the public interest, where, owing to special conditions, a literal enforcement of the provisions of the ordinance will result in unnecessary hardship, and so that the spirit of the ordinance shall be observed and substantial justice done."

Illustration: California's enabling legislation provides: "Variances from the terms of the zoning ordinances shall be granted only when, because of special circumstances applicable to the property, including size, shape, topography, location or surroundings, the strict application of the zoning ordinance deprives such property of privileges enjoyed by other property in the vicinity and under identical zoning classification. Any variance granted shall be subject to such conditions as will assure that the adjustment thereby authorized shall not constitute a grant of special privileges inconsistent with the limitations upon other properties in the vicinity and zone in which such property is situated. A variance shall not be granted for a parcel of property which authorizes a use or activity which is not otherwise expressly authorized by the zone regulation governing the parcel of property."

Illustration: The zoning ordinance of the District of Columbia provides that its Board of Adjustment may grant a variance "where, by reason of exceptional narrowness, shallowness, or shape of a specific piece of property at the time of the original adoption of the regulations or by reason of exceptional topographical conditions or other extraordinary or exceptional situation or condition of a specific piece of property, the strict application of any regulation would result in peculiar and exceptional practical difficulties to or exceptional and undue hardship upon the owner of such property * * * so as to relieve such difficulties or hardship, provided such relief can be granted without substantial detriment to the public good and without substantially impairing the intent, purpose and integrity of the zone plan as embodied in the zoning regulations and map."

b. *Rezoning (Amendments)*

A property owner may seek relief from the existing ordinance by attempting to have it amended. A text amendment is an amendment to the text of the zoning ordinance, such as lowering the height limit or changing the list of activities permitted in a given zone. A map amendment is an amendment to the zoning map that reclassifies a single parcel from one zone to another. Amending the zoning ordinance or map is a legislative act by the city council, as opposed to the board of adjustment's administrative action in granting a variance. The distinction may be significant for purposes of judicial review, since courts generally defer more to legislative acts than to administrative acts. On judicial review, see page 404. However, some courts do not apply the same presumption of validity to rezonings as to the enactment of the original zoning. When a small parcel is rezoned for its owner's benefit, rather than for the general welfare, a court may characterize it as spot zoning and invalidate it. Many statutes require a supermajority vote by the legislative body, such as a two-thirds vote, to rezone property when a specified percentage of the neighbors have filed a protest against the proposal.

Illustration: Fawn Township, Pennsylvania rezoned an eighty acre doughnut shaped parcel from residential, so that its owner could operate a motorcycle racecourse. All the neighboring lands, including the parcel surrounded by the doughnut, still were zoned residential. A court invalidated the rezoning as illegal spot zoning because that parcel did not differ in any relevant way from the surrounding properties. *Appeal of Benech* (1977).

Illustration: Prince George's County, Maryland rezoned a parcel from low density residential to mixed commercial and residential. A court invalidated the rezoning because there was no showing that the original zoning classification was mistaken or that any change had occurred in the area since the original classification. *MacDonald v. Board of County Comm'rs for Prince George's County* (1965).

Illustration: A court invalidated the rezoning of a parcel of land in Washington County, Oregon from single family residential to "planned residential" to permit a mobile home park. The court held that the rezoning applicant had not established a public need for the rezoning or that any such need was best served by changing the classification of that particular parcel as compared with other available property. *Fasano v. Board of County Comm'rs of Washington County* (1973).

c.   Contract Zoning (Conditional Zoning)

Local government may grant a request to upzone a parcel if certain restrictions are imposed on the intended use to reduce its adverse effects on other land or if the owner offers certain inducements that are sufficiently valuable to the community. This type of rezoning may be referred to as contract zoning or conditional zoning. The restrictions imposed on the parcel may relate to physical conditions, such as reducing the maximum lot coverage, or to the use, such as limiting the owner to the particular use intended though numerous other uses would be allowed under the new zoning classification. Inducements offered by an owner might include dedication of land to the community or special beautification of the property, such as landscaping along the front lot line. The community may require that a recorded deed include the agreement, that covenants made by the owner in favor of the community be recorded, or that the zoning amendment be made conditional on the owner's fulfillment of the promises. Contract zoning generally is granted on an individual basis, although the general zoning ordinance explicitly may provide for it.

Some courts do not permit contract zoning because it violates the principle of zoning uniformity since restrictions are applied to one parcel in a zoning class that are not applied to the other parcels in that class. Courts also have invalidated contract zoning because it amounts to a bargaining away of the local police power or because it is not authorized by statute. When a court upholds such zoning, it usually observes that the property could have been rezoned without the additional restrictions and that neighbors cannot object to the restrictions because they are benefited by them and the affected property owner cannot object because she consented to them.

Illustration: Peoria County, Illinois rezoned a five acre tract from agricultural to commercial to enable the owner to construct a dance hall after obtaining the owner's agreement to restrict the premises to that use only and to dedicate land to provide access to the highway. The agreement was set forth in a recorded restrictive covenant. The court invalidated the rezoning. *Ziemer v. County of Peoria* (1975).

B. SUBDIVISION REGULATION

Local government may impose additional requirements when land is subdivided into individually saleable or buildable lots. When a large parcel of land is converted into individual lots, the community has an obvious interest in ensuring that the new streets tie into existing city streets and are not too narrow for fire trucks and sanitation vehicles. The same concern exists concerning linkage with all other municipal services, including water and sewage, parks, playgrounds, and schools. Local government often control these features of the subdivision's development by prohibiting the sale of subdivided lots until a subdivision map has been governmentally approved and recorded.

Illustration: The Standard City Planning Enabling Act provides that the local "planning commission shall adopt regulations governing the subdivision of land within its jurisdiction. Such regulations may provide for the proper arrangement of streets in relation to other existing or planned streets and to the master plan, for adequate and convenient open space, for traffic, utilities, access of firefighting apparatus, recreation, light and air, and for the avoidance of congestion of population, including minimum width and area of lots. Such regulations may include provisions as to the extent to which streets and other ways shall be graded and improved and to which water and sewer and other utility mains, piping, or other facilities shall be installed as a condition precedent to the approval of the plan." These provisions often are included in a state's Subdivision Map Act.

1. What is a Subdivision

The state subdivision enabling act usually specifies the type of land division that is subject to local subdivision regulation. Many land divisions are treated as subdivisions for certain purposes and not for others. Subdivisions of fewer than five parcels commonly are exempt from regulations imposed on larger subdivisions, although special provisions may prevent subdividers from evading the regulations by periodic "quartering" of land. Subdivisions of very large individual parcels, such as one, two, or forty acres, also often are exempted from regulation. An apartment building generally is not treated as a subdivision, even though "the division of the property for lease, sale or financing" is a common definition of "subdivision." However, condominium projects often are treated as "vertical subdivisions," and the conversion of an existing apartment building into a condominium may require local subdivision approval.

2. Subdivision Process

A subdivision is created when a landowner submits to the local government a tentative or preliminary map of a proposed subdivision that shows the location of individual lots, roads, public utilities, and other required elements. The map is reviewed by all interested agencies, such as the fire department to ensure that roads are wide enough for fire trucks and that buildings are spaced far enough apart to avoid a conflagration, the police department, the planning department, the parks department, and the streets department. Each agency can demand changes in the plan to satisfy its standards. If the applicant successfully accommodates these official demands, the proposed map is approved. After the applicant constructs the public improvements shown on the map, a final subdivision map is approved by the government and is recorded in the public records. The subdivider then can sell lots in the subdivision by deeds that refer to the recorded subdivision map for boundary locations. Building permits then are issued to the subdivider or to individual lot buyers if the building plans conform to the applicable zoning and other regulations. Sometimes, a development agreement will be executed between the developer and the government to assure the developer that the rules will not be changed during the lengthy approval process, because of an election or for any other reason.

3. Subdivision Exactions

A community may require the subdivider to make certain donations to it as a condition for approving the subdivision map. The subdivider may be required to dedicate the streets to the city, pay for utility line installations, dedicate land for parks, schools, or public buildings, or pay fees in lieu of dedicating land.

Illustration: The Minnesota Subdivision Act provided that municipal subdivision regulations "may require that a reasonable portion of each proposed subdivision be dedicated to the public for public use as parks and playgrounds." In residential subdivisions of less than thirty acres, the subdivider may be able to contribute an equivalent amount in cash. In determining the extent of the dedication, the regulations "may take into consideration the open space, park, recreational or common areas and facilities which the subdivider has provided for the exclusive use of the residents of the subdivision." Pursuant to this provision, the City of Bloomington required subdividers to dedicate ten percent of the value of the land to be subdivided. *Collis v. City of Bloomington* (1976).

Illustration: The California Subdivision Map Act provides: "There may be imposed by local ordinance a requirement that areas of real property be reserved for parks, recreational facilities, fire stations, libraries or other public uses." Another section authorized dedication of land or payment of fees in lieu "for classroom and related facilities for elementary or high schools" where existing schools are overcrowded. Under a related provision, the City of Walnut Creek imposed a dedication requirement of two and one-half acres of park or recreation land for every 1,000 new residents or an equivalent fee if no park was designated on the master plan and the subdivision was within three-quarters mile of a park or proposed park. *Associated Home Builders of Greater East Bay, Inc. v. City of Walnut Creek* (1971).

In *Dolan v. City of Tigard* (1994), the U.S. Supreme Court held that a subdivision exaction constitutes a taking under the federal Constitution unless (1) an "essential nexus" exists between a legitimate state interest and the exaction and (2) the exaction bears a "rough proportionality" to the projected impact of the proposed development. In *Nollan v. California Coastal Comm'n* (1987), the Supreme Court held that the California Coastal Commission's demand for an access easement over beachfront owners' property as a condition for permitting them to rebuild their house constituted an impermissible taking because there was no "nexus" between the demand (for parallel access from one coastal lot to the next) and the harm the Commission was attempting to alleviate (loss of coastal views).

State courts have not adopted a uniform standard for determining the validity of subdivision exactions. The strictest view requires that the exaction be specifically and uniquely attributable to the subdivision activity. The most lenient standard is that the exaction must be reasonably related to the use of the facilities to be made by the subdivision's inhabitants.

C. GROWTH MANAGEMENT

A community may regulate its rate of residential growth to reduce the burden that new population imposes on municipal services and budgets. Zoning and subdivision regulations often indirectly inhibit growth by reducing the supply of land available for development (e.g. open space zoning, large minimum lot sizes), by pricing out much lower-cost housing (e.g. exclusion of apartments and mobile home parks), or by restricting users (e.g. single family districts prohibiting more than a specified number of unrelated people from living together). Growth management regulations, on the other hand, deal with this issue directly by restricting the number of residential building permits that can be issued. Some of the numerous techniques for restricting growth are indicated in the following Illustrations.

Illustration–Moratorium: An initiative ordinance enacted in Livermore, California provided that no building permits could be issued until classrooms are not overcrowded, schools are not operating on double session, sewage treatment facilities meet regional quality standards, and water supplies are adequate. *Associated Home Builders of Greater Eastbay, Inc. v. City of Livermore* (1976).

Illustration–Cap: A court invalidated an initiative ordinance in Boca Raton, Florida that limited the city to 40,000 dwelling units. *Boca Raton v. Boca Villas Corp.* (1979).

Illustration–Points: In Ramapo, New York, a building could not be erected until the property owner acquired a specified number of points based on the availability of sewage, drainage, parks and recreation, roads, and firehouses. The developer could increase the point count by providing the services personally, rather than waiting for the town to supply them. *Golden v. Planning Bd. of Ramapo* (1972).

Illustration-Quota: Petaluma, California issued only five hundred building permits per year for residential projects of more than four units. Permits were awarded according to a point system similar to Ramapo's. Additional points were awarded for design and environmental amenities, low and moderate income housing units, and geographical balance of new development throughout the town. *Construction Indus. Ass'n of Sonoma County v. City of Petaluma* (1975).

Illustration–Percentage: Raymond, New Hampshire limited the number of building permits a person could receive to one a year for every ten acres of land he or she owned. For example, the owner of forty acres could obtain four building permits a year. *Beck v. Town of Raymond* (1978).

D. LANDMARKS AND HISTORIC DISTRICTS

Many communities protect their historic buildings and neighborhoods by specially designating them and subjecting them to stringent design control. The owner of a property designated as a landmark or located within a historic district is prohibited from altering its external appearance without obtaining a permit from the appropriate regulatory agency. In return, the owner may be given a property tax reduction or may be permitted to use the building in an otherwise unpermitted manner to generate an economic return. In some situations, the community may purchase a preservation easement in the facade or structure, thereby eliminating the owner's right to destroy its historic features.

Illustration: The Louisiana Constitution created the Vieux Carre Commission, which regulates historic architecture in the French Quarter of New Orleans. No building can be altered and no sign can be displayed without a permit from the Commission. The Commission also can grant property tax exemptions for such buildings.

Illustration: By statute, cities in New York are "empowered to provide by regulations, special conditions and restrictions for the protection, enhancement, perpetuation and use of places, districts, sites, buildings, structures, works of art, and other objects having a special character or special historical or aesthetic interest or value. Such regulations * * * may include appropriate and reasonable control of the use or appearance of neighboring private property within public view, or both." If the measure constitutes "a taking of private property it shall provide for due compensation, which may include the limitation or remission of taxes."

Illustration: Based on the above statute, New York City permits an area to be designated as a historic district subject to special regulation if it contains improvements that "(a) have a special character or special historical or aesthetic interest or value; and (b) represent one or more periods or styles of architecture typical of one or more eras in the history of the city; and (c) cause such area, by reason of such factors, to constitute a distinct section of the city." A landmark is "any improvement, any part of which is thirty years old or older, which has a special character or special historical or aesthetic interest or value as part of the development, heritage or cultural characteristics of the city, state or nation and which has been designated as a landmark * * *." Pursuant to the ordinance, the City refused to permit the owner of Grand Central Station to erect an office building over it. *Penn Cent. Transp. Co. v. New York City* (1978).

E.   ENVIRONMENTAL PROTECTION

State law may require local government to study the environmental effect of any action it considers taking, including granting approval for private land development. The appropriate agency may be required to prepare an environmental impact statement or report before approving a subdivision, rezoning land, or granting any other form of development permit. The requirement may be entirely procedural and require a study without dictating the agency's response to unfavorable data. Or the law may include a substantive requirement that the agency must avoid adverse environmental effects.

Illustration: The California Environmental Quality Act requires all agencies that regulate private individuals' activities, including "the issuance to a person of a lease, permit, license, certificate or other entitlement for use," to give major consideration to preventing environmental damage. An environmental impact report must be prepared that identifies the project's significant environmental effects, identifies alternatives, and indicates how the significant effects can be mitigated or avoided. An agency should not approve a project if feasible alternatives or mitigation measures would substantially lessen the adverse environmental effects, unless economic, social, or other conditions make the alternatives or mitigation measures infeasible.

The federal Comprehensive Environmental Response, Compensation and Liability Act (CERCLA, commonly referred to as Superfund) and comparable state laws impose a duty to clean up environmentally contaminated properties. The owner is absolutely liable even if he was not the polluter, unless he comes within the "innocent owner" defense by showing that the contamination was caused by a third party who was not his agent or in a "contractual relationship" with him. A deed creates a contractual relationship between a buyer and seller, thus making the current owner responsible for previous owners' activities. However, the owner is not liable if he acquired the property after it was contaminated but "had no reason to know" of it after making "all appropriate inquiry into the previous ownership and uses of the property," exercising due care, and taking appropriate precautions against "foreseeable acts or omissions" of third parties. This exception to liability effectively requires every purchaser to make a due diligence investigation or environmental audit of the property's condition and to negotiate with the vendor for appropriate contractual protections relating to liability for known or later discovered contamination.

Most litigation over cleanup costs (response costs) occurs between private parties, rather than with the government. Owners who are compelled to pay cleanup costs often attempt to recover from their sellers, who may attempt to rely on an "as is" clause for their defense. An owner also may try to compel her property insurance carrier to pay cleanup and defense costs, which requires a modern interpretation of policies written many years before liability for toxic wastes was a concern.

F. EMINENT DOMAIN

Government directly can control land use by acquiring property and exercising the prerogatives of an owner over it. Communities usually manage parks, civil buildings, airports, and similar public amenities and services in this way. If the private owner of a desired parcel is unwilling to sell, the government can compel its transfer through an eminent domain (condemnation) action. In such a proceeding, the government must prove a "public use" for the acquisition, but courts normally defer to legislative determinations as to public use.

Illustration: To break up concentrated land holdings and to facilitate the real estate market, a Hawaiian land reform statute requires certain residential landlords to sell parcels to their tenants in certain situations. The United States Supreme Court held that a valid public use existed, even though the statute required the transfer of property from one private person to another. *Hawaii Hous. Auth. v. Midkiff* (1983).

Illustration: Courts routinely hold that a valid public purpose is served by urban renewal ("slum clearance") projects even though buildings taken from private owners may be transferred to new private owners. *Berman v. Parker* (1954).

The government is required to pay "just compensation" for property it takes. A jury determines the amount after hearing evidence concerning the property's fair market value. In certain cases, the government can take land immediately and pay the owner later after the fair market value has been determined.

II. LAND USE REGULATION PROCESS

A. WHO MAY REGULATE LAND

1. Federal Regulation

The federal government regulates all land that it owns or administers, such as national forest land and Native American trust land. By virtue of its constitutional supremacy, the federal government is not subject to state or local control for land that it regulates. Although no comprehensive federal zoning or national land use plan exists in the United States, the federal government plays a significant indirect role in the regulation of land uses through its commerce and budgetary powers.

Illustration: Under the Federal Water Pollution Control Act, all dredging and filling in most of the nation's waters are subject to approval by the Army Corps of Engineers.

Illustration: Under the 1970 Clean Air Amendments to the Clean Air Act, state and local governments must submit plans for improving air quality to the federal Environmental Protection Agency. These plans include matters such as the location of shopping centers, sports complexes, sewer lines, and industrial developments.

2. State Regulation

Certain areas of a state, such as those of critical environmental concern, may be subject to a direct state permitting process in addition to or in lieu of the local procedure. Alternatively, a state may classify lands within its borders and limit local control to regulation within those classifications.

Illustration: In Hawaii, the State Land Use Commission classified all land as urban, rural, agricultural, or conservation. The State has restricted the permissible activities within those classifications. Counties may adopt more strict regulations in each district, but the State controls land use decisions in the conservation districts. However, enforcement is a county, rather than State, responsibility.

Illustration: In Vermont, a building or development permit must be obtained not only from the local agency, but also from a state agency, thus giving the state a veto over local development.

3. Regional Regulation

A regional agency that operates below the state level but above the local level may have authority to regulate certain lands. The communities within the region may create the agency, or the state may create it because of a statewide interest in the area.

Illustration: The Regional Planning Act in Minnesota provides that two or more counties, cities, or towns can enter into an agreement to conduct regional planning activities. The agreement must provide for a regional planning board that will prepare a regional development plan for review by the participating government units.

Illustration: A California statute provides that no significant development work can be performed along the San Francisco Bay coastline without a permit from the Bay Conservation Development Commission. This permit does not excuse the obligation to obtain all necessary local permits.

Illustration: The Tahoe Regional Planning Agency (TRPA) was created by California and Nevada statutes and was ratified by an act of Congress. The Agency must ensure that all projects in the area comply with its regional general plan, ordinances, rules, regulations, and policies. While local municipalities may enact their own land use ordinances, they may not be less stringent than those promulgated by TRPA. TRPA is composed of two separate state groups, CTRPA and NTRPA. TRPA cannot approve a project unless a majority of both CTRPA's and NTRPA's delegates to TRPA vote favorably.

Illustration: Under a circular used by the Office of Management and Budget, any local agency that sought federal assistance for a variety of enumerated programs, including land use activities, first had to submit its plans to the regional clearinghouse designated by the state governor for evaluation and comment. These clearinghouses often were the region's local council of governments.

4. Local Regulation

Power to regulate land is vested in the state. State legislatures generally have delegated land use regulation to cities and counties by means of a zoning enabling act, subdivision enabling act, or similar form of statutory authorization. These statutes both enable and set limits for the local regulation of land. A court will invalidate a land use regulation that is not authorized by the enabling act because the regulation is ultra vires.

Illustration: The Standard State Zoning Enabling Act, which was prepared by the United States Chamber of Commerce in 1928, provides that cities are empowered " * * * to regulate and restrict the height, number of stories, and size of buildings and other structures, the percentage of lot that may be occupied, the size of yard, courts, and other open spaces, the density of population, and the location and use of buildings, structures, and land for trade, industry, residence, or other purposes."

Illustration: The American Law Institute Model Land Development Code (1976) provides that each local government is " * * * authorized to plan or otherwise encourage, regulate, or undertake the development of land in accordance with this code."

Illustration: The California Government Code provides that counties and cities may: "Regulate the use of buildings, structures and land as between industry, business, residents, open space, including agriculture, recreation, enjoyment of scenic beauty and use of natural resources, and other purposes. Regulate signs and billboards. Regulate location, height, bulk, number of stories and size of buildings and structures; the size and use of lots, yards, courts and other open spaces; the percentage of a lot which may be occupied by a building or structure; the intensity of land use. Establish requirements for off-street parking and loading. Establish and maintain setback lines."

Since most local land use regulation requires state authorization, any novel regulation may be challenged on the ground that it has not been authorized. A variety of issues have arisen in interpreting enabling legislation, such as whether (1) delegated power to regulate land subdivision and building construction includes the power to control or slow down growth; (2) the power to regulate the bulk of buildings includes design or architectural review; (3) the power to regulate subdivisions includes the power to compel subdivision exactions; (4) the initiative and referendum process can be used; and (5) the requirements of mapping and of uniform regulations in a zone prohibit devices such as floating zones and planned unit developments. Courts resolve these issues based on the language of the state enabling acts and the court's attitude toward local innovation.

5. Citizen Regulation

When citizens are discontented with local land use decisions, they may take matters into their own hands. Voters may be able to use the power of referendum to nullify official actions that already have been taken or the power of initiative to enact laws. Many significant land use decisions have been made in the initiative process or have been repudiated by referenda. Height limits and growth restrictions often are created by the

initiative process. Referenda often are used to over-
turn the approval of a large scale commercial or residential project.

Illustration: The voters of Eastlake, Ohio amended the
city charter to provide that, for any rezoning granted by the
city council, "it shall be mandatory that the same be approved by a 55% favorable vote of all votes cast of the
qualified electors of the City of Eastlake at the next regular
election, if one shall occur not less than 60 or more than 120
days after its passage, otherwise at a special election." *City
of Eastlake v. Forest City Enterprises, Inc.* (1976).

Illustration: Article XXXIV of the California Constitution
provides: "No low rent housing project shall hereafter be
developed, constructed or acquired in any manner by any
state public body until, a majority of the qualified electors of
the city, town or county, as the case may be, in which it is
proposed to develop, construct, or acquire the same, voting
upon such issue, approve such project by voting in favor
thereof at an election to be held for that purpose, or at any
general or special election." *James v. Valtierra* (1971).

Initiatives and referenda cannot be used in every
state for land use regulations. The enabling act's procedural requirements concerning planning department
studies, consistency with the comprehensive plan, and
notice and hearing rights may prohibit use of an
electoral process that does not provide such safe-
guards. Some courts permit the referendum but not
the initiative because the required preliminary and
procedural steps are preserved in a referendum; it
merely adds voter ratification to the process. Other
courts permit both a referendum and initiative but
limit their use to matters of general land use regulation. In this type of jurisdiction, an initiative or referendum could not be used for small parcel rezonings,

because the action is more properly characterized as administrative, rather than legislative.

B. PLANNING PROCESS

1. Comprehensive Plan

State enabling acts generally provide that local land use regulation must be done in conjunction with planning. Some courts interpret this type of provision as requiring no more than some forethought and generalized consideration of the community's needs, rather than an impulsive response to an isolated development. At the other extreme, some courts invalidate land use regulations if they were enacted before the adoption of a master plan, general plan, or comprehensive plan that sets forth the community's goals and policies. Finally, other courts interpret a planning requirement as mandating that all future land use regulations must be consistent with the plan.

Illustration: The Standard City Planning Enabling Act, prepared by the U.S. Department of Commerce in 1928, provides that the local planning commission shall prepare "a master plan for the physical development of the municipality, * * * including, among other things, the general location, character, and extent of streets, viaducts, subways, bridges, waterways, water fronts, boulevards, parkways, playgrounds, squares, parks, aviation fields, and other public ways, grounds and open spaces, the general location of public buildings and other public property, and the general location and extent of public utilities and terminals, whether publicly or privately owned or operated, for water, light, sanitation, transportation, communication, power, and other purposes; also the removal, relocation, widening, narrowing, vacating, abandonment, change of use or extension of any of the foregoing ways, grounds, open spaces, buildings, property, utilities, or terminals; as well as a zoning plan for the control of the height, area, bulk, location, and use of buildings and premises. * * * The plan shall be made with the general purpose of guiding and accomplishing a coordinated, adjusted, and harmonious development of the municipality and its environs which will, in accordance with present and future needs, best promote health, safety, morals, order, convenience, prosperity, and general welfare, as well as efficiency and economy in the process of development; including, among other things, adequate provision for traffic, the promotion of safety from fire and other dangers, adequate provision for light and air, the promotion of the healthful and convenient distribution of population, the promotion of good civic design and arrangement, wise and efficient expenditure of public funds, and the adequate provision of public utilities and other public requirements."

Illustration: The ALI Model Land Development Code (1976) provides: "A local government may adopt a Local Land Development Plan (in words, maps, illustrations or other media of communication) setting forth objectives, policies and standards to guide public and private development of land within its planning jurisdiction and including a short-term program of public actions."

2. Planning Commission

Many communities' planning activities are conducted by a planning commission that is assisted by a planning department. The planning department consists of paid professional city planners. The planning commission is composed of community members who are appointed by the local legislative body. The planning commission is responsible for various tasks regarding the master plan and land use ordinances.

Illustration: The Florida enabling act provided that a local planning commission had to:

(1) Acquire and maintain such information and materials as are necessary to an understanding of past trends, present conditions, and forces at work to cause changes in these conditions. Such information and material may include maps and photographs of manmade and natural physical features of the area concerned, statistics on past trends and present conditions with respect to population, property values, economic base, land use, and such other information as is important or likely to be important in determining the amount, direction, and kind of development to be expected in the area and its various parts.

(2) Prepare, adopt, and from time to time amend and revise a comprehensive and coordinated general plan for meeting present requirements and such future requirements as may be foreseen.

(3) Establish principles and policies for guiding action in the development of the area.

(4) Conduct such public hearings as may be required to gather information necessary for the drafting, establishment and maintenance of the comprehensive plan and such additional public hearings as are specified under the provisions of this part.

(5) Make or cause to be made any necessary special studies on the location, condition, and adequacy of specific facilities in the area. These may include, but are not limited to, studies on housing, commercial and industrial conditions and facilities, public and private utilities, and traffic, transportation and parking.

3. Land Use Ordinances

The local legislative body usually enacts the land use plan and ordinances based on the planning commission's recommendation and on public hearings.

The legislative body also adopts the official zoning map and decides all proposed amendments to the map, zoning ordinance, or master plan. The legislative body usually is not involved in the approval of subdivision maps, applications for special exceptions, or variance applications, although it may review such decisions.

4. Interim Ordinances

The state enabling act may permit a community to enact a land use regulation without first drafting a comprehensive plan or holding public hearings to protect the regulatory scheme from premature land development, which is particularly likely when property owners know that regulations are pending. This emergency or interim power may be limited to certain periods of time, such as eighteen months, or to certain forms of governmental action, such as prohibitions rather than permissions. An interim ordinance also may require the approval of a special supermajority of the local legislative body.

C. ENFORCEMENT

Permitting and recording requirements are designed to stop impermissible land use activities before they begin. For example, a subdivider will not be permitted to record the necessary subdivision map if it does not satisfy the subdivision ordinance. Similarly, a building permit will be denied if the proposed building does not conform with the zoning and building regulations. Likewise, a permit will be denied to an owner who seeks to use land in a manner not permitted by local zoning and licensing regulations. Despite these precautions, a property owner may violate a land use law. In that case, the community may sue to enjoin an improper activity or to demolish an illegal structure, may seek criminal sanctions, or may employ self-help. Transfer of noncomplying property may be made unlawful or subject to a right of rescission by the transferee. A pre-transfer code inspection may be required, or the community may have authority to record a notice of an ordinance violation so as to cloud the owner's title. Enforcement of land use regulations usually is vested exclusively in local officials, although neighbors sometimes can sue to enjoin illegal activities or to recover damages for a violation.

1. Nonconforming Uses

Land use regulations generally apply only prospectively and do not apply to buildings or activities that already existed before the regulation's effective date. Originally, it was assumed that nonconforming uses would disappear naturally over time, but such structures and activities instead tend to endure by virtue of their monopolistic advantages. Consequently, many communities now attempt to apply their zoning regulations to eliminate them. Courts generally do not permit the immediate abatement of nonconforming structures or uses, but a community may be allowed to "amortize" the activities by giving them a limited amount of time to continue their nonconforming features. The community also may prohibit a nonconforming structure from being enlarged, altered, put to any other nonconforming use, or continued after a nonconforming use has been abandoned or a nonconforming structure has been destroyed.

Illustration: A New Orleans, Louisiana zoning ordinance provided: "No building or portion thereof or land used in whole or in part for nonconforming purposes according to the provisions of the Ordinance, which hereafter becomes and remains vacant for a continuous period of 6 calendar months shall again be used except in conformity with the regulations of the district in which such building or land is situated. Neither the intention of the owner nor that of anybody else to use a building or lot or part of either for any nonconforming use, nor the fact that said building or lot or part of either may have been used by a makeshift or pretended nonconforming use shall be taken into consideration in interpreting and construing the word 'vacant' as used in this section * * *." *Fuller v. City of New Orleans, Dept. of Safety & Permits, Bldg. Inspection & Permits* (1975).

Illustration: A Los Angeles, California ordinance provided: "The nonconforming use of a conforming building or structure may be continued, except that in the residential zones any nonconforming commercial or industrial use of a residential building or residential accessory building shall be discontinued within five (5) years from June 1, 1946, or five (5) years from the date the use becomes nonconforming, whichever date is later. * * * The nonconforming use of land shall be discontinued within five (5) years from June 1, 1946, or within five (5) years from the date the use became nonconforming, in each of the following cases: (1) where no buildings are employed in connection with such use; (2) where the only buildings employed are accessory or incidental to such use; (3) where such use is maintained in connection with a conforming building." *City of Los Angeles v. Gage* (1954).

Illustration: A Santa Cruz County, California ordinance provided: "A nonconforming use may be ordered to be terminated by order of the board of supervisors upon recommendation of the planning commission within a period to be specified in such order. * * * If the nonconforming user has not made a substantial investment, or the investment can be substantially utilized or recovered through a then permitted use, such order may require complete termination of the nonconforming use within a one year minimum after the date of the order. In making such recommendation, the planning commission shall consider the total cost of property and improvements, the length of time, the adaptability of the land and improvements to a then permitted use, the cost of moving and re-establishing the use elsewhere and other related factors. Where the nonconforming use involved the removal of natural products, the amount or percentage of depletion shall be deducted from the cost of investment, and the current need for the product and its availability elsewhere shall be considered." *People v. Gates* (1974).

III. JUDICIAL REVIEW

A. ROLE OF THE JUDICIARY

Courts consider the validity of local regulatory actions in a variety of contexts. Suit may be brought by (1) the government to compel an owner to comply with regulations; (2) an owner or parties supporting her, such as brokers and contractors, to invalidate the regulations; (3) a neighbor or neighborhood organization to force government to reject the owner's proposal or to enforce some restriction against the owner; or (4) interested outsiders, such as housing and welfare organizations, to invalidate neighborhood "exclusionary" activities. If the court is reviewing legislation, it generally employs the "arbitrary and capricious" standard and invalidates the legislation only if it is not a rational means to achieve a legitimate end. However, if the legislation infringes a constitutionally protected interest, courts apply a "strict scrutiny" test and require a compelling state interest to uphold the legislation. If the action is adjudicatory (quasi-judicial or administrative), rather than legislative, the standard of review generally is "abuse of discretion," and the court determines whether "substantial evidence" in the record supports the action. If a fundamental or vested right is involved, the court may make an independent judgment in the matter, rather than merely reviewing the agency action.

Many courts characterize a land use action as legislative if it was taken by a legislative body and is legislative in form. Thus, zoning and rezoning are legislative acts because they are performed by a city council or other unit of local government. In contrast, the granting of a special exception by a planning commission or a variance by a board of adjustment are adjudicatory. Other courts reject this approach as being too formalistic and instead examine the nature and content of the action. For example, rezoning a small parcel of land might be held to be adjudicatory under this analysis.

In general, courts attempt to avoid making substantive zoning decisions. They do not want to serve as super-zoning boards that substitute their judgment for that of experts and local officials. However, courts do not hesitate to intervene on questions of procedural fairness or protection of basic rights.

B.   GROUNDS FOR INVALIDATION

A person aggrieved by a land use regulation may judicially challenge the regulation or its application. Many of the bases for such challenges already have been discussed. For example, a plaintiff may allege a lack of authority under the state enabling act (ultra vires). Architectural review, historic preservation, and growth management activities frequently have been challenged on that basis. A plaintiff also might allege that the legislative body improperly delegated authority. This challenge often has been raised against design review boards and neighborhood consent ordinances, which require block or neighborhood approval as a precondition to granting a permit to engage in an otherwise lawful activity.

1.   **Arbitrary and Capricious**

Even when legislative, a land use regulation is invalid if it is arbitrary and capricious. This challenge often is made to the zoning classification applied to an individual parcel of land or to the distinction between permissible and impermissible activities in a zoning district.

Illustration: Lake Success, New York reclassified a parcel of property from business to residential. The court invalidated the reclassification because the only sensible use of the property was commercial and all the surrounding property was zoned and used for commercial uses. *Udell v. Haas* (1968).

Illustration: A court held that a Newark, New Jersey ordinance was unreasonable, because it prohibited pick-up or delivery service by launderettes in business districts but permitted the same service by bakeries, appliance repair shops, restaurants, cleaners, and drug and other retail stores. *Marie's Launderette v. City of Newark* (1955).

Illustration: A court invalidated the James City County, Virginia zoning ordinance because it made the following distinctions: " 'Hotels, motels, and theatres' are permitted; banks, office buildings, and grocery stores are prohibited. 'Antique shops' are permitted; shops selling antique reproductions are prohibited. 'Restaurants' are permitted; 'fast food' or 'drive-in' restaurants are prohibited. Gift shops are permitted, provided they are 'accessory to hotels or motels having fifty or more dwelling or lodging units' and are 'designed and scaled only to meet the requirements of occupants and their guests'; other retail stores selling identical gifts are prohibited." *Board of Supervisors of James City County v. Rowe* (1975).

Judicial invalidation in such cases is not always expressly based on the arbitrary and capricious standard. The court may hold that the government action is inconsistent with the comprehensive plan or is ultra vires. A court also may characterize the irrational distinction as a denial of equal protection or substantive due process for the affected owner.

2. Due Process

A person whose property interest will be affected by a government land use decision is entitled to procedural fairness. Procedural due process issues arise in numerous ways in the land use process. When notice is required, questions may exist concerning the form of communication (mail, publication, or posting), the persons entitled to receive notice (property owners only, tenants, local residents, or neighbors outside the municipal boundary), the adequacy of information provided (identifying the affected property or the proposed measure), and whether the government action is administrative, which requires individual notices to all affected parties, or legislative, which requires only general public notice. In terms of the hearing, questions may exist concerning whether the issues at the hearing are the same as those described in the notice, who has the right to speak and to present evidence, the right to cross-examine, the taking of unsworn or opinion testimony (including staff reports, field trips, and neighbors' opinions), and the adequacy of the hearing record. The decision-making process may raise questions concerning conflict of interest (personal involvement, campaign contributions, ex parte contacts) and bias. The initiative or referendum process raises an entirely different set of procedural questions.

Unlike most other areas of law, substantive due process is alive and well in the context of land use regulation. Based on this constitutional protection, courts will invalidate a land use action that is arbitrary, inconsistent with the general welfare, or too intrusive on personal liberty.

3.   First Amendment and Associational Rights

When a land use restriction infringes a First Amendment or other constitutional right, the normal presumption of validity and the attendant judicial deference may not apply. This is particularly the case with regard to regulations affecting speech, religious activities, and family associations.

a.   *Speech and Religion*

Signs and billboards clearly convey messages to their readers. Although communities may regulate their size, shape, illumination, and placement, other types of restrictions are less enforceable. For example, restrictions relating to political signs are allowed only when alternative methods of communication are available. Commercial speech is less protected than political speech, but the scope of protection for commercial speech has not been definitively stated. The leading United States Supreme Court decision on commercial speech, *Metromedia, Inc. v. City of San Diego* (1981), had no majority position and included five separate opinions. The Court invalidated an ordinance that prohibited off-site advertising (advertising that does not relate to goods sold on the premises) but permitted on-site signs.

Land use regulations affecting other constitutionally protected activities also may be subject to special scrutiny. For example, in some jurisdictions, churches have a preferred status and are exempt from many zoning regulations. Schools, bookstores, and movie theaters are similarly protected in differing degrees. However, judicial validation of special zoning treatment for sexually oriented theaters and bookstores appears to permit some degree of content regulation. On zoning for sexually oriented businesses, see p. 431.

Illustration: A Mount Ephraim, New Jersey ordinance excluded live entertainment throughout the borough. The United States Supreme Court invalidated the ordinance because it was an overbroad prohibition against protected forms of expression. The Court set aside the conviction of a bookstore proprietor for permitting nude dancing on the premises. *Schad v. Borough of Mount Ephraim* (1981).

b. Association

A court also may invalidate an ordinance that infringes on the right of association. For example, a court may hold that a single family residential district unconstitutionally intrudes on associational or privacy rights if it excludes occupants based on their relationship to each other, such as a group of unrelated persons living together, rather than based on the residential characteristics of the structure, such as the number of kitchens or the square footage.

Illustration: The single family zoning ordinance of Belle Terre, New York prohibited more than two unrelated individuals from living together, though any number of related persons could share a residence. The United States Supreme Court upheld the ordinance against charges that it infringed on rights of privacy and travel. *Village of Belle Terre v. Boraas* (1974). On the other hand, the Supreme Court invalidated an ordinance that was applied to prohibit a grandmother from residing with her son and two grandsons, who were first cousins rather than brothers. The Court held that the ordinance constituted an improper intrusion into family living arrangements in violation of substantive due process. *Moore v. City of East Cleveland, Ohio* (1977).

4. Taking

A land use regulation that imposes a severe economic burden on a property owner may be challenged as an unconstitutional taking of property under the Fifth or Fourteenth Amendment of the United States Constitution or similar state constitutional provisions. The courts have been unable to reach a consensus or single theory as to when a regulation amounts to an invalid taking of property.

Illustration: A 1921 Pennsylvania statute prohibited the mining of anthracite coal if removal would cause residences on the surface to subside. The U.S. Supreme Court invalidated the statute as an unconstitutional taking of the coal company's property rights in the coal that it could no longer mine. *Pennsylvania Coal Co. v. Mahon* (1922).

Illustration: A 1966 Pennsylvania statute prohibited the mining of bituminous coal if removal would cause residences and public structures to subside. The U.S. Supreme Court upheld the statute because it protects the public interests in health, the environment, and "fiscal integrity." The Court held that the statute did not cause a taking of property. *Keystone Bituminous Coal Ass'n v. DeBenedictis* (1987).

Courts consider a variety of factors when determining whether a taking has occurred. The most important factors are discussed below.

a. Nature of the Government Activity

Early cases concentrated on the formal nature of the government activity. If government physically took possession or took title to property, it had to pay just compensation. If government activity injured property, it might be liable in trespass or nuisance. On the other hand, if a government regulation merely caused the property's value to decline, a taking did not occur, because title, possession, and the physical condition of the property remained unaffected. Today, courts generally reject those distinctions and recognize that government may take land by severe regulation as much as by the institution of formal eminent domain proceedings.

Courts sometimes say that the more government activity resembles the acquisition of resources for itself, rather than the regulation of competing private interests, the more likely it is that a taking has occurred. Thus, downzoning property adjacent to the municipal airport may be viewed as an attempt by the community to avoid purchasing the property or paying nuisance damages to the owner. Thus, a taking has occurred. In contrast, the same downzoning might be valid if it is done to protect an adjacent residential neighborhood from industrial intrusion.

Illustration: A New York statute authorized cable television companies to install lines and boxes on the roofs of apartment buildings. The U.S. Supreme Court held that the landlord's property had been taken, because the statute authorized a permanent physical occupation. Even though there was only minimal physical interference with property, the owner's right to exclude was violated. *Loretto v. Teleprompter Manhattan CATV Corp.* (1982).

Illustration: A New York City landmark preservation ordinance was applied to prohibit a railroad company from constructing a skyscraper over Grand Central Station. The U.S. Supreme Court held that the owner had not suffered a taking of the right to exploit a potential property right (annual rental income of $3 million for the airspace) since the owner was earning a reasonable return on the existing structure. *Penn Cent. Transp. Co. v. City of New York* (1978).

b. *Nature of the Owner's Property Interest*

Not all losses of value are takings. Courts use phrases such as "distinct investment-backed expectations" or "vested rights" to indicate the most protected property interests. The loss of value when undeveloped property is downzoned is not as likely to be a taking as when an existing use or structure must be eliminated.

c. *Extent of the Loss*

A loss of property value due to a new regulation does not automatically mean that part of the property has been taken by the government. A taking occurs only when the reduction goes "too far."

Illustration: Imposition of a new zoning ordinance caused property values to drop from $10,000 to $2,500 per acre. The United States Supreme Court upheld the ordinance in its first case to consider the validity of zoning. *Village of Euclid v. Ambler Realty Co.* (1926). Restrictions causing losses of 87% and 95% have been sustained in other cases from the Supreme Court and the Ninth Circuit, respectively.

Illustration: Because the state's Beachfront Management Act prohibited the owner of two beachfront lots from building houses on them, the state trial court found that he was deprived of all economic use of his property. The state Supreme Court nevertheless upheld the Act. The United States Supreme Court ruled that a complete destruction of value constitutes a taking of property unless common law nuisance rules would have caused the same result. *Lucas v. South Carolina Coastal Council* (1992).

The duration of the loss often is considered to be relevant. For example, a temporary moratorium on land development may be upheld, even though the property may have no economic value during the moratorium. Courts often uphold growth management ordinances that postpone an owner's right to develop for several years on the ground that the loss is only temporary.

d. *Public Benefit*

Courts sometimes employ a balancing test and compare the owner's loss with the public benefit. If the benefit is of dubious value or favors only a few, a court is less likely to tolerate a significant economic loss to an owner. It is sometimes said that property may be regulated to eliminate a burden it imposes on others but not to compel the owner to confer a benefit. However, critics say that this is a circular statement.

e.   Sharing the Loss

A court is more likely to uphold an ordinance that similarly restricts everyone, such as a uniform height limit over the entire community, than an ordinance that subjects one parcel to an economic loss for the sake of the others. Landmark designation, by virtue of selecting individual buildings, sometimes is attacked on this basis. Courts uphold landmark designation when it is part of a comprehensive plan or when the landmark owner benefits by the designation of other landmarks within the community. Reverse spot zoning—the downzoning of one parcel for the benefit of others—may be invalidated on this ground.

f.   Mitigation and Compensation Measures

A major purpose for variances is to provide an administrative mechanism for avoiding the taking of property. If a variance is available for a hardship situation, a property owner may lose his ability to contend that the ordinance causes a taking of his property. On variances see p. 438.

Other land use ordinances may provide offsetting compensation. For example, tax abatement is common for buildings designated as a landmark. Some communities have "transferable development right" systems that permit an owner of restricted property to transfer the unused development potential to other land in the community.

g. *Relief*

Although a court may invalidate an overly restrictive ordinance, owners fear that officials merely will enact a different, but similarly repressive, alternative. Therefore, aggrieved owners often seek to recover damages instead of or in addition to invalidation. In *First English Evangelical Lutheran Church v. County of Los Angeles* (1987), the United States Supreme Court held the Constitution requires payment of compensation for the time during which a regulation denies an owner use of her land.

5. Exclusionary Zoning

Many communities enact land use regulations or operate their land use permit processes to prevent certain classes of persons from residing there. Such exclusion may be motivated by racial discrimination or by a desire to save money by keeping out the poor, who may pay little in taxes but may require extensive social services. Many conventional land use devices, such as minimum lot sizes, costly building code requirements, and elimination of apartment and mobile home districts, can produce this effect while appearing facially neutral and ostensibly justifiable on environmental and public health grounds. Civil rights and welfare organizations often bring actions challenging such exclusionary devices on the ground that communities are attempting to avoid housing their fair share of the region's lower income residents.

a.   Federal Courts

(1) Constitutional Protection

The United States Constitution does not expressly prohibit a community from exercising its land use powers in an exclusionary fashion. However, if the exclusion is racially motivated, it may violate the Equal Protection or Due Process Clause.

Illustration: A Louisville, Kentucky ordinance prohibited a person of color from residing on a block that was predominantly white and vice versa. The United States Supreme Court held that the ordinance constituted an unconstitutional interference with property rights. *Buchanan v. Warley* (1917).

The federal Constitution has not been an effective tool for challenging exclusionary devices in all but the most blatant cases for three reasons. First, courts have interpreted the Constitution as requiring more than a disproportionate impact on one race. The challenged activity must have been undertaken with a discriminatory purpose or intent. Second, income level, unlike race, is not a suspect classification. Poverty triggers the strict scrutiny standard of review only when the poor are absolutely deprived of a meaningful opportunity to enjoy a necessary benefit. Finally, the standing requirement for exclusionary zoning litigation in federal court is difficult. A plaintiff must prove that some specific housing would have been available but for the exclusionary community action.

Illustration: A court held that a one-acre minimum lot size ordinance in Los Altos Hills, California did not deny Mexican–Americans equal protection even though it tended to exclude them. The town was not required to show a compelling interest to justify its ordinance, because there was no showing that adequate low-cost housing was unavailable elsewhere in the county and because wealthy Mexican–Americans were not excluded. *Ybarra v. Los Altos Hills* (1974).

Illustration: Arlington Heights, Illinois refused to rezone a fifteen-acre parcel from single-family to multi-family, so as to permit construction of a federally assisted housing project of 190 units for low and moderate income tenants. The U.S. Supreme Court held that the Village had not violated the Fourteenth Amendment, because there was no showing of discriminatory intent or purpose. The evidence demonstrated typical and legitimate zoning reasons for the refusal. Under the circumstances, disproportionate racial impact was not enough. *Arlington Heights v. Metropolitan Hous. Dev. Corp.* (1977).

(2) Statutory Protection

The federal Fair Housing Act (Title VIII of the Civil Rights Act of 1968) prohibits discrimination in the sale or rental of housing based on race, color, religion, sex, handicap, familial status, or national origin. The Act does not directly address the question of economic discrimination in zoning. However, unlike a constitutional challenge, the Act does not require proof of discriminatory intent. A discriminatory effect is sufficient.

Illustration: To halt the construction of a racially integrated townhouse development in an unincorporated area of St. Louis County, Missouri, the residents incorporated it and created a planning and zoning commission. The commission immediately enacted a zoning ordinance that barred all apartment construction. The court found that the ordinance had a racially discriminatory effect and had not been enacted to promote a compelling governmental interest. Therefore, it violated the Fair Housing Act. *United States v. City of Black Jack, Missouri* (1974); *Park View Heights Corp. v. City of Black Jack* (1979).

b. State Courts

Several state supreme courts have interpreted their state constitution to invalidate exclusionary land use regulations even without proof of discriminatory intent. Other states have reached the same result based on the state zoning enabling act. The holdings often are based on the principle that local land use regulation must serve the general welfare, which includes the housing needs of all residents of the region and not just the needs of upper income residents.

Illustration: The only type of housing permitted under the Mount Laurel, New Jersey zoning ordinance was single-family detached dwellings with a restrictive maximum number of bedrooms and excessive minimum lot area, lot frontage, and building size requirements. The Township also allocated more land for industrial use than was necessary. The New Jersey Supreme Court held that the ordinance violated the obligation of every developing community to provide low and moderate income housing for a "fair share" of the regional housing needs. *Southern Burlington County NAACP v. Township of Mount Laurel* (1975).

Illustration: Madison, New Jersey zoned disproportionate amounts of land for high cost residences, imposed excessively high subdivision and PUD exactions upon developers, and had an extremely expensive permit approval process. The court held these practices to be impermissible because "whether or not so intended, [they] operate in fact to preclude the opportunity to supply any substantial amounts of new housing for low and moderate income households." With regard to growing municipalities, the court held that a trial court need not "devise specific formulae for estimating their precise fair share of the lower income housing needs of a specifically demarcated region." Instead, the trial court should concentrate on "bona fide efforts toward the elimination or minimization of undue cost-generating requirements. * * * [I]t is incumbent on the governing body to adjust its zoning regulations so as to render possible and feasible the 'least cost' housing, consistent with minimum standards of health and safety, which private industry will undertake, and in amounts sufficient to satisfy the deficit in the hypothesized fair share." *Oakwood at Madison, Inc. v. Township of Madison* (1977).

INDEX

References are to Pages

CDLXXXI

ZONES AND ZONING